The Choice Is Yours!

How one man's journey prepared him
to survive and thrive on life's challenges.

DONALD GORDON ROSS

Print ISBN: 978-0-9919032-0-7
Ebook ISBN: 978-0-9919032-1-4

For my grandchildren Kody, Kylie, Lukas, Norah
and those who follow...

Dedication

This book is dedicated to the health care professionals at Sunnybrook Health Sciences Centre who saved my life, and to the health care professionals at Providence Healthcare who helped give me back my life— dozens of compassionate human beings without whose perseverance, skill and superb care I would not have been able to survive, let alone write this book. Allison and I will be forever grateful, and they will always be in our hearts.

Contents

Prologue..9

"Life Is A Highway"..9

1948 – 1964 A Young Lad..............................11

"We Are Family"...11

"A Whole New World" 21

"Those Were The Days" 25

"Those Lazy Hazy Crazy Days Of Summer"..........33

"Hello Muddah, Hello Fadduh" 39

"Oh! My Papa!"...43

"Send In The Clowns"..49

"Be True To Your School"......................................53

"Yesterday's Songs" 57

1965 – 1974 A Young Man 63

"Life In A Northern Town" 63

"Wonderful Summer" 69

"Summer Of '69"...75

"Working On the Chain Gang" 79

"My Dad"..83

"Ya Got Trouble"...91

"When The Going Gets Tough, The Tough Get Going"..................95

"I'm Getting Married In The Morning" 99

"Show Me The Way" 103

"Get A Haircut And Get A Real Job" 107

1974 – 1998 A Responsible Man 109

"Leader of the Pack" 109

"The End of the World" 117

"This Old House" 121

"Teach Your Children (Well)" 127

"(I Can't Get No) Satisfaction" 131

"Two Out of Three Ain't Bad" 135

"Love on the Rocks" 139

"Back On My Feet Again" 143

"The Twist" 149

"I Left My Heart In San Francisco" 153

1999 – 2011 A Man in Love! 159

"Take A Chance On Me" 159

"(You're My) Soul and Inspiration" 163

"Unforgettable" 169

"In My Life" 173

"Mr. Businessman" 179

"I Get Around" 185

"No Surrender" 189

"The Kids Are Alright" 199

"Drive" 204

"Spookie" 211

"Memories" 217

2012 A Fighting Man! 223

"Against All Odds" 223

"White Rabbit" 229

"That's What Friends Are For" 233

Dionne and Friends, 1985 233

"It's My Life" 239

"Walk Like A Man" 243

"Laughter In The Rain" 251

"Ac-Cent-Tchu-Ate the Positive" 255

"Alone" 257

"I'll Be Home For Christmas" 261

2013 A Repurposed Man! 265

"Homeward Bound" 265

"The Gift" 269

"Talk To Me" 275

"Que Sera Sera" 279

"Little Children" 283

"Life's Lessons" 287

Epilogue—A Contented Man 293

"The Homecoming" 293

Donald Gordon Ross
born July 9, 1948 - and counting

Prologue

"Life Is A Highway"
Tom Cochrane, 1992

Perhaps the first question to ask is why? Why take the time to put down on paper (or, in this age, the computer) my memoirs of my life's journey so far? I have been thinking about doing this for several years as a way of recording some of our family history so that it would not be forgotten. I feel that to know where you came from, what your roots are, and who you are, is important, particularly in a day and age that is so fast-paced that sometimes the truly important things in life get brushed aside. I have been interested in history since I was a youth, and I was an English Major in university, so I like history and I like to write.

I had wanted to do this initially just for myself, but it's no longer quite that simple. I thought it would be valuable for my children, Matt and Kate, to have a history of their father that would include many details they may not be familiar with, or might have forgotten about—significant events and experiences, people who influenced me on my life's journey, and life's lessons I've learned. And now that I have four young grandchildren–Kylie, Lukas, Kody and Norah–whom I cherish very much, I would like to impart a sense of what their grandfather is all about. Realistically I may not live long enough to do that by the time my grandchildren are old enough to truly appreciate it, or to hear it directly from me! Don't we all wish one of our grandfathers, or great-grandfathers, had written a personal history—particularly after the events of the past year?

I am now only too acutely aware of my own mortality, and that I won't be around forever. I look at genetics and realize that I may not live to see my grandchildren married. Over the past four years, my wife, Allison, and I have attended the funerals of many dear friends who departed far too soon and far too young. So disproportionately many that if you made a bell curve of these passings you would come to the statistical conclusion that the rest of us might have to live to be 100 just to hit the life span average that is so often quoted, and supposedly increasing, according to medical "authorities"! I realize that my generation has moved to the front of the queue, and that's not a line you wish to be at the front of!

Also, as I have now reached the esteemed status of a senior citizen, I realize that I have actually created a history of my own to relate. When you have been on the planet for 65 years, you have experienced much of what life is all about. Indeed, I have experienced happiness and joy... grief and sorrow...success and failure...pain and regret...ordeal and recovery ...and perhaps, most importantly, *love*.

My life experiences have been filled with challenges. And, with each challenge that I faced, a choice had to be made. Sometimes I made the right choices; sometimes I made the wrong choices. And choices most certainly always have consequences. Sometimes a door closed; but, more often than not, a door opened. My journey has been one of discovery, and finding answers. It is a story of profound awareness!

But, my reasons for writing are still not quite that straightforward. A big part of the answer as to why I want to write my story, for which I do not yet know the ending, is that the 12 month period from March, 2012 – February, 2013 was an incredible watershed experience in my life. The personal events of that year have had a dramatic and revealing impact on me. It was a year that saw me face a life-threatening illness where I stared down death and had a remarkable, if not miraculous, recovery. It changed my outlook on life. It remolded me as an individual. It made me realize that perhaps my whole life to that point had been about preparing me to at first survive, and then to thrive, through such a life-altering experience. It gave me a new sense of purpose.

They say that life is all about the journey. So, is this a novella...a family chronicle...a portrayal of the times...an autobiography...a fight for survival...or a journey of life and revelation? Well, I guess it has all of these ingredients. Let's see where the journey takes us...

1948 – 1964   A Young Lad

"We Are Family"
Sister Sledge, 1979

So…"Where should I begin? And, how should I presume?" That's a line from *The Love Song of J. Alfred Prufrock* that has stuck in my mind since a high school English poetry class. It seems to me to be an appropriate way to start writing down recollections of my life's journey to date. Another more practical line which comes to mind is "start at the beginning", and being both a practical and chronologically-minded person, I will.

I was born on July 9, 1948 in Toronto East General Hospital on a hot summer day—the first son of Gordon Wallace Ross and Norma Ellen Waters. The first Donald in our family was Donald Daniel Ross who lived in Scotland from 1743 – 1841. However, my parents decided to name me Donald, honouring my late uncle, Donald Alexander Ross, my father's brother, who died in World War II. But, before I begin *my* story, and to provide context, there is the story of those who came before me.

My paternal grandparents and family

My namesake, Donald Alexander Ross, was born on December 12, 1915 and was the eldest son of seven children born to my grandparents, Bruce Dow and Mary Elsie Virgo who were married early that same year on January 20. His younger brother, Wilmot (Bill), died at only 15 years of age of heart complications, and one sister died in infancy at only three months. That left my father, Gordon Wallace Ross, as Don's only remaining brother. My Uncle Don was a good looking man who, I am told, had a wicked sense of humour and loved to torment his younger siblings. Don was an all-round athlete who captained the Riverdale Collegiate football team. He also played hockey and was a very good amateur baseball player with the Webbers and Riverdale Kiwanis team. He was a deft pitcher at what would be considered a semi-pro level today. A love of fishing and hunting rounded out this all-Canadian man. And, amazingly, Don could also play the piano by ear. "Everyone thought the world of him," says his sister, my 92 year old Aunt Jean.

Don joined the Royal Canadian Air Force on June 20, 1940 near the start of World War II and decided right away that he wanted to be a pilot. He trained extensively in Regina and Calgary, where he graduated and won his commission in October, 1942. He took an instructor's course at Trenton and instructed for two years at Saskatoon, and later Pearce, Alberta. However, Don was very disappointed when his colour blindness prevented him from being given active duty. He had to settle for becoming a flight instructor. But Don wanted to be involved in World War II in active duty, not just as a flight instructor. Finally, he somehow finessed a way to get posted overseas to serve in the European Theatre of Operations. He was a Flight Lieutenant attached to RCAF Tiger Squadron #424 as a bomber pilot and squadron leader. His posting saw him arrive overseas on February 15, 1944.

My uncle, Donald Alexander Ross (Circa 1943)

My Uncle Don flew 13 bombing missions as the pilot of the now famous Lancaster bomber airplane. On that fateful night of March 5, 1945, Don led a bombing mission into Germany. There were many planes on the bombing mission that night, and many did not return. Over Chemnitz, Germany my Uncle Don's Lancaster bomber was either strafed by enemy fire or hit by another aircraft. My uncle gave the order for his four Canadian and two U.S. crew members to bail out, as he tried to keep the plane stabilized until everyone was out. Before he could jump the plane exploded.

Miraculously, one crewman, the tail gunner Cass Antonek from New Jersey, parachuted safely and survived being a prisoner of war. Cass indicated in his debriefing report that his bomber was hit by another fighter aircraft. Cass was also forced by the Germans to try to identify the remains of the flight crew from the body parts strewn around the wreckage—a most gruesome task! Only two men were identified, neither of whom was my uncle.

I have an air mail letter from Cass Antonek addressed to my father, Flight Sergeant Gordon Wallace Ross, when he was stationed in Ottawa. On the accompanying air mail envelope is, ironically, an 8¢ postage stamp featuring an airplane. The envelope is postmarked from Newark, New Jersey and dated July 2, 1945, less than four months after Donald Ross, my uncle and namesake went missing in action at only twenty-nine years of age. I recall as a very young child (perhaps six or eight years old) that Cass Antonek visited our home on Rykert Crescent in Leaside in the mid-1950s.

My Uncle Don had married Catherine (Kay) Mary Robertson on July 12, 1942 before going overseas. In July, 1944, his daughter, Beverley Dawn Ross, was born. Uncle Don did not live to see his beautiful blonde-haired, blue-eyed daughter before his plane went down. In the wake of his supreme sacrifice, Donald Alexander Ross left a devastated wife, a daughter without a father and a grief-stricken family of parents and siblings. He gave his life for his country and left a legacy of remembrance through generations. I am extremely proud to have been named after him. I have, from the family archives, several letters sent by my Uncle Don to my father in the months leading up to his tragic death and these help me to feel like I know him.

Now fast forwarding almost 70 years after my Uncle Don's death, I was able, with the willing and able assistance of my cousin Bev—yes, my Uncle Don's daughter—to identify a seven generation Ross lineage that spans 179 years. It reaches back to the birth of my great-great-grandparents in 1834 and 1846 and moves forward to my four grandchildren today in 2014.

My paternal great-grandparents and their families

My great-grandfather on my father's side was Alexander Christie Ross who was born in 1846 in Scotland and was a wool spinner. He married Mary McCulloch in Aberdeen and at some point they moved near Glasgow in order to gain employment in the wool mills. Mary had been born in Dunblane, Perthshire, Scotland, in either 1852 or 1854, depending on which records one believes. Economic times were tough in Scotland though, and in 1881 Alexander and Mary immigrated with their three children to Harrisville, New Hampshire, to obtain work in its renowned wool mills. They didn't spend all of their time working however, as they had four more children while in the United States!

In 1888, the family again immigrated, this time to Toronto, where work was again secured in the wool industry. Fertile ground was again found, as they produced three more babies before calling it a day after 10 children! The Toronto census records of 1901 show that the family was of the Presbyterian faith and that my great-grandfather made the whopping sum of $780 in the previous year! I know money went farther then, but still…

Alexander Ross died of La Grippe and a "failure of compensation of the heart" in 1909 at age 63. An interesting historical footnote is that his wife, my great-grandmother, Mary McCulloch, who lived into her 80s, acted as a mid-wife, and in later years became president of the Women's Christian Temperance Union in Toronto!

My grandfather, Bruce Dow Ross, was the first Ross born in Canada—

in Toronto on December 15, 1889, to be precise. The 1911 Toronto census indicates that Bruce was employed as a "Lamplighter for the City" and as a "Census taker". And indeed, his signature does appear on the top of the 1911 Census page that enumerates his own family. Today, that may be considered a conflict of interest! On January 20, 1915 Bruce married Mary Elsie Virgo in Toronto. My grandmother (Elsie, as she was called) was the daughter of William George Virgo (1862 – 1926) and Maria (pronounced Mariah) Danby, born in 1866 – both born in Toronto. And they too had ten children!

So, both my grandfather and grandmother had nine siblings! William Virgo was a fruit peddler and owned a horse and wagon. He bit the dust (literally) when he fell off his fruit wagon and sustained a head injury! Maria came from United Empire Loyalist stock and the famous Pillsbury family (think Pillsbury Doughboy) in the United States. And, apparently, going way back to the 1600s, one of our ancestors was a witch accuser in the Salem, Massachusetts witch trials! George Edwin Virgo, my great-great-grandfather and father of William George Virgo, was born in 1834 in Gloucester, England in either Awre or Alveston and immigrated to Canada in 1861.

Historically, large families were the norm 100 years ago, although family sizes started to reduce somewhat heading into the 20th century. Surviving infancy was not by any means a "slam dunk" in those early days of limited medical capabilities. My grandparents, Bruce and Elsie Ross, had six children who survived infancy—three sons and three daughters, including my dad and Uncle Don. My three aunts were Jean, Margaret (Marg) and Shirley. My dear Aunt Jean is living in Ottawa and she is the only one of the six children who is still living today. She's 92 years old.

Aunt Jean was able to offer me a few tidbits of information for this undertaking. For example, my grandmother, Elsie, had a reputation as a wonderful cook and passed these stellar attributes on to her daughters. Grandma Ross, as I recall her being referred to, was particularly renown for her Ross shortbread which she served at Christmas and her sausage rolls which she brought to the family reunions which were held occasionally at a farm in Agincourt, now a part of Toronto. Aunt Jean also notes Grandma Ross' culinary skills included a mean goulash. A

Sunday noon meal was always prepared by Grandma Ross while the rest of the family attended church. Then, later in the day, she hustled off to service at St. John's Presbyterian Church.

Much to my surprise, when I recently visited my Aunt Jean at her seniors home in Ottawa near her daughter, Dianne Tomkins' home, she rattled off the street addresses of 93 Kingsmount Park Road and 290 Glengrove Road in Toronto as two of the family residences in the 1930s and 1940s. Aunt Jean recalled visiting her grandmother, Maria (Danby) Virgo, at her Woodbine Avenue home in the east end of Toronto as a child. In the summer, Jean and her friends would change there and go swimming at Woodbine Beach in Lake Ontario which was very close by. And, she laughingly recalled how she and her friends would make their way up to the third floor attic of Grandma Virgo's house in order to secure an excellent vantage point from which to watch the thoroughbred horses race around the Woodbine Racetrack in the Queen's Plate!

My grandfather, Bruce Dow Ross

My great grandmother, Mary McCulloch Ross (Circa 1939)

**My father, Gordon Wallace Ross, his sister, Shirley, my paternal
grandparents, Bruce and Elsie (Virgo) Ross (Circa 1941)**

Grandpa Ross (Bruce) had spent over 30 years working for Rexall
Drugs, starting as a stock boy and working up to vice-president at the
time of his death at age 61. It is my Aunt Jean's opinion that her
father's (my grandfather's) death was hastened by the devastating loss
of his eldest son, Don, in World War II—a not uncommon toll that the
war kept taking years after it officially ended!

My maternal great-grandparents and family

I have less history on my mother's side of the family—the Waters—but
what I do have is again very much thanks to my cousin, Bev Raino,
who knows her way around the ancestry research process after doing
so much work on the Ross family. With Bev's touch on a computer,
birth and marriage certificates, immigration documents and census data
from a century ago appeared as if by magic to this not so tech-savvy
writer, furnishing me with specific dates and some fundamental

information on our Waters ancestors.

Because of the very special relationship that I had with my grandfather, Reg Waters, I have devoted a whole chapter on my "Poppa", as we lovingly called him. He greatly influenced me, particularly as a young boy. This account comes later in my memoirs.

Reginald Joseph Waters was born on April 9, 1894 to William Frederick Waters (b. 1861) and Sarah Louisa Philpott (b. 1862). Reg was one of two sons and two daughters, all born in England. However, the interesting fact is that each of the four children was born in a different town within a 10 year span. Emily was born in 1891 in Henshaw, Middlesex; Charles was born in Leeds, Yorkshire in 1893; Reg was born in 1894 in Manchester; and Olive was the last to be born, a footnote, in Folkstone, Kent in 1901. So, for whatever reason, presumably work, the family moved around a great deal. My grandfather and his sisters immigrated to Canada in 1904 from Folkstone, England and arrived together in Toronto when Reg was ten years old.

The 1911 census shows my grandfather as a Toronto Centre resident and at 16 he had a full-time job as a bell boy in a hotel. In fact he worked 60 hours a week and made $314 in total annual wages in 1910. His father, William, worked as a cabdriver and earned $384 in the same year, while his older brother, Charlie, worked as a labourer on a boat. All of the men worked to generate household income while Louisa, my great-grandmother, looked after the household, and the girls attended school. On May 12, 1916 Reg married Blanche Mary McDonald. Reg was 22 and Blanche was 23. On their marriage certificate Reg listed his occupation as "Traveller", whatever that meant, and Blanche listed her address as 15 Spruce Street in downtown Toronto near Yonge and Gerrard Streets.

Blanche, my "Nana" as we lovingly called her, was born on November 19, 1892 exactly 9 ½ months after her parents were married (February 9, 1892). What else are you going to do when you get married in the middle of a bitterly cold Canadian winter! Blanche's father, James McDonald, born on Christmas day in 1863, was a blacksmith by trade from Amaranth, Ontario, northwest of Orangeville and had an income of $575 according to the census of 1900. Her mother was Nellie (Ellen) and she was born on St. Patrick's Day, 1871—most fitting for an Irish lass whose parents had emigrated from Ireland. How novel that both of my great-grandparents celebrated their birthdays on special holidays!

My maternal grandparents, Reg and Blanche (McDonald) Waters (circa 1928)

My grandmother Blanche Waters, my great grandmother, Nellie McDonald, and my mother Norma Ellen Waters (Circa 1934)

My grandmother, Blanche McDonald (centre) with her father, my great grandfather, James McDonald, along with her siblings (Circa 1912)

Over 40 years ago, Poppa, knowing how much I appreciated antiques and all things historical, presented me with my great-grandfather's cigar box which has his initials "*J. McD*" inscribed on the lid. But the real treasure was in the cigar box. There lay James McDonald's pocket watch and fob, handed down to Reg by his father-in-law. Now, that is truly a special gift that I was entrusted with. It is much cherished and will be handed down as a family heirloom for future generations.

My great grandfather, James McDonald's pocket watch and cigar case with his engraved initials

"A Whole New World"
Peabo Bryson and Regina Belle, 1992

Backtracking a little from my birthday of July 9, 1948, my parents, Gordon Wallace Ross and Norma Ellen Waters, who had grown up in the balmy Beach area of Toronto had married on March 21, 1942 at Glenmount United Church in Toronto. Dad was twenty-three and Mom was twenty-four. I have both their marriage certificate and their marriage vows contained in their marriage book, which also includes the signatures of all of the wedding guests, a rather unique and historical family document. Mom and Dad enjoyed a brief honeymoon in Montreal at the Hotel de la Salle. Their total bill, which I have, for their three night weekend stay was a whopping $12.40!

Now, let me set the stage for readers who are younger than I, which will likely be most of you. In 1948, the year that I was born, William Lyon Mackenzie King was our Prime Minister and Harry S. Truman was the U.S. President. Queen Elizabeth II gave birth to her first son, Charles, currently heir to the throne of England. Our average life expectancy was only 62.9 years. The average income was $2,936 and a new house cost $7,700! A movie ticket cost 60¢, gas was 16¢ per gallon and bread was 14¢ per loaf. Fewer than 100,000 households in our country owned TV sets, and in 1948 a prototype machine used the first ever stored computer program.

Also in 1948, the Toronto Maple Leafs won the Stanley Cup (oh, for the good old days!), the Calgary Stampeders won the Grey Cup and Ben Hogan was the U.S. Open Golf champion. Dinah Shore and Nat King Cole topped the music charts. Columbia Records introduced a 33⅓ rpm vinyl record with a whopping 30 minutes of music on each side! Orson Welles, Humphrey Bogart, Lauren Bacall and Rita Hayworth lit up the movie screens with *Key Largo* and *Citizen Kane* as the top box office contenders.

I was raised in Toronto and first resided as an infant at 78 Highcroft Road in the east end with my parents and grandparents. I naturally have no memories of my early years until my parents bought their first home at 4 Astor Avenue in a newly developed east end suburb called

Leaside in 1949. They bought the house that cornered on Moore Avenue with savings my father sent home when he was in the Air Force during the war. That tiny little bungalow was demolished in the 1990s, and in its place was constructed one of the first new large rebuilds that spearheaded a trend of individual home redevelopment among the now highly desirable and expensive Leaside properties.

My very first friend was Peter Hishon who lived next door to us on Astor Avenue. As we were one of the first families in the neighbourhood to have a television, with all of three channels that were just black and white, of course, our house did become a repository for four year olds watching the likes of Howdy Doody Time, Hop-a-long Cassidy, The Cisco Kid, Bugs Bunny and Superman.

My only sibling, Allan Bruce Ross, was born on June 25, 1952, also in Toronto East General Hospital. Four years my junior, Al was named after my mother's brother, Allan Waters. Bruce was our paternal grandfather's name (Bruce Dow Ross), a great Scottish name which resonates with our Scottish ancestry. Both my brother and I became part of that famous cultural phenomenon, Leading-Edge Baby Boomers, babies born in the post-war era from 1947–1956. Boomers grew up in a time of dramatic social change—political unrest, the walk on the moon, anti-war protests, the civil rights movement, sexual freedom, drug experimentation and Woodstock. Baby boomers found that their music, most notably rock and roll, was an expression of their generational identity. We are now becoming senior citizens!

As many backyard Astor Avenue and later Rykert Crescent family photos will show, our family socialized a great deal with my aunts, uncles and cousins. On my father's side were his sisters Jean, Marg and Shirley. Marg lived in Kingston, Ontario, with her husband, Bob Roantree. So, while we didn't see them as much, we did still visit back and forth occasionally in either Kingston or Toronto. My three Roantree cousins, Doug, Nancy and Rob, still live in the Kingston and Morton area today.

Grandma Ross, me, Poppa and Nana in the backyard of our Astor Avenue home

We did see more of Aunt Jean and Uncle Murray (Longbottom), and their children (my cousins, Dianne, Carol and Ross) as we grew up. Dianne and Carol were the same ages as my brother and me. Ross was the youngster. Dad's youngest sister, Shirley, married Ron Kampers and they added two more cousins (Steve and Elaine) as playmates for my brother and me. The families were close and getting together was always fun.

We were equally close with the Waters on the other side of the family, but Mom just had one sibling. How times have changed over the generations!

My mother's brother, Al, and his wife, Marge, married in 1942 before Al went to war. Notably, my Uncle Al was a radio technician in World War II which piqued his interest in electronic media and predicted his venture into business entrepreneurship and future success in building a renowned Canada-wide radio and television empire called CHUM.

Al and Marge had three children, Sherry and Jim (who corresponded in age to my brother and me) and Ron. Being together for Christmases, birthdays, Easter and other social events was a must. Our families frequently alternated Sunday dinners at each other's houses. As kids, we had great times playing together. Sherry and I laughingly remember, after Sunday dinners, dressing up in our parents' clothes and acting out skits while the parents howled! And so the importance of family and family relationships was ingrained in my brother and me from an early age. My nine cousins on the Ross side and three cousins on the Waters side went on to have over 20 children between them (my second cousins) and they in turn have already produced several children to date.

My cousin Sherry and me at our Astor Avenue home in 1951

Riding my tricycle

"Those Were The Days"
Mary Hopkins, 1968

In 1952, the year my brother was born, my parents decided that they needed a larger home for their growing family. As they liked Leaside they bought a home at 80 Rykert Crescent which backed on to the Don Valley in the north end of the community. It was a typical two storey home of the time in a burgeoning area of Toronto. That was to remain our family home until 1966, remembered fondly to this day as my childhood family home, teeming with many great memories for me as I grew from a young boy of four into a young man of seventeen.

Leaside, and particularly Rykert Crescent, was a very close community. It was clearly very WASPish (White Anglo-Saxon Protestant), as was all of Toronto at that time, for the city did not begin to transform itself into one of the most culturally diverse and cosmopolitan urban centres in North America until the 1970s. Culturally, ethnically and religiously, all Leaside families had much in common.

All of the families had young children, and we all formed great friendships, many of which continue to this day. I was good friends with Frank Hewick, Geordie Colvin, Kenny Stephens, Maureen Kempston, Jim Beagley and Heather Moore, to mention a few. We all got along and played together. At Trace Manes Park we skated on the outdoor rinks in winter and played baseball in summer. We tobogganed and skated. Playing ball hockey or football on the street and yelling "car-r-r!" was the norm.

We went to church together; we played in the "wilds" of the Don Valley; we went to Cubs and Scouts together. That's where I met Doug Magee and Bill Devitt, friends still to this day. And there was a great tobogganing hill at the top of our street where every winter day after school at 4:00 kids from all around the neighbourhood would congregate. We'd bring sleds, flattened cardboard boxes and garbage tin lids and hurtle down the long incline to the valley floor until darkness descended, often flying through brush and snow to be disgorged in a tangle of bodies at the bottom. Great sport!

My parents, my brother, Allan, and me

Our Rykert Cresent home in Leaside

As first a Cub and later a Scout, we sold Christmas trees door to door every year for $2.50/each as a fund-raiser. And these Christmas trees were far from the perfected shapes of today. They were Scotch pine, not spruce, and the object was to find a tree without too many glaring gaps in the branches. I remember one year having to repeatedly keep sawing the bottom of the trunk at unusual angles in order for the tree to fit in the base to give the illusion that the tree was straight. That ended up being one of the shorter Christmas trees we ever had! And, decorating the tree often helped develop my creative skills, as I had to strategically hang ornaments to fill in the gaping bare spots that were always evident once the tree branches fell out!

Usually, we ended up having to place the tree in a corner of the recreation room so that we could tie it to each wall with fishing line, lest it topple over. And when the Scotch pines dried out by New Year's, their long five-in-a-cluster needles felt just like steel needles as they pierced our hands when we took down the tree. I suppose there's something to be said for the perfect shapes, straight trunks, soft needles and conservation arguments of today's artificial trees, but they definitely don't have the fragrance and reality of bringing the woodsy outdoors inside! However, I don't miss my hands looking like I have measles from the thorny jabs of the sharp needles after taking down the tree.

After Christmas we built forts out of the discarded Christmas trees which we collected from around the neighbourhood, dragging them to our backyard and playing in them until they became too prickly as they dried out. Then we waited and watched the forts until spring when rabbits would make a home and a family of bunnies appeared.

Allan, Dad, and me

As I have mentioned, we were still one of the first families on our street to have a black and white TV, although within a few years the number of channels had doubled to six! And we certainly didn't mind that we had to get up off the couch to change the channel manually! We were also one of the first families to get a colour TV in the early 1960s. There were no such things as flat screens, computers, iPads, cell phones, microwaves, or even fax machines. I remember the telephone number of our old rotary dial telephone as being first Mayfair, and then Hudson 5-2141. We rarely called long distance, as the charges were very high, unless one called after 11:00 p.m. Instead we wrote letters in longhand on paper (not on a computer). It took a week for mail delivery and another week to get a response, assuming the recipient wrote back immediately, and the letter didn't get lost in the mail! In the 1960s this was our generation's version of texting!

Imagine…every home received daily milk delivery! You left your empty glass milk bottles in the milk box built into the side of your house by the side door and the milk man left you your standard daily order. There was a bread truck that came around selling breads and other related products, and I recall fruit trucks as well. The "Ding Dong" man walked the streets to sharpen knives, ringing his clanging bell as he approached. And all children looked forward with wild anticipation to ice cream and Popsicle trucks and bicycle carts which came by in the summers! Everyone shopped at individual retailers or went downtown to shop at the Eaton's or Simpson's department stores until Yorkdale became the first large indoor shopping mall in Canada in the mid-1960s.

My dad had always been in advertising and sales promotion. After his discharge from the war in 1945, and at the urging of his father, my dad joined Planned Sales Limited as a sales rep. He was promoted to General Sales Manager in 1954 and by 1958 he had been promoted to Executive Vice-President in charge of a staff of 40. In 1961 he moved to Individual Sales as Vice-President and General Manager and became its President in 1969. Dad personally handled the "big league" accounts of such business icons as American Airlines, American Motors, BP Oil, Goodyear Tire and Rubber, Labatt's Breweries, Laura Secord Candy, Motorola, Reynolds Aluminum, Tamblyns, Uniroyal , Warner Lambert and Xerox. Name brand products such as Dr. Ballard's pet food, Noxema creams, Arrow shirts, Planters Peanuts, Bayer Aspirin and Philips Milk of Magnesia were all part of the portfolio.

Dad preparing an advertising pitch

The current TV series, Mad Men, nails how the advertising business operated in those times. It was a time that I've never seen the likes of, or the camaraderie of, since! Between spending time with friends in their social circle and entertaining Dad's clients, it never seemed that a week went by that my parents didn't go out for dinners at restaurants, attend cocktail parties, go to dances at the Royal York Hotel, or host parties and dinners—it was all a part of their life and the times! Friends, neighbours and relatives always looked forward to their annual Christmas Eve party. As they say, a good time was always had by all. This tradition started in the late '50s and continued for over 20 years until my father's death in 1979.

Times were different then. It was a rare exception if a mother worked outside of the home in those days. Mom did all of the shopping, laundry and house cleaning, although at times we had a cleaning lady. But, moms played bridge, belonged to a bowling league, joined the Parents-Teachers Association, did church work and helped out in the community, and as well took primary responsibility for raising the children. Every Thursday about 3:45 p.m. when I arrived home from school, I would look on our street to see where all the cars were parked. That's how I knew where the ladies were having "tea" after attending their Thursday afternoon bowling league activities on Eglinton Avenue. I would trudge up to the neighbour's door to get our key from Mom to let myself in our house. Dad "brought home the bacon".

I hated to get dressed up in a suit and go to church every Sunday at Northlea United Church. Nothing against church—I just hated to get dressed in a suit. To this day I hate tight collars and shirt cuffs and can't even abide wearing a ring! I always maintained that church attendance would increase if they relaxed the dress code; but, I never won that argument. Kids never talked back to their parents in the 1950s. Parents were firm disciplinarians—always. "Spare the rod and spoil the child," was the mantra.

My first good buddy, Peter Hishon, and me, 1954

Dad, Mom, Allan and me – ready for church! 1955

Speaking of which, I received more than one spanking from my parents in my childhood, and I was a pretty well-behaved kid who didn't get into trouble often. Although once, for some unfathomable reason, I threw catsup on my mother's nightgown that was hanging on the clothes line to dry. Mom definitely was not amused, and I did get a deservedly harsh spanking for that little infraction. Give a spanking today and Children's Aid would be called in! Go figure! But, I got the message, and the spanking certainly didn't cause me any psychological damage (I don't think)!

There were a couple of times when a legitimate case of mistaken identity got me into trouble. They say everyone has a double somewhere in the world. Wouldn't you know that mine lived down the street! Alan Smith and I looked so much alike that we were often mistaken for each other. He was a bit of a trouble maker so that didn't help my rep any!

I attended and enjoyed Northlea Public School (Kindergarten – Grade 8) from age 5 - 13. I was a good academic student, usually with a 75 – 80% average. I well remember each and every one of my grade school teachers, such as Miss Harris, Miss Reesor, Miss McAnless, Miss Hall, Miss McIntyre, Miss Laidlaw and especially my Grade 8 teacher, the much feared Louise Mackenzie. Most of the teachers seemed to be spinsters in those days. And then there was the principal, Mr. Wright, who all of the students called "Lefty". I fondly remember meeting my Grade 4 teacher, Miss McIntyre, when I returned as an adult 35 years later for Northlea's 50th reunion. When I asked if she knew who I was I was dumbfounded by her response as she, without hesitation, replied, "Of course, Don, and how's your brother, Allan?"

I participated in track and field, volleyball and the choir, although I had a terrible voice. I remember with embarrassment the year my voice changed, as I tried to quietly croak out the harmonies. Often at noon we would hurry home for lunch, which was about a one mile walk, down a quick bite, and rush back to school for 12:45 p.m. for choir practice or to watch movies featuring Abbott and Costello and The Three Stooges in the gym before school started again at 1:30. Occasionally though, I would go around the corner to my grandmother's house at 104 Donlea Drive for lunch. This I loved. Her house backed on to the school grounds so I was never late returning for afternoon classes. That was a big improvement over walking a mile each way to and from home for lunch, which is what I usually did.

Starting in Grade 8, our class had our own dance parties every couple of weeks with each student taking turns at hosting. We jived to the likes of Bobby Vee, Freddie Cannon, Neil Sedaka and Dion and slow danced to Bert Kempfert, The Highwaymen, Paul Anka and The Shirelles. We threw ourselves into all the latest dance crazes such as The Twist, the Mashed Potato, the Bristol Stomp and The Locomotion.

But, our parties were nothing compared to the partying that our parents did! Saturday night parties rotated around the neighbourhood. Betty and Max Strang, Connie and Bob Burgess (my mom used to hide the Scotch from Bob), Betty and Somerville (Brownie) Brown, Len and Div Brooks, Ham and Agnes Mateer, Cliff and Muriel Moore, Bill and Flori Fraser, George and Bea Jeffrey, Jack and Marg Beagley, Bob and Grace Miller, and the list goes on. Hard alcohol was the drinking norm, and consumption was frequent and generous. What would my great-grandmother, Mary McCulloch, President of the Christian

Temperance Union have thought of these goings on?

The Ross', Pearces, Browns and Moores partying! 1959

"Those Lazy Hazy Crazy Days Of Summer"
Nat King Cole, 1963

Before we had the cottage, our family took summer vacations in "cottage country". Actually, my grandparents (on the Waters side) started this tradition, usually renting a cottage in July with their kids (my parents) at Thurstonia Beach on Sturgeon Lake as early as the 1930s. They went on to frequent Birch Point Lodge in Haliburton from the 1940s to the 1950s, as did my parents (then young adults) from the 1940s on. Mom and Dad met Cy and Isobel Pearce at Birch Point Lodge in the 1940s, as well as Marge and Bill Brown, and they all became lifelong friends. They were like aunts and uncles to my brother and me as (unusual for the times) they didn't have children themselves.

Mom and Dad at Birch Point Lodge, 1945

Mom and Dad always rented a cottage for the month of July each year, so my brother and I were introduced to cottage life from infancy. My earliest recollection is at a summer cottage on the water at Jackson's Point on Lake Simcoe. Perhaps I was about seven at the time. What comes to mind more are the two cottages we rented on Snake Island off Island Grove on Lake Simcoe when I was eight, nine and ten years old.

The first cottage that we rented on Snake Island was from the Johnson family in 1956. The Johnson cottage was on the island about a half mile from the mainland, facing the mainland. You always had to prearrange for a water taxi to take you over, or pick you up. Of course, there were no phones on the island. Great summers ensued with the next door neighbours' kids, the Colemans.

I was really into playing with my "men". These were 2" high toy figures modeled in plastic or tin after western cowboys, soldiers, Indians and frontiersmen—the equivalent today of Star Wars, Teenage Mutant Ninja Turtles, and Marvel comic characters. Davy Crockett (King of the Wild Frontier) and his band of men, accompanied by the requisite palisade and battlements, was my favourite set. One day, while building a fort for my men, I fell and a big rusty nail went through my knee. I was literally wounded in battle at The Alamo. Somehow we raised the water taxi and got me into the Sutton hospital to get me patched up.

Me on my raft at Snake Island

There was one terribly stormy day when a sea plane made an emergency landing in the middle of the night. My parents were roused by the pilot banging on the door, asking for assistance. He was out in the wild weather battling driving rain and fierce winds trying to tie down the plane to our little dock so it wouldn't break up on the rocky shore. After the storm had passed the next morning, my brother and I were allowed to explore the fascinating bubble-like cockpit of the Seabee amphibian. The pilot was most appreciative that our family had helped to save his plane. At last he hopped into his seaplane, taxied out into the channel, turned the plane into the wind, and then, after the boat traffic had cleared, set the prop to maximum pitch. The engine came alive with a deafening roar as the plane leapt forward, gaining speed to get airborne. The pilot, named Ray, circled around and dipped his wings in salute and farewell to the good Samaritans below. Two weeks later Ray showed up at our home with a crystal vase—a thank you gift to my parents.

And, it was on Snake Island where my father built the family picnic table for the backyard of our new home on Rykert Crescent in Leaside. The lumber was transported over to the island by water taxi where my father first assembled and then disassembled the picnic table. Then he transported it back the same way to the mainland, and reassembled it at home. It sat under our backyard cherry tree for a few years until it was reclaimed when our own Haliburton cottage was built. Dad refinished the picnic table and it remains in use as the cottage dining room table today—over 55 years later!

The following year we rented a cottage on the other side of Snake Island next door to the Brooks, our neighbours on Rykert. This one had a boathouse with sleeping quarters over it and a basket full of comics. I was a voracious reader as a youth and lived in that boathouse reading comics and adventure books I had brought from the library. What a fantastic getaway to hide in up over the water—waves lapping at the shore below, wind whistling through the maples and birches! It was secluded, private…my own domain. What an adventure for a nine year old!

It was also that summer at the island sand pit, under the unfortunate influence of Brad Brooks, a thirteen year old, that I smoked my first cigarette. I was certainly green in more ways than one! It reminds me of the line from the song, *"It's My Life"*, by The Animals: "I smoked my first cigarette at 10, and for girls I had a bad yen." I was a bit young for that last part though.

It was Mr. Brooks who, a few years later, let me drive his car on the highway in Haliburton, before I ever had any kind of Beginners Permit license. I hadn't even had a lesson; he just said, "Here, you take a turn." It wasn't long after that Mrs. Brooks shocked our street by committing suicide by placing a plastic bag over her head one afternoon at home. A few months later, Mr. Brooks, who could not bear to go on without her, also committed suicide, using a gun in his car by the side of the road near Island Grove, leaving money on the top of his dresser to cover the funeral! How that double tragedy of an endearing couple shook the idyllic life of Rykert Crescent!

The Brooks tragedy was not the only one to befall a Rykert family though. One morning when I was eight, my dad came into my bedroom to tell me that our neighbours, the Carruthers, had had a tragic event occur. Their three year old boy, Brian, nicknamed Pudgy, had fallen off a dock into the lake and drowned. This, unfortunately, was not the end of the tragedies for the Carruthers as many years later, their son, Ian, a Rhodes Scholar no less, committed suicide. He was 21. That left them one remaining child, their daughter, Margo.

Our third summer on Snake Island we travelled back to the Johnson place facing the mainland. By then, our parents would let us walk down the road towards the far end of the island to a small convenience store for a candy bar—a mysterious "hole in the wall' run by the natives—our first exposure to an "Indian".

My parents' best friends, Cy and Isobel Pearce, always came up for a weekend or two. One day when we were fishing, I inadvertently dropped the stringer full of bass and perch over the side. Dad and Cy were not impressed. Another time, my dad was casting and the whole rod flew out of his hand into very deep water. Again, he was none too pleased; but, I, at least, had nothing to do with that one. Cy, the ever persistent and thrifty Scotsman, didn't give up that easily and insisted they troll back and forth to try and retrieve the rod. And they did hook it, reeling it back in. Definitely the catch of the day!

Continuing occasional weekend visits to Birch Point Lodge, my
parents' love affair with the Haliburton area continued to flourish.
They would rent one of the lakeside cabins that had dark brown wood
siding. There was nothing fancy about the cabins; but, the lodge meals
were something else! As a family-run lodge, the owners Jean and Earl
Casey believed in lots of good home-cooked food. Bowls of food were
served to your designated family table, and, as you sat on the
uncomfortable carved spindle chairs, which you didn't mind at all
doing, you helped yourself to heaping piles of roast beef, turkey, ham,
or whatever was being served for dinner—as much as you could eat!
Delectable main dishes were complemented with plenty of mashed
potatoes, gravy, vegetables, homemade rolls, pies and tarts. Cookies
were served in the lounge every night at 10:00. We never went to bed
hungry!

Poppa and Nana at Birch Point Lodge

Lake Simcoe never became a summer retreat option again as the rugged
beauty of the Haliburton Highlands was too beckoning to my parents.
For three consecutive Julys in 1959, 1960 and 1961, our family rented

the Wynn-Jones cottage on the Donarvon Road on Boshkung Lake. The Pearces shared the cottage for two weeks each year. Our retreat was a three bedroom cottage that came with a nice cedar strip boat for fishing, which the men did frequently.

Cottage life was taking shape for the Ross family. We had three fun summers with lots of fishing, swimming, boating and BBQing. We would trek down the road to get buckets of spring water. My dad worked in the city during the week for the first two weeks of our month's vacation and then took his holidays. We would walk down the road and across the highway to the one Bell telephone in the area on Thursday nights to call my dad and give him a list of what to bring up on Friday. My parents would often invite friends up for the weekend, a trend that really moved into high gear when we built our own cottage.

In July, 1962, we stayed at Hart Lodge on Hwy. # 35 beside Mountain Lake in Haliburton for two weeks. This was the last rental summer vacation our family took before our cottage was built. We took trips over to our cottage lot about 25 minutes away to start clearing the beach and casting an eye as to the exact site and positioning for the new structure. Little did I know at the time, when we were staying at Hart Lodge, that directly across the lake, and well within sight, was Harold and Phyllis Gould's cottage, and their neighbours and good friends, the Gadways. Only a few years later our paths would cross and be a major turning point in my life's journey!

Our family up north at Thanksgiving

"Hello Muddah, Hello Fadduh"
Allan Sherman, 1963

My parents thought it would be a good idea for me, as a young boy, to go away to an overnight boys' camp for a couple of weeks in the summer. They didn't ask me; they just decided. The first time I went I was nine years old and it was 1957. To their credit, they hatched a plan whereby I went with a school friend, Neil Hollingshead. This part was good, as Neil and I were good friends and in Cubs together. However, being born under the sign of Cancer, I am a home and hearth kind of person, and was shy and introverted at that age.

I still remember being driven north to Big Doe Camp on Big Doe Lake near Burk's Falls in Muskoka. And then my parents left me alone for the first time in my life, and for two whole weeks! I quickly learned the meaning of homesickness. I was desperately unhappy and so miserable that I just wanted to go home. I remember looking down the road every day in hopes of seeing my parents drive in for me. This was the first time in my young life that I had really faced change and being on my own, and I didn't like it one bit! But, I stuck it out, suffered in silence and started to participate in activities that I had never tried before.

There was horseback riding, canoeing, archery, riflery, swimming, arts and crafts, water skiing and nature lore. I believe Tuck Shop was my favourite. While we had assigned programs in the morning, I chose my favorites of archery, riflery and canoeing whenever I could from the optional activities offered in the afternoon.

What I didn't like was being roused out of bed every morning at 7:00 a.m., along with the 100 other campers, to the sound of a bugle blasting morning reveille. We all had to assemble by cabin number on the central camp grounds in the morning mist for morning ablutions and then charge into the lake skinny for our daily cleansing. I still to this day will only go in the lake when I am very hot, the water is very hot and the air is very hot!

That first year I was assigned to Cabin #6 and my counsellor was a wonderfully compassionate Japanese fellow named Ron (to whom I felt very attached) who helped me to get through my homesickness. I remember arriving home at Union Station by train and proudly introducing my new friend, Ron, to my parents.

Big Doe Camp had a huge impact on me, and not just in a negative way! In particular, I quickly developed a passion for canoeing which has carried on my whole life and which is my preferred conveyance on water. It is so quiet and peaceful on a lake in the placid calm of morning before the wind comes up. I deftly paddle through the lily pads and around the submerged logs of marshlands.

As a teenager, I became quite adept at gunnel bobbing, the rather gymnastic feat of standing on the gunnels of the canoe, using a gently rocking (up and down) motion to propel the canoe forward—an extremely tricky balancing act. And then, other times, balancing carefully, and with the sun just right, I would stand in the canoe which allowed me a glimpse of a large musky lying in the shallow waters close under the sprawling branches of the low hanging willows.

But what I really love most about canoeing is fishing, especially, casting into the shallows for bass. I love the challenge of using a spinning rod to cast with precision beside a clump of lily pads, a dock or a fallen tree. And I love the bang and splash when I occasionally get a strike.

Aside from being introduced at camp to homesickness and canoeing (as well as many enjoyable camp activities that I might never otherwise have had the opportunity to experience) I got over my horrible fear of putting my head under water. Where that seemingly unfounded fear originated from, considering my cottaging experience, I have absolutely no idea to this day. When I arrived at Big Doe Camp, I was petrified to hear that swimming lessons, including bobbing and diving, were mandatory activities! I couldn't swim a stroke and putting my head under water was just not something I could do. However, you didn't say "no" to the fear inspiring camp director, Aubrey, and after two weeks I had earned my Beginners Swimming Certificate. My parents were astounded. They just couldn't believe it, as they stared at each other with jaws dropped!

My friend Neil, a new camper friend and me at Big Doe Camp, 1957

I will never forget how the camp song sung to the tune of *Bye, Bye Black Bird* immortalized the feared camp director.

> Pack up all my beer and fags
> Here we go, down the Mag
> Bye, Bye, Big Doe.
>
> Where somebody waits for me
> Glen Bernard, yes sir-ee!
> Bye, Bye Big Doe.
>
> No one here can love and understand me,
> Least of all the camp director, Aubrey.
> Make my bed and light the light,
> I'll be home late tonight.
> Big Doe…Bye, Bye.

I went to Big Doe Camp for four more years until I was thirteen. Each year I enjoyed the experience more and more, particularly the three day canoe trip called The Mag. We headed down the Magnetawan River through Burk's Falls and Lake Cecebe, camping at Hobo Junction by the railway trestle, and ending at the historic village of Magnetawan.

By my last year, I was actually quite sad to leave at the end of the two weeks, knowing that I would never return, for our cottage in Haliburton was about to be built that fall. Each year, I earned a more advanced swimming certificate—Junior, Intermediate, Senior, and then in the last year I was learning Life Saving. And, I had received my Senior Certificate at the youngest age allowed! I'd come a long way! Ironically, as I write my memoirs 52 years later, I have just received another senior's designation, except this time for an entirely different reason!

Big Doe Camp was founded in 1946 by Aubrey and Marjorie Rhamey and was operated by the family for more than 50 years. Often the Camp did not break even, but for them it was as much about giving back to the community and helping boys grow into young men. Sadly, Big Doe Camp closed its doors in 1998.

"Oh! My Papa!"
Eddie Fisher, 1953

I remember nothing about my paternal grandfather, Bruce Dow Ross, as I was only two when he died. And all I recall about my paternal grandmother, Mary Elsie (Virgo) Ross, who passed away when I was 8, were the times that I went around the corner from the school to have a lunch she prepared for me. However, I do know that every time I went there I thought that it was great sport to hide the toothbrushes in the towels in the bathroom closet.

I was, however, fortunate enough to know my maternal grandfather, Reg Waters—my Poppa—well into adulthood. I adored Poppa. He was everything you could imagine in a grandfather, the one family figure I regret my own children never had. We had wonderful times together. I was his first grandson, and I know that I was special to him.

I would occasionally stay at my grandparents' home for weekends and these trips were always great adventures for me. On a Friday afternoon I would await Poppa's arrival in wild anticipation of all of the adventures we would have for a weekend sleepover. In the car, we would always play, "I saw it first"—a game where we each tried to spot "For Sale" signs on houses. Poppa would always purposely drive by an abandoned, gothic-looking wood frame house on Queen Street which he maintained was haunted.

Nana and Poppa had built their house in 1948 at 47 Lynndale Road down near The Beaches just south of Kingston Road and east of Victoria Park. This amazing little bungalow backed on to the spectacular Toronto Hunt Club golf course. One of the most amazing things of all about their house was the laundry chute which was hidden in a sitting room closet. I could drop all sorts of items down to land in a laundry basket placed under the chute in the basement. You can just imagine all of the household items that Nana and Poppa found missing after my visits!

One of the other places of mystery in their house was Poppa's office in the basement. It was a forerunner of today's "home office", I guess, but there was certainly no technology in evidence. Poppa would show me his "samples" that he pronounced as "somples". My grandfather was, as he liked to say, in the haberdashery business. He sold socks and ties, and men's accessories, and regaled me with his wide array of fashionable items. I particularly remember the Happy Foot brand of socks that is still around today! He knew everyone in the business and was extremely well respected.

Poppa had a sun room built on the back of the house that looked out onto a well treed backyard of pines and maples and backed onto the golf course. He beautifully hand finished the special textured and grained panelling that he had put on the sun room walls. On Friday nights the boxing matches were a must to watch on the old black and white TV in the sun room. Poppa and I would eat those little round peanuts that had to have the little skins peeled off. And weekend breakfasts were always served in the sun room to take advantage of the wonderful view of nature that the forested backyard and golf course afforded.

Pops would tell me bedtime stories that he made up, such as "The Man With No Head", and a story about his father who had been in the 96th King's Hussars in England. Once my grandparents took me to the show to see "Old Yeller", a very sad western movie in which the dog dies at the end. And, because the dog Old Yeller is covered in blood, the Ross family genetics of passing out at the sight of blood kicked in. I was so embarrassed.

I fondly remember swinging on the swing that Poppa made out of rope and a board in the backyard between two of the many pine trees. We would rake leaves together in the fall, collect acorns from the giant oak in the front yard and golf balls from the back yard, and go for walks on the Boardwalk. Each summer we would count the number of tomatoes on a single tomato plant that he always grew at the side of the house. I remember 42 tomatoes one year!

And at Christmas time, I would anxiously await that day in December when Poppa would pick me up at home and take me, and sometimes my cousin Sherry, downtown to see Santa Claus at Eaton's Department Store. I stared fascinated at all of the magnificent mechanical Christmas displays beautifully decorated in the department store windows of Eaton's and Simpson's If it sounds like something out of a 1950s' movie…well, it was. These were some of the best times of my childhood. Somehow, I actually knew it then, and I love to think back on those memories!

Poppa and Nana, 1941

My cousin, Sherry, and me at Eaton's

My grandparents home at 57 Lynndale Crescent

My maternal grandmother (my Nana) also passed away when I was young, only seven years old, and, sadly, I have only vague recollections of her. I just know that I loved her dearly the same way that I felt about my Poppa. Much to everyone's surprise (no one saw this coming) Pops remarried only a couple of years after Nana passed away. I recollect my mother reeling in shock at the news when she hung up the phone one summer day after speaking with her father. Poppa's new wife, Madeleine, was always very kind to me, but it wasn't quite the same warm fuzzy feeling as with Nana.

I cherished my time with Pops as I grew into my teens, and then into adulthood. My wife, Pam, and I went to Pops and Madeleine's for dinner, and they came to our home. When at Lynndale, we would reminisce about my childhood adventures and inevitably make our way around the house and grounds to the basement office where Pops continued to regale me with stories and still show me his latest "somples". On occasion he entrusted to my care certain old treasures as he knew I appreciated antiques. Included in these gifts were his Windsor chair, a 1920's floor lamp with a beautiful sculpted base, his father-in-law's timepiece and personalized cigar box, as mentioned earlier, as well as other odd and unique items that he had collected along the way.

Pops and Madeleine enjoyed occasional visits to our family cottage. One day Pops stood on the beach to practice casting, as his hand co-ordination and timing for release wasn't what it used to be. He flubbed a cast badly and it sailed off at a right angle landing just off shore under a tree beside the dock. We were all flabbergasted when a largemouth bass bit the lure with a resounding splash. We all laughed uproariously while he reeled in his prize.

Poppa was actually in my life longer than my own father was. I was 34 when he passed away. I was about to visit him again in hospital on the afternoon that my mother called me with the sad news. It wasn't long before that I told him on an earlier hospital visit that Pam and I were expecting our first child. He said, "That's wonderful, Don!"

Poppa with my brother, Allan, and me and my model cars

Poppa and Madeleine

Poppa lived a good life. He was much loved, and loved much. His quiet manner dovetailed with my own. He was a kind, loving soul and I never saw him lose his temper. Pops was always interested in all things about me whether it was Cubs, school or career. And he had great stories to tell! Poppa was a wonderful role model. He appreciated everyday pleasures, his family and the little things in life.

Poppa once told me in later years, "Don, everyone should have three friends in life. A friend who is older from whom you can learn, a peer of your own age with whom you can relate and enjoy camaraderie, and a much younger friend whom you can teach." He was the consummate example about what grandfathering and teaching is all about.

Towards the end, when age took its inevitable toll, our roles started to reverse, as I became more the adult and he became more the child. My grandfather had a tremendously positive influence on me, and I miss him still, as I could certainly tell by the emotion I felt as I wrote this chapter.

"Send In The Clowns"
Frank Sinatra, 1973

In my Grade 7 class, I "fell in with a bad crowd", as they say. It was "bad" only in the sense that we clowned around a lot together in class, joking and laughing uproariously. It was so much fun; my most fun year in public school. However, great fun comes at great cost, as my concentration dropped and I lost focus on my studies…my grades slipped badly. My parents were not amused, nor was my teacher, Mrs. Russell, who deserved much better, as she was one of my favourites.

To correct my errant ways, so that I could better realize my academic capabilities and not be distracted, Mrs. Russell decided that the best course was to move me into the "brain class" for Grade 8. The "brain class", as the rest of the school called it, was a group of carefully selected students who were identified out of Grade 4 as having the most aptitude (smarts) academically. The educational thinking of the time suggested that these students' collective interests would be best served by grouping them together in the same class for the balance of their public school education (Grades 5 – 8).

I reacted with horror at the prospect of being catapulted into the brain class! My academic qualifications had always been on the borderline at best—hardly qualifying me for inclusion with this group whose marks were 85 – 90% and up! My usual marks, averaging 75 – 80%, had always put me near the top of my class no matter what mix of classmates I had from year to year, and I liked that. Now I would be clearly at the bottom of the "brain class" with my lowly Grade 7 average of only 68%!

It was awful enough to feel academically inadequate to be part of that group; but, what was even worse was that, feeling socially awkward at that age, I was going to have to break into an extremely tight clique of very bright students. They were all good friends after several years of being together, and held dance parties rotating from house to house every couple of weeks! The immensity of this social challenge was almost overwhelming for me! This was the equivalent of being dropped off at Big Doe Camp alone for the first time! I was apoplectic! And, I had all summer to fret about it!

This kind of educational thinking would never be considered today to be in the best interests of a 12 year old boy, on the verge of puberty, without a careful evaluation of the student's personality, his emotional development and his relational abilities to handle such a major social change, not to mention without discussing this option with him, or his parents! This was the second major traumatic change in my life that I had been thrown into without consultation, and somehow I had to deal with it.

Fortunately, my good childhood friends—Maureen Kempston and Heather Moore—were part of the "brain class", and peripherally, I knew a few others, such as Janet Crawford and Judy Sanmiya, from church. This certainly helped facilitate my entry into this esteemed group. I was forced to put my nose to the grindstone to keep my marks up and to maintain some kind of academic respectability with the other students so as not to embarrass myself. I have always been the type of person who has to work very hard to get good marks. Nothing came naturally to me. If I didn't work hard, I didn't get the marks—period!

My parents always led by example, and so I kept working at acceptance and inclusion, trying to emulate and develop some of the social skills that I so envied in them. Change had been forced on me. I had already learned at camp that I don't like change. However, I was also learning that I was a survivor and that I could adapt to change. How little did I know then how well that quality would stand me in good stead time after time in future years! I had no way of recognizing then how instrumental these life experiences were going to be in my ability to survive my greatest personal challenge 50 years later!

In Grade 8 my neighbor Maureen Kempston, who lived across the street at 81 Rykert Crescent, became my first girlfriend. My dad always called Maureen, Hoppy, and me, Skeeter, when we were young childhood playmates after we first moved to Rykert. We dated through part of Grade 8 and Grade 9, mainly evolving out of the Grade 8 parties our class so often held. I was incredibly shy and it took months before I worked up enough courage to give her a first kiss. I don't think that's the way it works today. Parents of that era would not leave you alone with a person of the opposite sex, let alone mention the word sex! Maureen would go on to acquire a law degree and have a very successful business career, breaking the glass ceiling as the first female President of General Motors Canada! My dad always jokingly said, "You should have married Maureen!"

Also in Grade 8, I played the lead role of Artaban in *The Other Wise Man* for the Christmas pageant. I didn't ask for the role; my classmates voted me into it! It was a big acting job with a ton of memorizing as I was in almost every scene. We had three performances. For a shy and insecure 13 year old I was way out of my comfort zone; but I accepted the role, persevered to do my very best, and performed the role quite well, I was told. At our Grade 8 graduation, I volunteered to host the dance party afterwards. We danced away the night in our basement recreation room, and my father cooked hamburgers and hot dogs for us at midnight on the BBQ. I had successfully made the transition to the "brain class". The "clown" had made his exit!

Grade 8 Graduation – John Mardall, Heather Moore, Maureen Kempston and me

Donald Gordon Ross

"Be True To Your School"
The Beach Boys, 1963

I grew up in my teens in one of the most iconic eras ever—the 1960s! I attended Leaside High School from Grades 9 – 13, from 1962 – 67 when I was between 14 and 18 years old. Going to high school was a big change from the relative security and predictability of public school. I seemed to be a little fish in a big pond.

High school courses were, by and large, mandatory with few choices. The subjects were very traditional and hadn't changed for years. There had been no recognition or advanced thinking to develop and offer course options that would prepare you in a practical way for the variety of careers that are available to students today. I took English, French, Latin and German in various years. I enjoyed history, geography, shop and even math and algebra; but sciences were my downfall. No interest and no aptitude! I failed physics and chemistry big time!

All assignments were handwritten, as there was no such thing as a computer then. You were not even allowed to bring in this new fangled invention called a calculator to your math exams, because not every student had one. It would give those who had one an unfair advantage. So, all calculations had to be completed manually; but, at least we learned the methodology behind the calculations! My marks in high school weren't as high as in public school, but I remember a 66% average in Grade 13 did get me accepted into the University of Toronto. Today that would be nowhere near good enough!

Many of our teachers we loved, some we feared and most we immaturely and disrespectfully made fun of in one way or another. The cast of characters included "Dipper Don" McLeod (history/math), "Teddy Bear" Rosevere (math), the "Welshman" Richard Lewellyn (English), "Arty" Williams (history), "Sex on Stilts" Miss Eaton and Sarah Pallett (Latin). My nemesis was Mr. Shankman whom I never forgave for always putting me on the spot in history class to answer questions for which I never seemed to have answers!

There were some teachers whose monikers would be so socially and politically inappropriate today that legal action would now have been a

certainty! They shall remain nameless. But, who could forget the
reverend Dr. Maura conducting a reading of the Bible every morning at
9:05 a.m. during opening exercises. His heavily accented voice
resonated over the public address system like it had been drawn from
the bottom of a deep well, as he unfailingly droned, "Let us hear-r the
wor-rd of Go-od!"

The 1960s was the decade of rock and roll. We collected 45 rpm single
records and 33⅓ speed record albums and played them endlessly on
our record players. No other decade of music affected our culture the
way that the '60s did. To this day, my favourite radio stations are the
ones that play music from that era.

As the 1960s progressed, everyone started to grow their hair long like
The Beatles, and versions of the hippy look took over fashion. I
dressed in Levi jeans, Madras shirts, and mukluks, and often sported a
Mexican style roped vest! I'd go downtown by subway with friends to
cull through an army surplus store called *Thrifty's* on Yonge Street to
find unusual attire that was "cool". The Yonge Street strip became a
favourite haunt as every teenager shopped for records at Sam The
Record Man or A & A Records at Yonge and Dundas. We'd have our
favourite haunts on our circuit throughout downtown, which included
Kresge's and Eaton's College Street store with its unique art deco
design, never-ending aisles, wooden escalators and basement bargains.
Hamburgers could be bought for a quarter!

I didn't play organized sports in high school, but I certainly watched
them. Leaside had a proud heritage of competitive sports teams.
Groups of us cheered on the Leaside Lancers from "the hill" in the
autumn afternoon football games against our school rivals. Our
hockey team was anchored by one of my best friends, Sturdy, who had
transferred from another school and played awesome goal. The
dancing done on the gridiron and ice was only exceeded by that done
in the gym at Friday night dances, often to the likes of Little Caesar and
the Consuls or The Ugly Ducklings. The highlight of the year was the
Formal which was held at least once in the fairytale setting of Casa
Loma. Students didn't go all out with their dress, tuxes and limos the
way that they do today, but the boys wore suits and the girls wore

formals and corsages. A big difference from today, however, was that you didn't go to the Formal unless you had a date.

In 1966, my parents decided to move from Leaside north to Bayview Village in the Bayview and Sheppard area. I wasn't at all keen to move away from Leaside and my friends, having grown up there for the past 14 years on Rykert Crescent. There's that resistance to change again, although I don't think many teenagers, even today, want to move when it means leaving their friends and changing schools. However, the move would bring me much closer to my girlfriend whose family lived in Bayview Village too. I was also able to strike a bargain with my parents. They agreed that I could finish Grade 12 and attend Grade 13 at Leaside High School, as long as I didn't mind trekking out the one mile to Bayview Avenue to do a bus commute. A done deal!

So, in March of 1966 our family moved to 12 King Maple Place, a sprawling ranch bungalow with a huge finished recreation room with fireplace and bar, and another room that we developed into a games room where we spent much time playing pool and billiards with friends. Well over a million dollar property today, I believe my parents paid $47,000 for it after selling our Leaside home for $32,000. It was a great house. My father was doing well in his own advertising business, and my parents were always entertaining friends. They were "moving up".

I remember my parents had a big 25th wedding anniversary party at our home in 1967. And in 1969, a 21 birthday party bash for me. Mom and Dad allowed me to host a party in Grade 13 for all of my Leaside friends. I hired a three piece band of school chums to play music. Word travelled fast and the turn-out was huge, far beyond the number I had invited. It was jam-packed; everyone had a terrific time, and the party was the talk of the school. Good for my parents for allowing this; but, then again, they were party people! It was an easy sell!

Is it any wonder that my generation speaks so nostalgically of the 1950s and 1960s? The tranquility of that idealistic childhood was only interrupted by the assassinations of John F. Kennedy, Bobby Kennedy and Martin Luther King. Every one of us from that era remembers those horrible days as if they happened yesterday, as those shocking tragedies shattered our idealism and changed our outlook on life forever!! Just like with the 911 terrorist attacks, everyone of my generation remembers exactly where they were and what they were doing 50 years ago on November 22, 1963, the day that John F. Kennedy was assassinated. I was just 15.

"Yesterday's Songs"
Neil Diamond, 1981

Music is something that has been important to me all of my life. It's been a backdrop to my life. Melodic tunes wafting over the air waves have been a source of immense enjoyment, and occasionally of painful reminders. How often do we play a song over and over in our heads, and frequently can't stop thinking about it! "I think I'm going out of my head!" In particular I'm all about the rock 'n roll music of the 1960s. This era of music will not be replicated again, at least in my lifetime. You hear the 1960s' tunes in movies and on retro radio stations more than any other decade of music history. This decade of music bound together a generation who did not have iPhones, iPods, CD's, computers or even videos!

Okay, of course I am a baby boomer and grew up on rock 'n roll; but, for me the five year period of 1963 – 1967, when I was between the ages of 15 – 20, was the best of music with the likes of Leslie Gore, The Four Seasons, The Beach Boys, The Righteous Brothers, Sonny and Cher, Simon and Garfunkel, The Grass Roots and The Mammas and Pappas. Some of my favourite tunes included *Like a Rolling Stone*, *The Eve of Destruction*, *Light My Fire*, *White Rabbit*, *Blue Velvet* and *Surf City*. I remember rushing out one day to buy a 45 rpm of *Mr. Tambourine Man* by The Byrds. I played it 50 times in a row until finally my parents forced me to give them a break!

And, if those groups and hits weren't enough to audaciously accost the auditory senses, in stormed The British Invasion with The Beatles, The Rolling Stones, The Dave Clark Five, Procul Harem, Dusty Springfield and The Zombies. Who could ever forget *Ruby Tuesday*, *The House of the Rising Sun*, *Tired of Waiting*, *Glad All Over*, or *Nights in White Satin*! Every Sunday evening at 8:00 p.m. we watched The Ed Sullivan Show on TV to see the latest British groups. Who would have guessed that four mop tops would change the world of music!

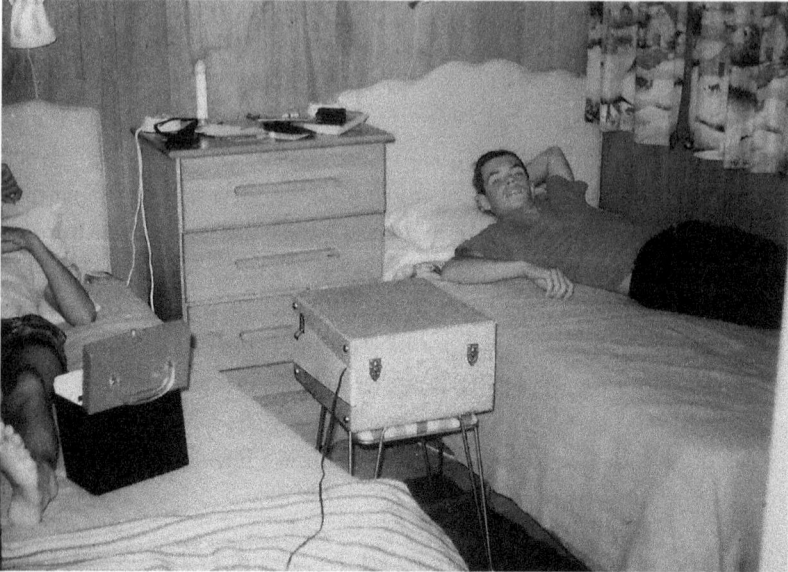

Listening to my 45's

1050 CHUM was the top rock n' roll radio station in Toronto, if not the country, and that's where the dial of my radio station was permanently turned to. I would play my 45 singles and 33⅓ albums endlessly on the turntable of my portable record player which also came with me to the cottage every summer. I would meticulously follow the hits on the CHUM Chart Top 50 and anxiously awaited its weekly publication, running over to a Bayview Avenue music shop from my classes at Leaside High on Thursday noon hours to grab the latest compilation to see how my favourites were rising up the chart. To this day I still have my CHUM Chart collection.

I always grabbed two CHUM Charts and sent one by mail to my good friend from the cottage, Dave Beardslee, who lived in Royal Oak, Michigan, a suburb of Detroit. Dave followed the music scene almost as fervently as I did. In return, Dave sent me the local Top 40 charts from the Detroit radio stations which would often give me a preview of which records would likely be hits in Canada once they were released here. Dave would tell me to watch for new groups I had never yet heard of, such as The Supremes and The Ronettes. What was all the fuss about *Where Did Our Love Go* or *Be My Baby*? Then, when I heard them I knew, and started listening to Dave's insistent suggestions more closely. I was also able to listen to and buy records through Dave that weren't ever released in Canada, such as those by The Dynamics and Richard and the Young Lions. Great tunes I surely would have missed otherwise.

CHUM Charts

I analyzed the progress of all of the hits and became quite adept at predicting the rankings of the year-end Top 50 hits. Here was the first evidence of my analytical abilities which were to stand me in good stead years later in business. I would religiously listen every night to 77-WABC in Boston to Cousin Bruce Morrow who even today still disc jockeys a weekly retro 1960s' radio show on Sirius Satellite Radio. And, through airwaves crackling with static, I rarely missed tuning in to WLS in Chicago for their Top 3 Most Requested Songs broadcast every night at 10:00 p.m. Then I really knew the hottest tunes that were bound to be sure fire hits!

Now it didn't hurt that I had a relative in the broadcasting business. My Uncle Al (Waters), my mother's brother, left the pharmaceutical business in 1954 to buy a struggling Toronto radio station. That radio station was CHUM 1050 and my uncle built it into a Canada-wide media empire. Uncle Al took his time learning the radio business and

in 1957 made the "insane" decision to radically change the station's
format from religious programming to Canada's first 24 hour Top 40
hits format, basing his rationale on a successful format developed by a
Nebraska family business. Even my Aunt Marge, his wife, criticized
him on this decision. But, as became his way, his defiance of
conventional wisdom and willingness to take chances made him a
legend in broadcasting. What Uncle Al had was vision!

Within a year CHUM was the number one radio station in the city.
And so was born the CHUM Chart, the CHUMbug Club, CHUM
Chicks and CHUM disk-jockeys, such notables as Al Boliska, Jungle Jay
Nelson and Bob McAdorey. My uncle "built this city on rock 'n roll",
as Jefferson Starship later sang. Over the years Uncle Al parlayed the
success of CHUM into 23 radio stations, 12 TV outlets, including
CityTV and 21 specialty TV channels, including MuchMusic, Bravo and
Space. He remained the Chairman and President until 2002, and sadly
passed away in 2005.

My uncle was a modest and private man who always referred to himself
as "just a salesman". But he was a damn good salesman! He was
persistent and he was prudent. Generous and loyal to his employees,
Uncle Al knew how to pick people who knew how to run the business,
and gave them the authority to do so. How enlightened is that! How
many businesses could learn from that model! You can learn a great
deal listening and watching people lead by example. I listened, I
watched and I learned.

Now there were a few perks that, as his nephew, came my way. More
than once in my teens I enjoyed attending a Toronto Maple Leafs
hockey game with my cousin, Jim, in their rink side season ticket red
seats. And, also more than once, my uncle dropped off the entire TOP
50 collection of records from the CHUM Chart! Did that make me
popular, or what! And once, Uncle Al arranged for CHUM disk-
jockey, Dave Johnson, to be the "dj" at one of our class parties in
Grade 9. And now…wait for it…yes, I did get floor seat tickets to the
1965 Beatles Labour Day weekend concert at Maple Leaf Gardens.
Could it get any better for a 17 year old? Probably not, but yet one of
my earliest and fondest memories of my Uncle Al is one winter
Saturday when he took my cousin, Sherry, and me down to the Cherry

Street railway station. We squealed with delight as the trains rolled by flattening the pennies that my uncle had laid on the railway tracks for that express purpose.

Uncle Al, Sherry and me

I have already complained that, sadly, there is no other decade of music like the 1960s. The charts were always filled with songs I liked. Alas, the music of the 1970s, for me at least, had very little to recommend itself. Nor did the advent of 8 track tapes! I mean, yes, there was the saving grace of The Bee Gees, Elton John, Supertramp and Neil Diamond, and a few hits from continuing stars of the previous decade, but, by and large, the music of the 1970s was a bitter disappointment for me, and I had tuned out by the end of the decade. And then, just when I thought that good music was down for the count, along came the 1980s.

Exactly 20 years after my favourite five years of music, my flagging interest in music was revived. I loved the songs of the five year period from 1983 – 1987. I really enjoyed Bryan Adams, Madonna, Simple Minds, Duran Duran, The Pet Shop Boys, Michael Jackson, Bonnie Tyler and David Bowie, and hits like *One Night in Bangkok*, *St. Elmo's Fire*, *Alive and Kicking*, *Relax*, *(I've Had) The Time of My Life*, *Nothing's Gonna Stop Us Now* and *Total Eclipse of the Heart*. Music was back! And then, as the '80s decade moved towards its close, the window closed too. There's been no music trend to turn my crank since. Grunge, hip hop, *alternative* rock, *rap—alternative crap*! I guess I'm getting old as the music of Rod Stewart, Diana Krall, Josh Groban, and even Tony Bennett now appeal to me! Love the old standards, which, ironically enough, many of the hits of the 1940s - 60s have now become…soft jazz, a little sex…I mean a little sax.

My uncle and his family played an instrumental role in bringing rock 'n roll music to not just Toronto, but all of Canada. So, in acknowledgement of our family's important contribution to our country's culture, and because of the impact of music on my life, I decided that it would be fitting to title each chapter of my life's journey after a song title that related in some way to the subject matter of the chapter. For some, the titles are more obvious than others; but, I will let the reader make the connections as you journey with me on the *soundtrack* of my life.

1965 – 1974 A Young Man

"Life In A Northern Town"
The Dream Academy, 1985

The natural evolution of vacationing at Birch Point Lodge and then renting summer cottages was that we would one day have our own family cottage. My Aunt Marge and Uncle Al had already built a cottage on Buckhorn Lake in the 1950s. Mom and Dad began looking at cottage lots as early as 1959 or 1960, and preferred a point. They had almost bought one on Boshkung Lake in Haliburton. It was in 1962 that our Rykert neighbours, Cliff and Muriel Moore (my friend Heather's parents), who themselves had a cottage on Lake Kashagawigamog in Haliburton, brought a new development of lots to my parents' attention. They were on Peninsula Drive on Grass Lake just outside of the town of Haliburton.

My parents' good friends, Cy and Isobel Pearce, whom they had originally met at Birch Point Lodge, were also looking for lakefront property. On a spring Saturday, Cy and Isobel came, saw and bought the lot now known as Pearce's Point. My parents had been unable to get away that weekend to go with them. The following weekend my parents came, saw and bought the lot next to Cy and Isobel. It wasn't a point, as Cy and Isobel had secured that property; but we had "visiting rights" and 144' of beautiful shoreline. And so began one of the greatest neighbour relationships ever. Cy and Isobel built their cottage that same year, and we spent the first ever Thanksgiving weekend on Peninsula Drive. I was 14.

Late that fall a bulldozer began putting in our driveway and clearing our lot. The foundation and floor joists were built before winter set in. There was a natural level clearing close to the water, and despite the property being heavily treed with maples, cedars and balsams, only about three trees had to be taken down! I remember standing firmly in two different spots with my arms around small birches to save them from the bulldozer. One flourished for 35 years; the other still stands. I love birch trees. A debate lodged over the fate of the maple by the back corner of where the cottage would be positioned. The conservationists won that one too!

My parents knew from long cottaging experience exactly what they wanted in a cottage design and worked for months to get the plans right. The developer was Bob Bishop Jr. and the carpenter was Ron Sisson. Prerequisites for inclusion in the cottage design were big windows, a panoramic view, a fieldstone fireplace, a screened-in porch, three bedrooms, a generous-sized bathroom, a storage room, lots of pine and a central bar!

My parents' design was very forward-thinking for the times, and it has stood the test of time for over half a century. It boasted one of the most advanced designs in the area and was a well-appointed cottage all around. They didn't build four season homes then, and call them "cottages", as they do today; and cottages certainly weren't winterized. They were cottages in true form. The lot cost $2,200 and the cottage itself $10,000—a great deal of money for a cottage in 1962! The building of the cottage was completed in June, 1963. A siding called Haida Skirl clad the structure. A bulldozer created a beach, and truckloads of sand were brought in. Crushed white stone (Eagle Lake rock) was laid over the driveway. That first summer I built a stone retaining wall around the earth that had been brought in to form a terrace under where the deck is today.

Our cottage – The Trossachs

A small dock only 4' x 16' jutted out from the beach and floated on a metal barrel. Too many people standing on one side and you got a soaker, or worse. My 12' silver and red aluminum boat with a 5 ½ hp Johnson motor sat tied beside the dock and was only, with great reluctance, retired about 10 years ago. My father bought a 16' molded plywood boat with a 40 hp Evinrude motor for skiing and boating and christened it the *Norma Ellen*, after my mother. Soon a red cedar strip canoe appeared—from where I don't know. And, it wasn't long before Dad showed up with a little styrofoam Sea Snark sailboat to satisfy his yearn to sail. Life couldn't get any better for children growing up in the 1960s!

The cottage had to have a name, and my parents christened it The Trossachs within a few years of its completion. They had visited the highlands of Scotland on one of their travels. An area called The Trossachs that they drove through reminded them of Haliburton. The title also had the happy co-incidence of having our surname of Ross contained within it.

That first summer was special. It marked the beginning of a lifelong best friends' relationship with Dave Beardslee who lived in Royal Oak, Michigan. Bob Napier, a neighbor three lots down, had bought a point property that my parents almost purchased, but decided against because the lot price was double that of the other lots. Bob brought down his nephew Dave to meet me, as we were both going to be up at the cottage for the summer. We instantly connected, became fast friends and spent the entire summer together.

We both loved to fish and went casting for bass every day, often in the evening or at night in the canoe. We caught our fair share and the occasional lunker! We had a routine where we would motor down Kashagawigamog in one or the other's aluminum boat to play nine holes of golf at the Haliburton Highlands Golf Course in the late morning as the lodge guests went back for lunch. It was such a rugged course that Dave and I would joke about banking shots off rocks and trees in our creative efforts to reach the greens. Often we would get mad, because sometimes those shots weren't planned, and the result would challenge even the skill of Tiger Woods. Dave and I referred to ourselves as Arnie and Jack—Arnold Palmer and Jack Nicklaus, the two greatest golfers on the planet at that time!

We would then come back to the cottage for lunch and go water skiing in the afternoon before heading back to the golf course for another nine holes of punishment in the later afternoon.   After dinner we would usually fish, although if there was a good movie playing at the Molou Theatre in town we might take it in before or after we fished.   I remember seeing *Dr. No*, the first James Bond film starring Sean Connery, and will never forget Ursula Andress coming out of the water! But, there was also *Stagecoach, If It's Tuesday It Must Be Belgium* and *The Pink Panther*, to name a few titles. On a rainy day, and one particular summer there seemed to be a never-ending number of those, we would play Monopoly, Risk, cribbage or Hearts. And we loved to play our 45s on my record player in my bedroom. We both followed the record charts religiously seeking out our favourites.

Dave, Al and me beside the 'Norma Ellen'

The first year Cy and Isobel had a nephew from Scotland staying with them for a while and we hit it off well. He kept telling us about all of the English recording artists who were making it big across the pond, none of whom had ever cracked the North American market. He raved about one particular English group that he assured us would imminently soar to the top of the charts here; but, we gave his impassioned prediction no credence whatsoever. I mean, how could a long-haired group of guys with such a stupid name be successful here? No way. It was 1963 and the group he was referring to was The Beatles! They took over the music charts in the fall and the British Invasion was on!

My parents, as the reader by now realizes, loved to party, and the cottage was party central! The sign which now hangs over the counter, and that reads "Gord's Bar", is both testament and tribute to my father and the extensive use that was made by that counter as a bar. Dad and Cy would start the morning off with their "eye openers" of vodka and OJ. Dad would often cook kippers (a smelly fish) on the BBQ, as my Mom wouldn't allow them to be cooked inside. I love fish, but kippers—yuck!

Everyone would keep an eye out for the "'sun to be over the yard arm" for the gin and tonics to begin at midday; after all, it was summer, and it was hot. Before you knew it, it was Happy Hour as 5 p.m. approached. This meant another libation adjustment, and cocktails, such as Manhattans and Whisky Sours, were served, usually along with some hors d'oeuvres such as clams, sardines or cheese on crackers. A BBQ appetizer favourite was wiener sections and pineapple chunks on skewers.

And a BBQ was the order every Saturday night. Often the entrée was a two inch thick sirloin steak that took two good men to lift to the BBQ. Dad would slice it into 3/8" slices. It went a long way. Those first days were when charcoal and lighter fluid were all that was used for the BBQ. We started it manually using the stove pipe method. Later, electric heating elements came along and were set under a pile of briquets to facilitate getting the fire going. Propane was two decades away yet! Pork chops, chicken, hamburgers and hot dogs were regular fare.

Most weekends we had guests, friends of my parents, such as the Browns, the Strangs, the Russells, the Chisolms, the Croots, the Glasscocks, and the list went on. I thoroughly enjoyed their company, as most were like family. We often went golfing and fishing together.

As I grew older, I could interact with them more and, except for the drinking obviously, I participated in many social hours. It probably helped me to become more socially adept and overcome my inherent shyness, and fostered my ability to get along with older people. I started to come out of my shell. I had a blast with them. Those were great times!

Cy and Isobel Pearce were like second parents to me. I loved them dearly. Cy flew the Scottish flag on a flag pole that we all helped raise with great fanfare and, of course, appropriate toasts at the end of their point. Isobel never liked staying at the cottage alone, so often during the week, I would sleep over at the Pearce's and Is would make me a mighty fine breakfast of bacon and eggs. She was a great cook and made fantastic peanut butter squares. If Dad or Mom weren't to be found at our cottage, they were usually next door. There was a huge hole left in our lives when Isobel passed away less than a decade after she and Cy had built their cottage.

Catching breakfast!

Cy and Isobel Pearce

"Wonderful Summer"
Robin Ward, 1963

Everyone has had that one special quintessential summer experience, the one they recall all their lives as being the best ever, perhaps even life changing! My dad clearly felt that his son was having far too much fun spending the summers golfing, swimming, water skiing and fishing, and decided that I should get a summer job. What a bummer! A Rykert neighbor was a yearly guest at a local Haliburton lodge called Chateau Woodland on Lake Kashagawigamog, the next lake over on our cottage's five lake chain. My dad got our neighbor, Mr. Mateer, to write a letter of recommendation in my application to Chateau Woodland for my first ever job. I got the job and became their waterboy. It was 1965 and I was 17.

In late June, I was enjoying a week at the cottage with my friend, Bill Pattie, before I started my summer job at Chateau Woodland. Bill's parents were good friends of Cy and Isobel Pearce, and that's how we had met. Bill attended high school in Etobicoke. Now everybody has a friend who is a true ladies man, and that was Bill. Definitely not shy about approaching a girl, or being on the lookout for girls. Not a bad friend to run interference for you, if you were somewhat shy yourself about "cold calling" the opposite sex. That would be me!

We were having a great time at the cottage. Bill kept trying to hit on Helen of Helen's Bun Shop fame. What an unfortunate name for the business! Helen actually ran a bakery for her mother off the South Kashagawigamog Lake Road and used to sun on her dock with her girlfriend. If she was in a two piece, Bill spotted her! Bill had her picked out from 500 yards as we cruised by in the boat. If I remember correctly, Helen dusted off Bill's overtures, but that never fazed Bill one bit!

Anyway, one night Bill had gotten wind of the Golden Slipper Dance Hall down Lake Kashagawigamog, and insisted we go to see what we could "pick up". I had never been there before. "Picking up" was not quite my style, if I even had a style at 17! The place was packed with a combination of local teenagers and young adults, cottage youths and summer student imports from around the province who were up in

Haliburton about to start summer jobs at one of the many lodges—
Birch Point, Chateau Woodland, Halimar, Bonnie View, Holiday Inn,
Deer Lodge, Wigamog or Locarno. Today, sadly, only Bonnie View
and Halimar remain as testament to those glory postcard years of
family summer vacations for a week or two on the "American Plan" in
a cabin at a northern lake getaway lodge.

Going to the "Dirty Boot", as the Golden Slipper was disrespectfully
called, turned out to be one of Bill's most brilliant ideas! We had an
absolute blast! Didn't Bill run into a girl named Callie Gadway from his
high school! And hadn't Callie just started work as kitchen staff at
Chateau Woodland—of all places the lodge where I too would be
starting to work the next week? Callie was there with a few of the
other Chateau staff who had already started work and introduced us
around. This was a great intro for me personally to many of the people
I would be working with that summer, and it eased me nicely into this
new group.

We danced and danced all night to great rock and roll music and even
tried square dancing. Did I ever think I would use those skills again
when they forced us to do square dancing in public school?! That night
probably ranks in the Top 25 fun nights that I have ever spent. A
group of strangers thrown together and having a fantastic time! Boy, I
was now actually looking forward to working that summer!

Bill got on very well with Ms. Gadway. I should mention that many
years later Callie reverted to her more formal given name of Carolyn
and became a dear and lifelong family friend. Anyway, the next night
Bill suggested we drive over to see Callie at Chateau Woodland, and
she, in turn, suggested that we drive down to the far end of the lake to
visit her childhood friend, Pam Gould, who was working at a small
lodge several miles down the road. Why not? I remember driving
into this tiny lodge in my dad's 1964 sea green Ford Galaxy XL 500
convertible with bucket seats and the roof down. That's when I really
saw living proof that this vehicle was truly a chick magnet!

Pam was an attractive blonde who fawned over the car, played a little
coy and caught my attention right away. It was love at first sight. We
were attracted to each other immediately, and I was smitten! The four

of us hung out together for the evening and left in time to get Callie home by curfew without incurring the wrath of the ever vigilant Mrs. Dean, den mother and cook at Chateau Woodland. In perhaps the most unexpectedly quick and out of character conclusion I think that I have ever come to, I decided that night that I would ultimately marry Pam. I was in love pure and simple. And several years later we were indeed married!

Pam 1965

My job at Chateau Woodland consisted of three completely different responsibilities. My first task was to be in the kitchen at 7:00 a.m. each morning to butter toast, using a paint brush! How gauche! Then, I would pump pails of fresh water from the well and carry them to the many outlying cabins along the cliff, the shore and in the woods. There was no running water. Actually, there was lots of water, but I provided the running! I swear my arms grew in length by 2" that summer! Then, and this was the good part, I was the lodge bellhop on Saturdays as the guests changed over. It was hard work schlepping their bags across the paths to their cabins, but the tips were great! I remember a couple of Saturdays making $25 or $30 in tips mid-season. That was huge money!

The whole summer was just one fantastically good time! The staff got along great and there was a crazy bunch of characters, mainly girls. But the guys were close. I shared the boys' staff cabin with John Humble from Port Hope and Mark Wiggins from Burlington. Everybody partied a lot. Carolyn Gadway, who, as noted, went by the name Callie and was a close friend of my girlfriend Pam, worked at the lodge as part of the kitchen staff. Mrs. Dean, the Chief Cook, ruled the roost. You didn't mess with Mrs. Dean! Late at night you had to slip right by her cabin to get back into Chateau if you were past curfew, and not much got by her notice. You paid dearly if you were caught. Many was the night that I tore along the road in my dad's car "hell bent for election" as I tried to make it back before the midnight curfew after seeing Pam at the lodge she worked at several miles down the road.

What followed was the most socially active summer one could imagine. The staff at Chateau all became great friends. We partied together, went to the Molou together, spent our days off together and danced at the Slipper together. I often would bring our boat over and take everyone water skiing. There were some pairings, but we hung out as a group all the time.

While the lodge discouraged fraternization with the guests, there was Gabrielle Hortzendorf, a German beauty of 19 with her golden tresses, who wanted to meet on the staff dock late one night to go "*swimming*"! There was one of the older attractive staff they called "Nickels" and we won't go into why she was called that.

There was Mary Pat and Jan from Petrolia, a real sweetie called June Cousens, Liz from Listowel and Marnie from Sarnia. Marnie had a big crush on me which wasn't reciprocated! She and a couple of the others met me at Maple Leaf Gardens when we all convened to see The Beatles after the summer. She brought me a great looking wooden No Parking sign she had scooped from somewhere out on the back roads, as she had always kidded me about the fact I liked to go "parking" with my girlfriend. I still have that sign somewhere. I must find it and put it up at the cottage! It's a great sign!

Saturday nights we would all go to the Dirty Boot. This was actually the dance hall on Lake Kashagawigamog that my parents had also gone to in the 1940s when their family stayed at Birch Point Lodge. Although a couple of times we paddled by canoe, we would usually go in my parents' iconic Ford Galaxy convertible. You just know I had it made. Those nights were the best as we danced the night away.

I was always very youthful looking and that got me a feature role in the Haliburton Rotary Parade—my second role in life on stage after playing Artaban, *The Other Wise Man*, in Grade 8. Only, in this case, I was not exactly on stage, but rather on a *barge*! All of the lodges created floats to enter in the August Rotary parade. The Chateau Woodland staff had to come up with the theme and create the float. Again I was elected as the central character. What is it about this Ground Hog Day type repetition of events?

The theme was Cleopatra—decadently reclining on a barge and being fed grapes by Mark Anthony. Guess who played Cleopatra? Yep, me again! A mop was died black for a wig, red lipstick was applied and two balloons were propped up under my yellow print moo moo dress. John Humble played Mark Anthony and fed me the grapes. And, yes, there are a couple of photos I have. I looked so-o-o cute! I guess this was the closest I have ever come to cross-dressing! I had a blast laughing and waving at friends who lined the main street. Of course, wouldn't you know that one of my balloons burst during the parade. I guess today that would be considered a wardrobe malfunction!

As Cleopatra in the Haliburton Rotary Parade

73

The dilemma for me was to balance this continuous social activity at Chateau Woodland with seeing Pam and developing that relationship, so I was a very busy boy! What a summer! I spent a lot of evenings travelling several miles down the road to her lodge. It was a new burgeoning relationship and, as Pam and I wanted to spend time together, just the two of us, we didn't socialize as much as a couple with the Chateau gang as we could have. I tended to keep the two lives somewhat separate which necessitated a challenging balancing act. And so began the relationship with Pam that summer which would irrevocably change my life in a variety of ways forever—both good and bad!

It was a summer I wished had never ended. It was the summer of some of the best rock 'n roll music ever with fab hits such as *I Got You Babe, Satisfaction, You've Lost That Loving Feeling* and *Like a Rolling Stone.* It was a summer that I came out of my shell and experienced an almost once in a lifetime circle of instant friends. It was a summer of love. While my innate nature will always be that of an introvert, I finally started to develop more socially extroverted behaviour. This was learned and emulated behaviour as a result of my environment, namely exposure to my parents and their friends. It also resulted as I gained self-confidence so that I could develop my own social circle. It was a coming of age in many, but not all, ways.

"Summer Of '69"

Bryan Adams, 1985

Actually, it was the summer of '67, but I love that song! As the author, I can take artistic license. Couldn't beat Chateau Woodland for the summer experience of a lifetime, but I came close two years later. I was just graduating from Grade 13 and I was successful in getting another summer job in Haliburton. This time I worked at The Driftwood restaurant which is now the Country Rose Garden Centre at Industrial Park Road. In 1967 it was both a restaurant and gas station and owned and run by Mrs. Marion Moffat, a school teacher from Bancroft. I seamlessly moved between pumping gas outside one minute and serving food inside the next. Can you imagine that happening today! I don't think so.

Mrs. Moffat had recruited some of her Bancroft students to run the operation, so here I was again breaking into a social group who all knew each other and were from a small town to boot. I was the city guy. But I was getting better at this fitting in game, and I fit like a glove here! Another fantastic summer ensued with the friendships of Dan and Bill Price, Donna Stephaniuk, Lynda Hawley, Diane, Gerry, and Anna Mae McCeachran and her boyfriend Bill White.

Boy, did we have a blast that summer! I motored over to work in the aluminum boat. We partied a lot at night. We went to the Molou. I still got to hang out and fish with my good friend, Dave Beardslee, who continued to come up to Haliburton in the summers. I had to juggle all this with Pam, who was still my girlfriend and was working at Locarno Lodge next to Wig-a-mog that summer. I don't think that I was as successful at juggling as I needed to be. If I recall, Pam strayed a bit, and I rather favoured Donna.

I remember Pam and I double dating one Saturday night with Dennis Casey and his girlfriend. Dennis was a son of the Caseys who ran Birch Point Lodge, where my parents and grandparents had vacationed 20 years before. Dennis ably represents his community as an elected Municipal Councillor today. Talk about your six degrees of separation. We took my dad's big black New Yorker that had a honking big 375 hp engine and powered up Highway #35 from Haliburton to the dance pavilion in Bala in Muskoka. We were pulled over by the police on the way. They were thinking teenagers and power car spells trouble…after all, it was the decade of sex, drugs and rock'n roll. We certainly had the rock'n roll part down pat, but I will be more circumspect about the other two, as this is a family read. Anyway, The OPP didn't *find* anything. However, what we found was one of the loudest and most crowded dance pavilions I had ever attended. It was a blast! Two great bands—The Turtles and The Yardbirds—were playing, and both had big international chart hits. It was a chaotic scene—the crowds, the drinking, the smoking, the weed!

The Driftwood gang and I had hilarious times hanging out together. That was the one summer I actually smoked cigarettes, because they all did, although I don't think my parents ever knew, and we certainly drank. That was also the one summer that I got into serious trouble with my parents—and quite rightly, as I acted very irresponsibly. I found out that Pam was seeing someone else and I was really upset. Of course I wasn't exactly an angel anymore myself, and in retrospect, summer romances where kids work together at resorts are the norm.

Anyway, I was really pissed and sought solace with my Bancroft friends as we smoked and drank the night away. A bunch of us ended up at Skyline Park, the popular spot for couples, and the night slipped away into dawn. My cardinal sin was not calling my parents at the cottage to let them know I was staying out, or over, or something—anything!! This was totally uncharacteristic behaviour on my part. Mom and Dad, of course, thought the worst and had notified the police, and checked the hospital. They were up all night worried sick! By that time I was feeling pretty sick myself. But, that was nothing compared to the reaming out and dressing down I received when I tried to slink down the driveway at 7:00 a.m.! Grounded—I learned my lesson well though, as an incident at university proved the next year.

The friendships with the Bancroft crowd, unlike with the Chateau crowd who were dispersed all over the province, carried on for a couple of years quite closely. There was no text messaging, or computers or even cheap long distance to keep in touch the way one can today though! I often went to Bancroft and stayed with the Prices for a weekend, even Christmas holidays, to visit with everyone. We'd drive around the countryside and pick everyone up and hang out at the restaurant. I remember one time that they came down to Toronto and visited at our Willowdale home on King Maple Place.

I particularly remember a quintessentially gorgeous fall weekend that I spent with my Bancroft friends. I helped to decorate the high school for the Autumn Dance. Afterwards, several of us partied at a cottage and crashed for the night. I found out later that night, as one of the girls and I got somewhat friendly, that she was the principal's daughter! Yikes! I do often wonder how the journeys of these good folks with whom I have long ago lost touch have turned out? What twists in the road did life have for them?

Bill Price and me at The Driftwood

Donald Gordon Ross

"Working On the Chain Gang"
Sam Cooke, 1960

There were other summer jobs through the late 60s and early 70s. I sold Watkins Products door to door in Bayview Village. This was an age old door-to-door sales company that sold a spectacular oven cleaner, among other things, and which I was constantly demonstrating to bored housewives looking for answers to their cleaning challenges, and perhaps other woes. Wish I had a great story to tell about that, but, sadly, no excitement on that score. In fact there was no scoring at all! It was a fairly short-lived job, although because I racked up sales of a whopping $167.43 in two weeks, their sales newsletter promoted this "incredible" achievement under the caption Dynamic Don Ross!

One summer, I performed the traditional student job as a security guard, and some of those assignments, which included Collegiate Sports, Shoppers Drug Mart, an apartment building, an industrial plant and Eaton's, were the most boring I have ever had and murderous on the feet! And I hated shift work. On one assignment, I remember being so bored that I secretly read one of my cherished Charles Dickens novels in a shed in an outdoor gardening centre. A far cry from the activity and excitement at Chateau Woodland or The Driftwood!

I also had the dubious honour of being a "scab"! Honeywell Controls was on strike and they needed to keep the manufacturing plant operational. I knocked on the door of Mr. Bilodeau, the president of the company, who was a neighbor of ours, to see if there might be an opportunity for a student to help out. And so I became a strike breaker testing little mechanical control gizmos. Exceedingly boring, but the job lasted most of the summer and the pay was decent. I still have a personal letter from Mr. Bilodeau thanking me for my work and wishing me well.

Another summer I worked for Fraser Construction (a Rykert neighbour's business). After digging a ditch, which almost killed me in the heat, I was given a much easier job assisting a worker on a huge grouting machine for the rest of the summer—much easier. I also worked at OXO Foods one summer on Don Mills Road. This was in the plant that made batches of OXO flavour cubes. The smell of the batches was sickening.

There was one other job I had in Haliburton, which was in 1966 between my Chateau Woodland and Driftwood gang summers. That was working for Bill Emmerson of Emmerson Lumber for the princely sum of 75¢ per hour. I performed a variety of odd jobs around the Yard, as well as assisting customers. Stan Roberts, the foreman, assigned me to work alongside two long-time employees, Ron Davies and Harley Fader, local boys whom I thoroughly enjoyed learning from and learning about both the lumber business and small town living.

What I recall vividly to this day at Emmerson was unloading box cars full of lumber. Lumber was brought in by train to Haliburton and then shunted to the lumber yard for unloading. As I was the youngest and smallest, I was designated to crawl on my belly into the top of the box car in sweltering heat and pull the lumber out one agonizing piece at a time until the load was reduced enough in size for others to stand upright. Now those 2" x 12" x 20"s were tough slugging! Some of those larger pieces of lumber felt like they had come from the bottom of the lake in terms of their weight. Those were exhausting days! When I went home, I went directly to bed!

Probably the best summer job I had, at least in terms of money and continuous hours, was at the LCBO store on Grenville Street in downtown Toronto. I was attending Ryerson at the time, so it was close by for later day shifts after class. I worked two or three summers and part time during the school year. At that time Liquor stores were not self-serve, and there weren't many of them. Grenville was one of the only downtown locations.

I often worked the counter with many other employees fetching bottles to fill the order slips that customers would give us. I wrapped the bottles individually in paper and bagged them. I got to know all the codes and where everything was kept. We could all move at warp speed, but still we were often swamped with customers bellying up to the counter at Christmas, thrusting their order slips in our faces. Those few stores did a land office business! Being downtown, we had a lot of "winos" come in for the cheapest bottle of sherry or wine they could get. I always thought it ironic that the city ended up building the new morgue next door!

There was a real cast of characters working there, I can tell you. The likes of Kenny Spriggs, Len Cotton, Bruce Smith, Don Fanjoy, Dougie Smith, Jim Stoner, Ray Toy and Gordie King were a downtown mix of the craziest characters I have ever worked with. It was an eye-opening education, but they were great with me. Stan and Len, the two assistant managers were great, and actually Mr. Hargreaves, the manager, was okay although somewhat intimidating, as he exuded a very business-like and stern manner. I remember offering him condolences on the passing of his wife. Two other student part-timers, Mike Simon and Gerard Cosgrove, and I got on famously, although we were competitors for hours. I won the pool for the Kentucky Derby winner one year—Royal Chocolate—and I've been a chocoholic ever since!

The Grenville Street LCBO store, 1973

I experienced a wide variety of summer jobs and was thrown into working situations with a diverse cast of characters, many of who couldn't be scripted any better for a movie. And there's the key—*a real cast of characters*. Each job was a valuable learning experience as I worked with mostly wonderful people from many walks of life and learned about the ways of the world. Each job was an education.

People from all kinds of socio-economic and cultural backgrounds, and job experiences, provided me with a rich tapestry of valuable experience in interacting and getting along with others. I met people who I otherwise would never have met. Each time I became a little more comfortable in my own skin and got more adept at social and relational skills. I now find that there aren't many people with whom I can't get along.

"My Dad"

Paul Peterson, 1962

"He ain't much in the eyes of the world. He'll never make history. My Da-a-d. Now here is a ma-a-n!" These words are from the 1960's song by Paul Peterson. I always think of my father when I hear that song. The words weren't entirely applicable in my dad's case, as he was very "much" in the eyes of the world—his world ... of family and friends! He was well-esteemed, respected and loved. I adored him. He was my role model and hero, and taken from us suddenly and much too soon.

Dad (Circa 1940)

Gordon Wallace Ross was born, May 20, 1919. He died July 10, 1979 a few hours after my 31st birthday! Dad was likely the most predominant influence in my life, and I always wanted to be like him. My dad was born and raised in Toronto and went to Riverdale Collegiate Institute. He didn't take any post-secondary education and joined the Canadian Air Force in 1940. He was never posted overseas or saw action, as he was colour blind. But, he was stationed in Ottawa for two years. He was a good looking man by all standards, particularly those of the ladies, and he grew better looking with age. I always thought on that basis that there may be hope for me! Dad had definitely not yet reached his "best before date" when he passed.

My dad was certainly an extrovert who was wonderfully personable, and had lots of friends whom he kept as friends for life—such as Bill Russell, Bill Croot and Frank Chisolm from high school, Bill Brown and Cy Pearce from Birch Point Lodge, Gord Gasscock and Irv Wismer through business And dad made friends everywhere he went. Everybody loved his fun personality. He was always a friend and jokester with a keen sense of humour. He couldn't tell a joke to save his soul, so I come by that trait honestly. But he was a master of the quick quips, the off the cuff one liners, and we were always groaning over his puns. So there's another trait I came by honestly; after all, I spent 30 years around him. Some of that had to rub off.

As an active, participating man, Dad belonged to the Scarborough Golf and Country Club where he golfed and curled. He would organize friends and neighbours to come up to Haliburton each winter to go in the curling bonspiels. And, he was a regular churchgoer and was quite involved in the church as a young man. Fishing trips were always the order of the spring, usually with Frank Chisolm and Cy Pearce. As I got older, I went along to spend time with the boys. Friends, and particularly young people, sought him out for advice on their problems. He was just the kind of guy who everyone related to and would confide in. Dad was much sought after to propose toasts to the bride. He may not always have been a blood uncle, but he was an adopted one by many daughters of his friends.

Now this act was a tough one for me to emulate. I so much wanted to be like my father, yet as a youngster I was quite shy. Go figure. It took me well into adulthood before I fully realized that I should stop wishing to be like my father and focus on being myself. I realize now that there is a lot of my father in me. I learned and assimilated much from my father to help shape me into who I am today. I am finally comfortable *in my own skin*.

There is a reason that Gord's Bar at the cottage is named after him. The bar counter was always covered with various alcoholic beverages, or at least it always seemed that it was. Now, don't get me wrong, my parents were certainly not alcoholics. They just liked to have drinks with friends at the cottage on weekends. This was just a way of life in those times. My dad might have a cocktail when he got home from work. On the other hand, being in the advertising business, Dad did a lot of entertaining at lunches and dinners—martinis, manhattans, screw drivers. This was also indicative of the times when drinking was very socially acceptable, if not expected!

Mom and Dad's wedding, March 21, 1942

Dad taught me how to fish and play golf. We used to love going to the Haliburton Golf Course to play nine holes. The first year we had the cottage he paid a whopping $25 for the family—for a whole season's membership! Boy, did we get our money's worth that year! We would often have family golf outings on the weekend along with all the golf that my good friend, Dave Beardslee, and I played during the week. Dad let me hit a golf ball for the first time from what used to be the 2nd tee up on the hill behind what is now the 9th green at the Haliburton Highlands course. It was a blind shot to the green. I think his rationale was so that no one would see me because I was under the minimum age of 12 required to play on the course. Dad could hit the ball a ton. He often overshot the green on what was then the 8th, and is now the 7th hole! And he was often accurate at hitting the 9th green (now the 8th) from the scenic tee atop the hill.

Dad with Cy Pearce – Best Buds!

I have three pewter mugs awarded to my dad for golf tournaments that are a testament to his golfing prowess. The first was for Low Net in the 1950 Fall Advertising and Sales Club Golf Tournament. The second mug awarded to Dad was in the following year for 1st Low Net of the Planned Sales Golf Tournament. And, the third pewter mug says "Gord Ross—Planned Sales Golf Tournament—1952—2nd Low Gross."

Dad and Cy Pearce would always go out fishing at midnight on the opening day of bass season. By then there had been much consumption of alcoholic beverages as they whiled away the evening waiting. Casting was the norm for night fishing in between beers, so Dad and Cy usually got caught up in the shoreline trees and had to retrieve their lures in the morning—after their eye openers, of course!

Dad had a successful career in advertising and sales for 25 years. I have letters from my dad addressed to his father in 1945 discussing career and job possibilities to pursue once he was discharged from the RCAF. In these letters his father speaks of John Cakebread and a new company called Planned Sales that he had started in the advertising field. Further to these ongoing correspondence discussions about Dad's future, he joined Planned Sales and worked with them for many years. He was an account representative to start and worked himself up to Vice President of Sales. Life was good—a progressive career, marriage, two children and a nice house in an up-and-coming neighbourhood.

Dad had some notable accounts such as Noxema, Dr. Ballard's Dog Food and American Motors. I remember them because of all of the promotional materials such as Dr. Ballard towels and styrofoam floats in the shape of Noxema sun tan lotion bottles! At times he did some back and forth travelling to Montreal and Detroit. In Montreal he always found time to stop and buy a wonderfully fresh, triangular-shaped bakery bread that was a mix of brown and white swirls inside. We awaited his return with mouths watering!

In 1961 Dad decided to go into a partnership with Keith Robinson and start his own business in advertising and sales. The company was called Individual Sales. But, almost immediately, Keith developed tuberculosis. Dad had to do double duty to get the company underway in Keith's prolonged absence. It took a toll. What took a greater toll on him though a few years later in 1972 was when Dad's business went bankrupt. He didn't say much about it. We didn't lose the cottage, as it was protected; however, my parents had to sell their beautiful house on King Maple Place.

Mom and Dad lost a big chunk of the good life. Dad tried another executive sales position with a marketing firm, but that didn't work out. He ultimately took life insurance courses and entered that business starting as a life insurance salesman with Confederation Life. It must have been a difficult pill to swallow. He didn't talk much about it with me; my parents never talked about those kinds of serious matters—stiff upper lip and all that—even when I lived at home. In retrospect, I should have asked more about the business problems. On the other hand, I was brought up not to question my parents. Rightly or wrongly, it would have been a very difficult thing for me to have approached them on.

Mom and Dad's Silver Wedding Anniversary Party with Al and me

After I was married, and through the 1970s, I did not spend as much time with my father as I would have liked, and as I should have. By that time, I was married, not living at home, building a career and had my own preoccupations. And I saw my parents even less when Pam and I purchased our own small fixer upper cottage in 1977. I was to pay dearly for this omission. Dad and I both missed the boat by not spending more time together in his last few years. It is one of my major regrets that I can never erase.

By 1979 I realized that some of my priorities in life had become skewed and needed some readjusting. Pam and I were having some serious relationship problems, and I had actually decided to leave her upon returning from a trip to California in February. She persuaded me not to and we did stay together. But, one of the priorities that needed readjusting was the amount of time spent with my father. We just needed to connect more. I loved him very much, and you only get one father! Part of my still lingering feeling of regret today is certainly because he died so unexpectedly in 1979; but, I had recognized my omission a few months before his death, and we were getting together more often. I am so grateful for doing that!

Donald Gordon Ross

"Ya Got Trouble"

Robert Preston, The Music Man, 1962

What to do? What to become? What career path to embark upon? These are all good questions for someone graduating out of high school to be asking. Well, I didn't have a clue as to what I wanted to do. I wasn't alone, that's for sure! So, I did what every 18 year old was encouraged to do by their parents—go to university, the answer to everything! Post-secondary education would launch you on to a career and gainful employment!

Unlike some fortunate souls who seem to have known all their lives what they "wanted to be", there just wasn't any particular career choice which appealed to me, or that I knew enough information about to get excited. In high school guidance class I had completed a lengthy career assessment test, the esteemed results of which suggested that I would be best suited to become a funeral director! You can imagine my reaction to that revelation! Ironically, many years later in hindsight, I probably would have been well suited for that role because of the empathetic and relational skills which I eventually developed. Who would have thunk it!

And so, I applied to university. I submitted applications to Western, McMaster and the University of Toronto—all very highly regarded bastions of academia. I was hoping to be accepted at the latter for a couple of reasons. First, I wasn't keen to leave home and be on my own. Secondly, my girlfriend Pam was going to be attending Teacher's College in Toronto! Now there's a good reason for choosing a university!

Somehow I was accepted into the 3 year Arts program at the University of Toronto with the laughably low average of 66. They must have set the bar low that year because today those kinds of marks would not normally get you near the hallowed halls of Victoria College, except on a Sunday tour! So Vic it was, with me taking English, French, History, and, if one can believe it in this day and age, Latin! How useful was that! I took the line of least resistance with subjects I was comfortable with. Um-m-m.

Now, a little known fact about my personal history, or at least one rarely remembered, was that I failed my first year of university! That's right, I, Donald Gordon Ross, being of sound mind and body, after being a very good academic performer in public and high school, was an abysmal failure in my first year of post-secondary education! This was a low moment for me personally, and certainly not one that I was proud of. I was embarrassed. It dealt a blow to my confidence and my belief in myself

I know exactly why this happened though. First, I was a fish out of water. I had great difficulty making the huge jump from high school to university, both socially and academically. From a class of 30 in high school to sitting in Convocation Hall with 200 strangers was not my idea of a good time. The onus was solely on me to study and learn. I found the sheer volume of study, reading and learning to be done overwhelming—not at all an unusual reaction for many young people making the jump from high school to university. Combine this with the fact that I didn't possess what I call natural academic aptitude. In other words I had to work my butt off if I was to get just decent marks. And I didn't!

A huge contributing factor to my lack of academic success in first year was my participation in the annual Victoria College musical. One thing that I always wanted to do, when I finally got the opportunity, was to participate in a musical much like the ones I saw with Pam at her school, Earl Haig Secondary School. This must have been my arts and creative side beckoning to me, although I didn't recognize it at the time.

When I discovered that Victoria College was putting on a musical, I was there! I obviously just needed the right things to motivate me! And so, I became part of the cast of *The Music Man* production despite "stage fright" being my middle name! Shades of my performance as Artaban, *The Other Wise Man* in Grade 8! Being again one of the most youthful looking cast members, I was designated to play one of the town's young boys at the front of some of the song and dance numbers. Me with a horrible singing voice and me with two left feet! But, I did it and loved it. Perhaps I ultimately missed my calling, as I also perhaps did about becoming a funeral director! Two such diametrically opposed directions.

After months of hard work and rehearsing, we had three evening performances at Hart House in the winter. I will forever remember hiding behind Marian the librarian's table for a few minutes at the beginning of one particular scene. Then, to the audience's complete surprise, I smoothly catapulted myself from my hidden location over the top of the big library table to start the "Marian, the Librarian" dance sequence! The looks of astonishment and the applause were gratifying. I had pulled it off!

What a great time! This was like the Chateau Woodland and Driftwood gang all over again! The camaraderie amongst the cast was energizing. The cast parties were the best I ever attended! It was 1968. I was 19. These times were all about partying. I remember one particular party at a cast member's home on Blythewood Avenue. I made the unfortunate mistake of mixing my drinks and got very sick, spending much time calling Huey on the great white telephone.

I couldn't walk and I couldn't function. But, I had learned my lesson from the year before. In the most natural voice I could muster, I called my parents, waking them up—but that was okay. You see, this time I did call my parents to let them know that I would be staying at the director Rob Galbraith's downtown flat overnight, as we had a cast rehearsal at 9 a.m. the next morning at Victoria College. I hung up and bolted for the toilet!

The next morning, a Saturday, I woke up in Rob's flat. It was the ground floor of an old century home on Gerard Street near Church across from Allan Gardens, not exactly the high rent district of downtown. I had no idea where I was or how I got there, and there was nobody home. It was 9 a.m. I felt awful with a wretched hangover. I found a note by the bed with my car keys and directions as to where I could find my car on a side street around the corner. I dragged myself out to the car and drove to the rehearsal at Victoria College. When I stumbled in, I received my first ever standing ovation!

Again, at what cost did having a great time come? I had been skipping classes, rehearsing and partying. I certainly had not been studying. Frankly, I felt it was worth the price, for I had always wanted to be in a musical! I had fulfilled a dream! Put a price tag on that!

When it came time to write my exams in April, I thought I would have a nervous breakdown. I was ill prepared. I hadn't been to all the classes that I should have. Assignments had been completed, but I hadn't done all of the reading and studying that needed to be done. I was, to use the expression, freaking out! I knew history would be my Achilles heel, and indeed I knew I had flunked the exam when I wrote it.

So, I missed my first year. I ended up only failing that one subject—history—and only by a few marks! Unfortunately though, in those days, even if you failed only one subject, you failed your year. Unlike more recent times where you get credit for the subjects you pass; in those days you had to repeat your entire year. Boy, did that ever suck! My parents were apoplectic, and my dad spoke with the university administration because my marks were, oh, so close; but, they wouldn't budge on the decision. I paid the price. Another lesson learned!

"When The Going Gets Tough, The Tough Get Going"
Billy Ocean, 1986

I had fulfilled my dream of being part of a musical production. I couldn't put my education at further risk, so *The Music Man* was my one and only foray on to the stage in university. I had to buckle down and study. I couldn't screw up again—either for me, or my parents, for subconsciously we all want to please our parents.

There was never really much consideration given to not returning to university, as I knew I could do it if I applied myself. So I had three more years and had to start all over again. I ended up completing my Bachelor of Arts, or B.A., fondly referred to as the Bugger All degree! I majored in English, and experienced one of the greatest love affairs of my life—with revered English author, Charles Dickens. I loved reading his Victorian novels set in London, England, in which he created some of the world's most memorable fictional characters. His stories were composed with humour, a keen observation of character and society, great intrigue of plot and co-incidence, and they positively dripped with colourful description.

I can't tell you how many English essays I wrote. Some are still buried away in my personal archives. It was 1969 - 1971 and there was no such thing as a computer. Everything had to be written by hand. That was a lot of writing and terribly time consuming, as I had to write down my research, organize my approach, write a draft, and eventually, after editing, write the essay out in long hand for submission to my Professor. Often I was still handwriting the final version with the sun coming up. Essays had better be neatly written, or your Professor wouldn't be able to decipher it, and, if he couldn't read it, you were not going to get a good mark!

In my first year of university, I met one of my best friends, Craig Truscott, in history class, which I did occasionally attend. Craig loved history the way I loved Dickens. Craig has become a lifelong friend who has always been there when I needed a friend, and there were to be times going forward when I certainly did. Craig was dating a nurse at the time, and Pam and I double dated with Craig and Nancy occasionally. Craig and Nancy married and I was a groomsman. Both are wonderful human beings, real salt of the earth people.

Totally out of left field (I didn't see this coming) I joined a fraternity. Ken Wismer, the son of friends of my parents, Irv and Maxine Wismer, called me up out of the blue and asked me if I might consider joining a fraternity at U of T. Ken was a student there and was a member of Kappa Sigma fraternity. Not something that would normally cross my mind to consider, but I said I would be willing to come by.

The frat house was located at 218 Beverley Street, just south of College Street and was a fair jaunt across campus from Victoria College on the U of T campus. The long and the short of it was that I liked the group of students and felt it would give me a social base on campus, which, in retrospect, was totally consistent with my nature. I felt somewhat at sea, as I wasn't staying in residence, but rather commuting every day. Being a pledge, and then going through the initiation, was everything you read about. Although it was mostly harmless fun, it was somewhat degrading; but, it was what it was in 1969!

Being part of Kappa Sigma was quite social. I would go to the frat house for lunch or dinner when I could and certainly was there for the weekly evening meetings to conduct fraternity business. I learned to play bridge at the frat house and we all loved to go to Varsity Stadium to see the Varsity Blues play football. That was when they were competitive.

As time went on I held the equivalent positions of Vice-President and Grand Master of Ceremonies for our chapter. There were frat parties and their big Formal each year, usually up at the Aurora Golf and Country Club where one brother's family had a membership. One year we had some of the fraternity big wigs from the U.S. visit. One such nattily dressed "suit" whom I spoke with before having any idea to whom I was speaking, was Senator John. G. Tower. Senator Tower played a powerful role politically for many years in the government and was quite close to The White House. Many years later I read that he died in a plane crash.

I was now achieving As and Bs for marks, and never looked back.

However, I still didn't really know what I wanted to do so that I could earn a living. I thought that I might want to become a lawyer for which a Bachelor of Arts was a prerequisite. But, I eventually came to the conclusion that I had had enough of reading books and writing. I thought that there was just too much of that for my liking in being a lawyer. And I didn't want to teach, which was about all a B.A. was good for, other than being a prerequisite to getting into further specialized degree courses. You see, a B.A. gave you certain good skill sets such as the ability to articulate and to write, and university had taught me how to apply myself; however, it didn't prepare me for a specific career with practical application. So, where did that leave me?

I had a conversation with the son of my dad's business partner, Keith Robinson. He had gone to Ryerson Polytechnical Institute and took business studies, including marketing, general business and retail. This subject matter and idea caught my attention, and caused me to do my first ever strategic thinking.

Here's how my thought process evolved: Most students at Ryerson came in as high school graduates. So I would be somewhat overqualified, if I now went to Ryerson after university. However, and it was a big "however", I felt that my university education would give me a decided advantage over the other students, particularly my writing, application and expression skills. If that was the case, then I should be able to score high marks and gain the practical skills that I was missing for a career in business. That, along with the added advantage of a university degree in concert with my business admin diploma, should make me an attractive job candidate when I graduated. It was the big fish in the small pond idea, rather than the small fish in a big pond that I usually seemed to find myself in. I thought that this was a winning strategy, and it was!

Donald Gordon Ross

"I'm Getting Married In The Morning"
Stanley Holloway, 1956

Long blonde hair, a beautiful face and a beaming smile. Killer! Those were the physical attributes that attracted me to Pam. Actually her hair was short to begin with, but because I liked long hair, she let it grow. Pam was born on September 17, 1948, so was two months younger than I. Twenty-two years later that same September date was to become eventful, and then some 60 plus years later that same date yet again marked a significant event.

People often talk about coincidence, or six degrees of separation. Pam and her family lived in Leaside at the same time my family did, and we both attended Northlea Public School! In fact we were in the same Grade 2 class together, although I have no recollection of knowing her at that time. If not for Pam being absent on the day the class picture was taken, we really would have had a keepsake photo. Pam's family moved to 36 Millgate Crescent in Bayview Village shortly thereafter, and our paths were not to cross for another 10 years.

So, jumping forward again to 1965, when we were both 17, that was really when we met for the first time in Haliburton. Pam's parents, Phyllis and Harold, were great folk. Her mom was a very attractive woman and always very good to me. Pam's grandmother, "Dear", lived with the family. Sadly, her father contracted ALS (Amyotrophic Lateral Sclerosis, or Lou Gehrig's Disease, as it is called) and over the relatively short span of two years lost all muscle control and died on a last ditch effort trip to the Mayo Clinic in the United States. Pam had one brother, Bob, three years younger, and actually we became pretty good friends. In fact, I was Bob's best man when he got married.

Not only did our families both live in Leaside, we also both moved to Bayview Village; and, if that doesn't indicate that the fates were somewhat aligned, both of our families had cottages in Haliburton about 25 minutes drive apart. The Gould cottage was on Mountain Lake directly across from Hart Lodge where our family had vacationed in the summer before our cottage was built! And, Carolyn Gadways's family cottage was next door to the Gould cottage. Carolyn, of course, had been instrumental in introducing Pam and me when I worked at Chateau Woodland.

Pam and I certainly had a relationship that had its ups and downs. We broke up a couple of times. The truth of the matter was that I loved her and that overrode every other consideration in my mind. Unfortunately, I did not have the emotional maturity and relationship experience to realize that was a big mistake. You see, love, as I discovered much to my dismay, was simply not enough to sustain a healthy relationship; but, it took a painfully long time for me to admit to that realization—many, many years in fact!

Before Pam and I were married in the Anglican Church we took a course on marriage preparedness that engaged couples were required to participate in. Appropriately, it was called, "Fit to be Tied". My propensity for puns appreciated that title. We knew what answers the Reverend Bruton wanted to hear, and we gave them to him. It was that simple. Ironically, as the years progressed, we both became "fit to be tied" in the negative sense.

Pam was given several showers in advance of the wedding, and a couple of Jack and Jill showers, quite an innovation for the times, were thrown for us. Of course, the custom at the time was for the bride to have a trousseau tea where she put on display all of the shower and wedding gifts. All of the shower and wedding attendees came to her home on Millgate Crescent gushing with professed and predictable delight at the booty which included three fondue pots, two electric fry pans, three hot trays and multiples of many other household appliances checked off the Eaton's and Simpson's gift registries.

Friday, September 17, 1970—this was Pam's 22nd birthday and our wedding day. We were married in the late afternoon at All Souls Anglican Church in Bayview Village by the Reverend Bruton. As we exited the church there was a brief rain shower, perhaps portending things to come in our relationship. The bride wore her mother's white wedding dress from the 1940s with her long blonde hair down. Pam looked stunning! Carolyn Gadway was Pam's maid of honour. Dave Beardslee, in from Detroit, was my best man. My brother, Allan, and Pam's brother Bob were ushers in the wedding party. Pam had four attendants, including a young cousin. My good friend, Craig Truscott from university, also stood up for me, and my cousin, Sherry, was a bridesmaid.

September 17, 1970 - Pam and I marry

If memory serves, I think there were about 130 guests. It included aunts, uncles and cousins, grandparents, family, fraternity and other friends. We adjourned after the wedding ceremony to the Park Ballroom at the Inn on the Park at Leslie and Eglinton. Pam and I rode in a limo. A formal dinner and the requisite speeches ensued. We all danced the evening away until Pam and I changed into our "going away" outfits and bid adieu to the wild acclaim of the crowd. We had planned a brief honeymoon getaway to the cottage for the weekend, as I had to attend university classes on the Monday.

Pam and I set up housekeeping in a one bedroom apartment on the 5th floor of 130 George Henry Boulevard at Don Mills and Sheppard, just across from the recently built Fairview Mall.   Ironically, this lovely complex has just recently been torn down to replace the sprawling five storey structure with two 45 storey condominium towers. All apartments in 1970 were rentals. The condominium concept had not yet been introduced. Now, all one can get are condominiums; rentals are tough to find, unless they are older apartment buildings. What seems now to be a laughably low monthly rent of $166 was, at the time, a tough nut for us to crack.

"Show Me The Way"
Peter Frampton, 1975

Pam and I had been married in my last year of university, so during my entire time at Ryerson I was a married student. Pam was teaching and financially supporting us. I supplemented her income with part-time work at the LCBO store located within easy walking distance of Ryerson on Grenville Street, one block north of College just west of Yonge Street. The money and hours were good. Sometimes I had scheduled hours, and sometimes I got short notice calls to fill in for someone. I remember watching Game 7 of the historic 1972 Canada-Russia World Hockey Tournament on a Ryerson TV with many other students, the wild celebration that erupted when we scored that winning goal and then having to rush off to work up the street. An amazing feeling—not the rushing off to work part!

My Ryerson years (1971 - 1974) were relatively uneventful in terms of major life events. I enjoyed the practical business subjects after several years of arts studies. My academic learning, and the ability to write articulately, both of which I learned at university, stood me in good stead at Ryerson. They gave me the leg up on the competition that I had hoped they would on my assignments. I received As and Bs in all subjects. Accounting and finance were certainly not subjects which I had a natural inclination for, but I got through them. I quickly found that my interests lay in marketing, promotion, general business and retail, all of which I have used to advantage at various stages of my career.

I didn't socialize much after hours with the Ryerson students, largely because I was married and working part-time, as well as studying. A tricky balancing act! I did make a couple of good friends though. Len Jokovisch and George Beals were both on my marketing strategy team, my manufacturing simulation exercise and my retail outlet proposal. We worked together splendidly and aced projects when we worked together as a team.

George Beals, who was also married and had two kids, was ultimately going through to become a Minister, and later went on to Knox College at U of T to get his Bachelor of Divinity. His wife must have had the patience of Job. George had come to Ryerson because he believed that the church's problems were marketing related and that he could be more effective in the church by studying business and marketing. Actually, I found that thinking to be quite insightful in 1972, and felt the premise certainly had merit.

We lost touch over the years. But one day about 25 years later, as I was driving down Yonge Street in Richmond Hill I saw his name on the sign as minister of the Anglican Church. And, yes, I stopped and went in to visit. We had a wonderful reunion and catch up. But we didn't keep in touch, and now another 15 years have passed. Why is it that sometimes we don't keep in touch with people we naturally connect with? Why don't we maintain those relationships when they are found? Why don't we realize their importance? Is it a guy thing? We meet so many wonderful people with whom we become friends, even for a short period of time on our journey through life. I often wonder how the lives and journeys of all of these friends I met along the way turned out.

At one point during my Ryerson years, Pam and I decided, for financial reasons, to move into my mother-in-law's basement recreation room area which, in itself, was quite generous in size with a large living room/dining room area and huge bedroom. Phyllis' Bayview Village home was at 36 Millgate Crescent and backed onto the park. It was a lovely home and brought us back into the area where we had spent our later teen years. After a couple of years we moved to 24 Anvil Millway, a coach house at Bayview and York Mills. This was a very cool pad which we quite enjoyed.

In the spring of 1974 I graduated from Ryerson with my Business Administration Diploma with a major in Marketing and minor in Retail. Ryerson had not yet had the designation of university bestowed upon it; but, I had now twice the designation of "graduate" bestowed on me!

My graduation from Ryerson with Mom and Dad, 1974

Donald Gordon Ross

"Get A Haircut And Get A Real Job"
George Thorogood, 1993

So, at long last my lengthy scholastic education process came to an end and I now had to face the task of seeking gainful employment of a permanent nature—that's "gainful employment", not "painful employment". Everyone had been very patient with my scholastic endeavours, but now it was time to get busy and find a job. My strategic plan of furthering my studies at Ryerson in order to gain practical job skills with the decided advantage of a university degree in my back pocket did, as planned, place me in a competitively advantageous position compared to my fellow graduates. My strategy paid off!

I received job offers from Bank of Montreal, Confederation Life, General Electric and IBM! Four offers for a graduate and from top notch companies! Not bad at all! But, I ultimately turned them all down! I know...I know... my parents and Pam were getting exasperated. I got that, but I didn't feel that the job fit was right for me, or really what I wanted. Too bad I couldn't recognize this about my relationship! But, I do digress.

Uncharacteristically for me, I was feeling confident, if not a little cocky, about my job options. You see, I was initially turned down by General Electric for the position which I applied for. I didn't want the job but I applied so I could have the interview experience. When I was turned down in a boilerplate letter I received in the mail, I wrote them back (in longhand) pointing out my strengths and asking for an explanation as to why I wasn't offered a position! I had nothing to lose. I just thought that I would try this strategy and see what reaction I got.

Wouldn't you know they were so impressed by this approach that they came back to me with a job offer! You see, the position was for a sales representative, and I had just exhibited some of the key attributes that General Electric was looking for, namely that I didn't take "no" for an answer, and that I was determined and persevered. Now I felt a little guilty because I turned them down. But, I didn't want a sales position, and I didn't want to move to London, although many years later I quite grew to like London from my visits and, in retrospect, might well have enjoyed living there.

At Ryerson's Career and Employment Centre I had discovered a small ad for a Marketing Research Coordinator by a company called Upjohn HealthCare Services. I didn't recognize the company like I knew the names of the other big companies I had been interviewing with. I interviewed first with Myrna McMann and then with J.C. Leroux. I loved what I heard.

I had turned down Confederation Life. Ironically, my father joined that huge insurance company several years later. I didn't want the General Electric job, as it was sales. I kept Bank of Montreal and IBM dangling as long as I could. I had to make a decision on the IBM position by the end of the day on a Thursday. I was under a lot of pressure to accept one of these jobs. Thursday afternoon I had another interview with J.C. Leroux at Upjohn. High noon. High stakes.

I had played it very close, as I knew I would have to ask Mr. Leroux in the interview, if I would likely be offered the job. I was up against the wall. I had to give IBM an answer that day. I could tell the interview was going well. I wanted the job. At the end of the interview, J.C. offered me the position, and it was at the highest salary of any of the job offers, an astonishing $9,300 per year!

I hesitated all of 2 seconds before accepting with great enthusiasm. I was pumped. This was what I was looking for to get started on a career—a business and marketing role, perhaps with more of a risk going with a fledgling company in a new service business delivering nursing and home care services, but getting in on the ground floor. Pam and my parents were elated and I was out of the pressure cooker.

The Choice Is Yours!

1974 – 1998   A Responsible Man

"Leader of the Pack"
The Shangri-las, 1965

Let's be clear, your job is what you do to earn a living; who you are requires quite a different response and is much more complicated. Curiously, when most people are asked, "Who are you?" they respond by stating what they do—in other words they state their job or profession, what they do to earn a living. I say get your priorities straight. Be clear in your thinking. One should not be defined by *what you do*, but rather *who you are*! That's a big difference in perception—in how you perceive yourself, and in how others perceive you. I define myself as a husband, father, grandfather, brother and friend. My career is what I do to earn a living.

In some ways it is a good thing that the first company you work for is, in many ways, the best company you worked for. But, in other ways it is not. And so, I began my working career in May of 1974 with Upjohn HealthCare Services (UHCS), a new division of The Upjohn (Pharmaceutical) Company—a major player in its field and based out of Kalamazoo, Michigan, since about 1885, if I recollect correctly. This new division was originally started up in the U.S. and now they were gearing up to start a Canadian division. UHCS was to deliver nursing and homemaking services through a network of offices located in major cities across Canada.

My title was Marketing Research Coordinator. My responsibilities included market research, advertising and office furniture purchases for new office openings and expansions. I reported directly to Jean Claude Leroux (J.C.), the General Manager, a bilingual Quebec-born gentleman handpicked from the company's Pharmaceutical Division to do the start-up. What are the odds that your first manager is by far the best manager that you will ever have? But, in my case, that was exactly what happened! Somehow I recognized it then and appreciated it.

In his late thirties, J.C. was just a great individual to work for. Everybody agreed. He gave you direction and let you run with it. He gave you responsibility and authority. He shared the benefit of his experience and natural leadership ability. This sounds much like how my Uncle Al operated. I will always remember J.C. saying, "We may not always make the right decisions, but we make decisions!"

I particularly remember my performance reviews. He was extraordinarily perceptive and observant. He coached me, reinforcing the positive and helping me to identify my weaknesses, and gave constructive suggestions on how to improve. I felt motivated all the time. J.C. always exuded a very professional manner in how he treated people. He had great relational skills.

J.C. was a real mentor for me. I watched him and learned. Although he was my first manager, I felt that he portrayed all of the managerial traits that one needed to be successful—in business, and in life. I tried to emulate his approach. He had a fresh recruit to mould, and I was a sponge. He instilled in me the principle of treating people fairly. He taught me to listen to what employees have to say, to let them know that their efforts are appreciated and that they are making a contribution; to incorporate some fun into the workplace; to lead by example; and, to conduct myself professionally at all times. I would, throughout my career, draw upon what I had learned under Jean Claude Leroux's leadership.

One good thing about coming into a new start-up situation is that there can be opportunities for those who are proving their worth and going the extra mile. J.C. was travelling extensively around the country hiring and opening offices. Within a year my responsibilities had begun to expand. I became Marketing Coordinator, and then a year later Marketing Manager. I started to develop the company's marketing plan and work with Regional Managers on their plans too. J.C. then put me on special assignment—along with my other responsibilities.

I was asked to go to Winnipeg to see if I could assess what their problems were, as sales were dismal. I recommended a change in personnel and ultimately had the good fortune to hire a crackerjack. Initially, the company was hiring nurses—who hopefully had a little business experience to go along with their professional designation— for the position of Service Director (Branch Manager). We quickly realized that we had it backwards. Instead, we needed to be hiring individuals who were business people first and happened to have the nursing background. Big difference in focus!

I hired a new manager for Winnipeg and Heather Thom did a great job for us. Sales rose significantly. We're now talking 1976-77. Three years ago, and 35 years later, I ran into Heather at a Toronto consumer show. It was great to see her again after so many years! But, I do digress again. The success of the Winnipeg assignment led to another such assignment, this time to the other side of the country—Halifax. Same deal...problem office. Again there was the wrong person in charge. New hire—another crackerjack—and sales started to increase. Boy, was I looking good!

So I was learning the business—sales, budgets and how to manage people and operations. It looks good on the resume. Sometimes things seem too good to be true, and in one sense they were. In 1978, J.C. was promoted back to Upjohn International with an overseas posting in Belgium. Great move for him, but all of us in our growing division felt quite bereft at the thought of losing our much esteemed leader. But, as I was learning, the one constant in life is change. Hate that. But, we adapt, or face the consequences.

One of the biggest changes was our reporting relationship. The company did not replace J.C. with a Canadian General Manager. Each of us now reported directly to a U.S. General Manager named A.B. (Abe) Cook. All of the senior management of UHCS were originally pharmaceutical salesmen (whose more youthful days were in the 1950s and 1960s) with a product-based business, not a service-oriented one— quite a different approach to sales than the increasingly enlightened one of the late 1970s and 1980s! With their outdated 1950s' management styles some of them had clearly gone past their "best before" date! And, they had a disturbing tendency to view Canada as a fiefdom! Um-m-m!

Actually, I enjoyed reporting to Abe, and learned a lot from him. He listened to me and often went with my recommendations. He was very supportive. Many of us "direct reports" began travelling frequently to their Kalamazoo, Michigan head office, and we had a blast. We were much sought after by the U.S. managers. We knew how to grow the business while having fun, and they treated us with respect. We all got along well and partied hard after meetings in Kalamazoo, Los Angeles, Washington, Denver, Chicago and Phoenix, to mention a few locations. *"Wasting away in Margaritaville"* was our theme song. (No salt on mine, please.) I recall more than one meeting where we dragged our sorry hung-over butts into meetings just trying to make it through the day!

I will always be grateful to Abe for having the faith in me to give me opportunities. He promoted me to Marketing Director, as I was now the "go to" guy for him nationally in Canada and he relied on my advice. And, I received my first company car. Very cool! Then, when the disenchanted Ontario Regional Manager left UHCS, I was asked to take on management of his Ontario region. This was a huge load in addition to my responsibilities; but, you didn't look a gift horse in the mouth, as they say. It was also a huge opportunity for me!

I was now getting used to the fact that the one constant thing in business, as in life, is change. Our head office decided to restructure Canadian operations in 1981 and appoint a Manager, Canadian Operations. It basically boiled down to a choice between myself and one other individual, Andre Chamberlain, a Canadian ex-patriot who had made a name for himself on the accounting and finance side with UHCS in California, and who had been appointed Finance Director with the Canadian operation. Andre was older than I, had a long history with UHCS, and was bilingual and well connected politically. Nonetheless, I was offered the job. I was only 33 and I knew that it was really too soon in my career to hold such a position. I was not a natural leader and needed more seasoning in that regard. But, again you don't turn down such an opportunity; rather you grab it and run with it!

I remember flying down to the head office in Kalamazoo on the old North Central Airlines (we called it the Blue Goose) and being offered the promotion. Abe gave me a great vote of confidence and basically fought for my appointment over Andre, mainly, I think, because of my management style. Andre's was much more dictatorial, whereas my style was collaborative. As I met with Budd Norris, the president of

UHCS, in his office, he grudgingly said to me, "Well, Don, you are awfully young for this position, but we're offering it to you anyway." Not exactly a ringing endorsement! That's when I realized how hard Abe must have fought for my appointment over Andre, and in return, I was most appreciative, and had his back from there on in! That's also when I started to see firsthand examples of how not to manage people, and that can be as important a learning experience as good examples of effective managerial leadership. Boy, was I glad to have had J.C. as my first boss!

I spent four years as Manager, Canadian Operations, and thoroughly enjoyed the challenge. It was a sharp learning curve in terms of the broad responsibilities, Canada-wide span of operation and regional differences, and certainly in terms of the people management challenges. The 11 years I spent with UHCS were my training ground for everything that followed in my career. You develop skill sets. As I have well documented in this personal history, I was not an extrovert and definitely not a Type A personality, and not a natural leader. Some aspects of the role I found myself in we're challenging for me personally, but, at the same time, through learned behaviour, were a huge contributor to my personal growth in these areas.

As Manager, Canadian Operations with my Controller, Roger Peddle and Western Regional Manager, Pam McGowan

My reporting relationship changed again. Jerry Greer, the Vice-President of Field Operations, was my new boss. Jerry was also in his fifties and a product of the 1950s' school of archaic management and pharmaceutical salesmanship. It was a challenge to work with him and much tougher to "get his ear" than with Abe. Unlike Abe, it seemed to me that he did not see that Canada was different than the U.S. and that we had our own distinct, if sometimes subtle, differences. This perceived lack of recognition of Canadian individuality became extremely frustrating for all of us in Canadian operations. It was a prime example of the large American company managing a separate country just as if it was the 51st state! A not uncommon situation in the 1980s, and even today!

We were also going through a significant economic recession at that time. Interest rates were 18-20% and salary increases were a staggering 14%. It was a very tough time to manage a business. Can you imagine those numbers today! I learned a lot about managing profit margins in some softer sales years, and the bottom line (pun intended) was that each year our division actually became more profitable.

At one point, I had become so frustrated dealing with U.S. management that I had interviewed with our major competitor, Paramed Heath Services, a division of Extendicare, and was in serious discussions about running their division (it was a wholly-owned Canadian company with some U.S. operations). At the time, I was also making an important presentation to our senior management in Kalamazoo with strong recommendations on what we needed in the way of restructuring operations in Canada in order to grow the business for the future.

Larry Goff, a well respected senior Upjohn corporate executive, happened to sit in on the most important presentation of my career. I had worked hard consulting with my colleagues on these recommendations. I had decided to accept the position with Paramed if I didn't get what I wanted. Wouldn't you know, much to my surprise, and perhaps due to Mr. Goff's presence and international outlook and expertise, I got approval for almost everything I asked. In a way, almost reluctantly, and certainly with some regret, I declined the position with Paramed, explaining that after a decade of allegiance with

Upjohn, I owed them the chance to make good on what they had approved. It was, after all, what I asked for!

I worked away implementing the organizational changes. There were some personnel changes which I always found tough to make. Although they say (whoever "they" are) that if you don't find it hard to fire someone then you shouldn't be a manager. Though as 1984 rolled into 1985 I found myself becoming disenchanted more than ever with U.S. management. They continued to employ the same old pharmaceutical retreads in their senior management positions with the same old outdated management styles and attitudes. I was getting worn down. I wasn't as motivated as I should be. I felt I had done about all I could. Dare I have the arrogance to suggest that I might even have been becoming bored?

The final straw came when my newest U.S. manager spoke to me about accusations being made against me of taking personal time away from my job. (There was an ambitious ex-patriot pretender working in Kalamazoo, whom I had originally hired, by the way, who wanted my job. Politically savvy, he was insidiously working a campaign against me.). The whole scenario of events was pissing me off and, badly soured, I approached company management about negotiating my way out. I have to say that, after 11 years, I was very appreciative of Upjohn and the opportunities afforded me in my career advancement. I left with class and style, tying up loose ends, announcing and saying my goodbyes, and recommending my replacement. It was time to move on.

UHCS had prepared me well for whatever business opportunities I would face. It had been a great training ground, and I remember wondering why a smart organization would let a good employee get away when they had invested so much time, effort and dollars in him? Never mind how inefficient was that; rather, how foolish was that? But, then again, maybe they weren't so smart after all!

What a waste on their part! And, now that I think about it, perhaps it was a missed opportunity on my part. Maybe I should have approached Upjohn on that basis and made an effort to work things out to a career advantage for myself and investment advantage for them. After all, I, too, had invested a lot in Upjohn. However I didn't have that revelation and mature thought process until well after I had left their employ.

"The End of the World"
Skeeter Davis, 1962

In early 1979, I started to make a greater effort to spend more time with my dad. I specifically remember picking him up from the downtown Confederation Life head office to take him for lunch on his birthday in May. I also remember seeing Dad and Mom at the cottage on the Canada Day weekend. I dropped by with my friend Paul Gibson who was staying with Pam and me at our own cottage on Monrock Lake which we had purchased a couple of years before.

My mother confided in me that she was worried about Dad because of some mysterious chest pains he was having. This was the first I had heard of it, and he had already been to specialists and had tests! My parents typically keeping serious matter to themselves! Nothing was showing up in the tests, but the periodic mystery pains continued. Mom was worried, and, now, so was I! As I walked back up the drive looking backwards at Dad sitting at our round outdoor table repairing a heater, I worried and hoped that it would not be the last time I saw my father. But, it was!

On July 10, 1979, a few hours after my birthday, I got the dreaded call from the police at 2:00 in the morning from my parents' apartment. My father had had a massive heart attack and was on his way to North York General Hospital less than five minutes away. They told me he was alive when the ambulance left. My mother was at the cottage, as she was every summer. My brother was working out in Jasper Park, Alberta. When Pam and I got to the hospital, I could tell by the looks on the faces of the hospital staff that Dad hadn't made it! And so began the worst day of my life!

My world crumbled in an instant.

I was in a state of shock.

I was emotionally devastated.

I was inconsolable.

I was filled with regret.

Pam answered all of the questions that the hospital had while I vocally roared and raved in a state of complete denial. This was just not possible. There had to have been a mistake. My father was indestructible. I have relived that night thousands of times. I can see every moment still fresh in my mind, as if it happened yesterday! I was in an emotional state like I had never been in before!

Once I calmed down, Pam and I left the hospital, and I knew exactly what I had to do. After briefly taking time to pack, Pam drove us to the cottage at 4:00 a.m. At 7:00 a.m. I was tapping at my parents' bedroom window about to do the hardest thing I had ever had to do in my life. As devastated as I was myself, and still in a state of shock, I had to wake up my mom to tell her that Dad, her husband of 37 years, had died. No son should have to do this—but, then again, who better to do it?

I had probably assimilated my parents "do whatever you have to do" approach; but, I knew I had to suck it up and be there for my mother for she was going to need all the support everyone could muster. Every minute of that agonizingly long drive to Haliburton I was reliving the nightmare and dreading more than anyone can imagine what I had to do. I will never forget the look on her face, as I broke the news. How can you gently and humanely tell someone that her husband, who has virtually not had a sick day in his life, is suddenly gone?

Crying quietly, Mom took it as stoically as she could, as I held her tightly and uttered those useless, untruthful words that everything would be all right. Everything would not be all right. Everything would never be all right again! Whether I was ready or not, I had to step up. I had to try to suppress my own personal grief and shift into a supportive gear. I took over. The first order of business was that I had to take care of cancelling a business trip. I was due to be in Minneapolis that morning.

I walked next door dreading to tell Cy Pearce, my dad's best friend, that my dad was gone. Cy and his girlfriend, Bernie, were devastated. Then I had to make "the" phone calls. I had to relive that nightmare from hell again and again as I broke the news of my father's sudden death to relatives and friends. Reactions of shock and disbelief shook everyone to the core. No one could believe my dad was gone! Pam provided a calming influence as best she could, and she is good in these situations. Eventually, the critical calls completed, we all headed for home, and more calls! I was so emotionally exhausted by the end of the day that I couldn't think straight and fell into a fitful sleep.

My brother, Al, was out in Jasper Park working and couldn't be reached right away. I remember being woken up one morning when Pam returned from picking up my brother at the airport, and for a split second before I was fully awake and remembered what had happened, I believed that everything was all right. How I wished I hadn't woken up!

Al and I worked with Mom to set up the funeral arrangements—at Humphreys Funeral Home on Bayview Avenue in Leaside, of course. At the single visitation there was a sea of people offering condolences. I had never seen a room so jam-packed! What a tribute! I went through the motions on auto pilot. To this day I don't remember a single thing about the actual service. Al and I watched out for Mom, although she was swamped with support and kept up her spirits as best she could. My brother did not return to his job in Jasper and remained in Toronto to be with Mom for the next year. I admired his sense of responsibility and was thankful of that decision.

For months after my father's passing, I thought I saw him everywhere. I was very depressed. I had little interest in Christmas, a favourite time of the year for me. I came to realize that you don't get over a death; you only get used to it. And finally, years later, I did—get used to it, that is.

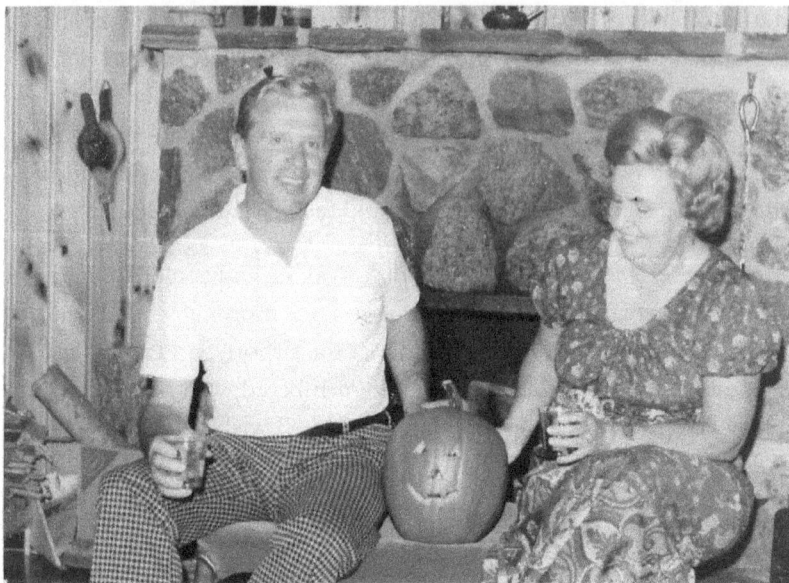

Dad and Mom at the cottage

"This Old House"
Rosemary Clooney, 1954

When I finished my last year at Ryerson, we had a celebratory graduation party at the Coach House at 24 Anvil Millway where Pam and I were living. We happily lived there until 1976 when we purchased our first home—a new housing concept being introduced at the time called a townhouse. The address was 20 Brimwood Boulevard, TH 56. It was just north of Brimley and Finch in a newly developing area of Scarborough. Our neighbours were great and we socialized a lot with them, and even took disco dancing lessons at our recreation centre to all of the hottest hits from *Saturday Night Fever*!

This was where we met our neighbours, Sally and Glen Loates, with whom we became very good friends, and whose continuing friendship became pivotal in a career change for me some 17 years later. In 1980 we actually bought Sally and Glen's townhouse when they decided to move to a much larger home in Maple to accommodate an expanding family and provide more studio space for Glen, an artist, to paint. Not too long before that they had the basement of their townhouse completely and beautifully finished into a show piece recreation room which included a reclaimed brick fireplace and a stainless steel vault, which Glen used to store his drawings and paintings in. Every square foot had been utilized. It really was stunning!

But, Pam, impulsive as was often the case, got it into her head to move again. I, of course, was a little resistant to change (surprise!) It was 1982. One weekend we drove out to look at a few out-of-town properties which she had found listed and we ended up looking at a century home in Claremont just north of Pickering. Now driving to and from Claremont was viewed as one hefty commute to work at the time, as there was not (for many years yet to be) a Highway 407 toll route to quickly connect one to Toronto and our respective places of employment—a minor detail to Pam. Pam did not exactly bolster our bargaining position when she blurted out in front of the real estate agent, "I want this house!" Thank you very much.

Claremont was a tiny, "four corners" hamlet with a post office, general store, public school and gas station/restaurant. And that was about it! The little village was smack in the middle of the region designated for the proposed new Pickering Airport which was to serve the greater Toronto area. While the locals fought an eventually successful campaign called "People or Planes" against the proposed airport, no development had been allowed for many years on the "airport lands". I'm not sure what illustrious committee decided on this ridiculous location for an airport when north of Highway #7 is one of the worst weather areas for fog and snow.

I hadn't minded our other housing moves, but this change was really giving me trouble. Pam really wanted this place and I mistakenly thought this move might help our marital troubles. Because I very much liked history and loved antiques, one aspect that really appealed to me was the fact that 1773 Central Street was a century home built in 1860! It was a former Baptist Manse situated directly across the street from the Baptist Church. It had 10 foot ceilings on the main floor, 18" baseboards, hardwood floors throughout, a big bay window perfect for a huge Christmas tree, a huge open kitchen and family room and three bedrooms. And it was on a large piece of property with big fir trees and a rickety garage originally used to stable horses. A lot of things appealed to this cottage boy. What didn't appeal to me was the fact that this was a definite fixer-upper with a ton of work and future expense in store. Plus the commute was definitely not an attraction.

We took possession on December 15, 1982 and, just before we moved, we found out Pam was pregnant! The timing was less than propitious. We had made the decision that we wanted children; we just didn't expect it to happen so fast, once we had decided. (It is interesting to note how history can repeat itself in that way, in future generations— leapfrog forward 25 or 30 years.) On the bright side, at least we found out we could have kids, as Pam was now 35. We had waited some time in our marriage for careers to get established and before actually deciding whether we wanted children.

So here are two city folk about to try country living—something akin to that 1960s' TV show, *Green Acres*. It was a very warm December that year when we moved in 10 days before Christmas and it rained heavily on Christmas Eve. In fact, it rained so much that our basement flooded! Of course, packed cardboard boxes from the move were strewn all over the basement floor. I had to find some high water boots and splash around in the dirty water moving boxes onto improvised platforms of hastily assembled wood. Merry Christmas!

Nevertheless, we had Christmas at our new home. I covered gaping holes in the wood lathe and plaster dining room walls with big pine boughs. With the lights dimmed, this looked cleverly festive while at the same time facilitating a happy, but temporary practical solution to the mess that the walls were in. On the bright side, we had a beautifully decorated ten foot high spruce Christmas tree from Quebec majestically holding court in our beautiful bay window in the living room.

r Claremont home, 1988

As we always pay for any good weather we get in this country, January proved to be the opposite of December in that it was a bitterly cold month. Shovelling snow by hand off our circular driveway was exhausting enough, but one day we came home to a house with no heat! Our oil tank had run dry. We didn't know enough to contract with a supplier who would regularly check and fill the tank. We had foolishly assumed that the existing fuel service would just continue! Needless to say we felt very foolish about this obvious oversight and had to do some quick scrambling. Welcome to country living!

When we discovered the absolutely exorbitant cost of heating this less than airtight and well-insulated old house, we had a load of firewood dropped at the side of the house for the brilliant idea we had of heating the two storey house with our kitchen wood stove. However, the pile of wood needed further splitting to fit into the wood stove. "How quaint," I thought, as I lay exhausted on the couch after swinging the axe for an hour!

And the weather extremes continued to play tricks on us. One day that first summer, we suddenly had no water! Because of almost drought-like conditions, our well had run dry. Hello, we have a well? We had to arrange for a truck to come in and fill our well up with water to tide us over until the well filled up by itself again. What's that expression about falling off the turnip truck yesterday? A couple of years later the government offered a subsidy to homeowners who would drill a well and end their reliance on shallow dug wells and on the possible contamination of the water. We took full advantage.

As the years rolled along at Claremont, we contracted to have the walls re-drywalled, the exterior brickwork tuck pointed, new front and back porches put on, custom screens made for the windows, and a second bathroom installed. I personally sanded all of the hardwood floors in the main floor and sanded down the painted floors on the second floor to reveal beautiful pine boards which I stained. Sanding down uneven floors that had several thick coats of hundred year old paint on them was no picnic though—a definite labour of love! I also painted or papered the walls of every room in the house, including the 18" baseboards, doors and mouldings.

Our plan was to authentically restore that historic home as much as possible, not renovate it. Big difference! How I grew to love every floorboard and nook and cranny of that old house. And I loved being in the country. And I didn't really mind the commute. It wasn't exactly a cottage feel, but it certainly wasn't a city feel either! And, as we added significant antique furniture pieces that we were collecting, the home started to take on a period piece feel. The whole project appealed to my artistic side and love of history.

The Claremont house had character! I reveled in playing historical detective to discover how the original rooms had been designed and for what purposes they had been used—all most intriguing because the house had been a manse and functioned as an office as well as the minister's family home. I found out that the matching red brick church directly across the street was actually built later than the manse. How could that be so? Well, it turns out that the original church building was a wood framed structure that was replaced after the manse itself was built!

And whenever there was a drought, the foundation of the old country kitchen (that at one point had been built on to the back of the brick house) was evident in the pattern of burned grass which abutted the current kitchen. Similarly, evidence of the concrete walkway from the front door of the house appeared in the grass. It led directly across the street to the church! And the front porch was used exclusively for parishioners to visit the minister, as it accessed what was originally his office, now our dining room. Because of its secluded nature, the minister's office could be discretely accessed for private meetings with confidentiality assured. All very fascinating to uncover the original design and purpose of each room and feature!

While the Claremont house remained our home for the better part of 10 years, it has always been a regret of mine that I never was able to finish restoring the home to its former stately glory. The years had treated it harshly during its time, not as a manse, but as a group home for children, among other prior uses. Unfortunately, full restoration would have taken a lot of money, as old homes are a money pit. But, the breakup of our family sealed its fate to ultimately be delivered into someone else's hands to carry on the privilege of historical restoration. It would have been a beautiful ending though.

"Teach Your Children (Well)"

Crosby, Stills and Nash, 1970

Our son, Matthew William Gordon Ross, was born on July 6, 1983, just seven months after Pam and I moved to Claremont. What a wonderful day that was! The miracle of a tiny baby! Matt was born in Scarborough Centenary Hospital by caesarean section. We had decorated a room for his arrival home. During the summer Pam wasn't teaching, but mothers were only allowed six weeks off work in those days, unlike the twelve months that today's moms get. We thought that was pretty generous, as maternity leave had been raised from two weeks not that long before! However, it is certainly a far cry from the full year of maternity leave available today!

Anyone will tell you that having a baby changes your life. And, they are right. It changes your outlook and your priorities, not to mention the time you have available to do the things you used to do without having to consider a small person. But, it's a labour of love. It's selfless. There is such a connection; such an instantaneous bonding. Your thinking and focus does a 180. Your child is so dependent. He becomes the focus of family life and activities. It is a 24/7 job, but it is a privilege, and a huge responsibility, to be entrusted with a human life. You would do anything for your kid, and you do. You want only the best for him and you try very hard to do just that.

Pam and I decided that we would like a second child, not quite as quickly as it happened, but that was okay. Twenty-two months later, on April 30, 1985, Kathryn Elizabeth O'Neil Ross was born, again by caesarean section (planned this time) and again at Scarborough Centenary, and by appointment this time. For both children we knew the sex ahead of time due to the necessity of amniocentesis because of Pam's age. I attended both births, and almost missed that of our second child, as the doctor seemed to forget about the husband and dad. I got called in just as our daughter emerged from the womb.

We always knew that she would be called Kate, and so she was; but, Pam and I had quite a spirited discussion over Kate's middle name of "O'Neil". It was the name of a young student who was special to Pam. I didn't like the name at all. In the final analysis, I thought that as Pam had gone through all of the difficulties associated with the birth, and they weren't easy pregnancies, that she should be able to call our daughter whatever middle name she liked. And so O'Neil it was! And frankly, with all of the unusual names bestowed upon newborns today, I now must admit that I find the name O'Neil quite unique!

Pam and me with Matt and Kate, 1985

Can one ever forget the first time their child is able to crawl, or stand, or take his first step? Does a parent care how many times their kid throws up on them, or how often diapers need to be changed? Matt and Kate each took a couple of years before they were able to sleep through the night, so that was about four consecutive years of getting up two or three times each night! You don't mind, but it was enough! Ironically, I am once again getting up two or three times a night, but now for an entirely different reason. I would gladly have played Mr. Mom, if we hadn't needed two incomes, or if convention at the time allowed dads to assume that role, or if I didn't have a corporate career to maintain.

So, fairly suddenly in quick succession, at the ripe old ages of 35 and 37, Pam and I had two children, a boy and a girl—one of each, a millionaire's family! Today that expression means that it costs a million dollars to raise them! Our course was now set for the next 20 years while we raised our children. It was a set course alright, but not necessarily a straight one!

Matt and Kate

"(I Can't Get No) Satisfaction"
The Rolling Stones, 1965

I had had enough of working for an American firm which treated Canada as a fiefdom. When I left Upjohn I had three Canadian companies in my sights. The three companies were Paramed Home Health Services, MDS Health Group and Tridont Health Care. I cold called all three. I had danced with Paramed before but not gone farther than that. They were quite interested in talking with me, but, unfortunately, they didn't have a suitable position open at the time. My discussions with MDS went well and there was a job offer to be had, although as yet unspecified, but then I got a strike from Tridont while I was in discussions with MDS.

Tridont had a different approach to hiring than many companies did. It identified good people for its organization, often without a particular position in mind, and hired them. MDS' approach was similar too, actually. However, Tridont offered the fresh challenge that I was looking for, and with a specific position in mind. It was a start-up company that was successfully taking Bay Street by storm by pioneering storefront retail dentistry, medical walk-in clinics, podiatry and optometry. This novel retail approach was at the time a brand new concept for the consumer. Today, it is commonplace. After 11 years with a very traditional corporate company (Upjohn), I was looking for a dramatic change. I just didn't expect the corporate pendulum to swing so radically when I found it!

I accepted the position at Tridont to head up a new chiropractic division. I would locate and sell license agreements to chiropractors with existing practices who would set up shop in the Tridont Health Courts (much like a Food Court) that Tridont was building in major malls across Canada. Latterly at Upjohn I had set up franchises, and this aspect had appealed to Tridont's management. I was quite torn between MDS and Tridont, and told my contact at MDS, the VP, Human Resources. He told me that I belonged with MDS but that at this point in my career I needed to try the more radical Tridont experience. He said to call him when I left Tridont, which he predicted I would after a couple of years. And, he was right!

My fancy title was Chief Operating Officer of First Chiropractic Services. It was meant to impress when the company was getting ready to go public and issue an IPO (Initial Public Offering) and it did. However, I quickly knew there may be a business management problem when I asked the Chief Financial Officer what my budget was and his response was, "We don't use budgets here. We're too successful. We keep making money and the banks keep funding us." Oka-a-y.

As Chief Operating Officer of First Chiropractic Care Centres, along with Brian Huggins, President of FCCC

The two dentists who had the brilliant idea to start the Tridont concept were Howard Rocket and Brian Price—great names for business entrepreneurs! These two bright chaps were unbelievably aggressive in how they went after business but could be inconsistent in how they treated their employees. For a few years they were the darlings of the business world—the wunderkinds! Howard I quite liked and could relate to; he had great relational skills and could sell ice cream to Eskimos! Brian was the business development guy and drove an Astin Martin. If he had a problem with you ... watch out, you could be gone!

Their expectations of employees were at times outrageous. I remember one night Howard called in to the office about 9 p.m. to see who was working. He had been over to the office of his buddy, Garth Drabinsky, the Canadian film and theatrical entrepreneur of Livent fame, and later infamy, where everyone was at work at that hour, so Howard expected his staff should be as well! I happened to answer the phone (a rare occasion when I actually was working that late) which was a good piece of luck on my part, but not so for a few other employees who weren't at work.

On the other hand Howard and Brian could unexpectedly be quite generous. They threw a huge corporate party at the exquisite La Maquette Restaurant on King Street in celebration of their IPO (Initial Public Offering). No expense was spared. I still have some unique, and perhaps now collectible, gifts from the occasion. One summer, Howard hosted a gigantic summer party at his posh summer home on Lake Simcoe. I also visited Howard at his home on The Bridle Path on more than one occasion. And, out of the blue, Brian had a jacket embroidered with First Chiropractic Services and anonymously left it on my desk as a gift. It took me days to figure out where it came from.

We were successful in establishing a few license agreements with chiropractors. But, there were two incidents that pushed the boundaries of my ethics. The first was when I was under a great deal of pressure to get a lady signed to a lease agreement for a location in a health court, for I was now handling some leasing responsibilities. Brian absolutely insisted that I go to the hospital where she was convalescing after an operation, and get her signature on the agreement. I thought this totally inappropriate but I did visit her as a concerned business partner. While we did discuss the agreement, she was not ready to sign, and I did not push to get her signature, as I had been directed.

The second incident was one that I regret participating in to this day. Again under tremendous pressure to get chiropractors signed up to the proffered success that practising under the Tridont banner "virtually assured them", I pushed a newly graduated chiropractor to sign and he did. I am by nature not a pushy person, so this did not sit well with me. However, the problem was really that my experience told me that this guy would not make it either as a successful chiropractor, or as a successful Tridont licensee. He was putting up a lot of money. I feel bad about that to this day.

By now I was severely questioning how much longer I should stay at Tridont. At the same time Tridont was starting to feel the significant pressures of expanding too fast and not using budgets. Brian told their General Manager to fire me allegedly for not selling enough license agreements and retail storefront space. But, I reported to Brian, not the General Manager. Brian didn't have the guts to face me! I tracked Howard down immediately, but, although he was empathetic, the deed was done and out of his hands. It wasn't that I didn't want to leave Tridont; it was that the reasons I was given for my dismissal were not valid.

However, a more than fair severance package was given to me, most likely to prevent legal action. I had spent two years there from 1986-1988, as my learning curve continued. Within a couple of years though, Tridont's initial meteoric rise to corporate success took an equally steep trajectory downwards.

"Two Out of Three Ain't Bad"
Meat Loaf, 1977

One down, two to go. So I had the Tridont experience; that brought me down to earth again. I called up my friends at Paramed, but nothing was happening there. I called up Ed Boyce, my MDS contact, and found he was just about to get in touch with me to see how I was making out at Tridont. This time I accepted a position at MDS Health Group as Director of Industrial Health Services. I had an industrial staffing service, industrial health clinic, executive health clinic, Workers Compensation evaluation service, audiometric testing, and occupational health service reporting to me. I was reporting to Ed Rygiel, VP, New Business Development, and one of the MDS founders. He wanted me to franchise this business.

I quickly ascertained that this was not a franchisable business. There were six quite different businesses here and three were not profitable. You couldn't go and franchise six distinct businesses that were essentially stand-alones, and not profitable ones! I had to convey this to Ed which quickly curbed his enthusiasm. My role now changed as I was charged with assessing each of these businesses and working with Doug Phillips, another MDS founder and the Chief Financial Officer, to find solutions as to how to handle these businesses—keep them, sell them, build them, spin them off, or what? The first thing I did was call up my old friends at Upjohn and offer them the opportunity to purchase the industrial nursing service, and they did. We also spun off the industrial health clinic, selling it to the resident health director on favourable terms.

And so it went...until I had finessed myself out of a job! But, MDS does try to take care of its own, particularly when they had asked me to deconstruct the business that I was to have originally managed and expanded. MDS is a class operation and all about treating its employees well. I was next assigned to manage OCW. What's with all of these companies that abbreviate to letters? OCW was the in house purchasing arm of MDS. It also included a manufacturing company, the company fleet, and a diagnostic imaging, mobile ultrasound and holter monitoring business.

Again under Doug Philips, I was charged with figuring out what to do with these entities, while managing OCW. I was based out of Mississauga and commuting from Claremont—now that's a long haul! Then I took over the diagnostic imaging business in the United States which was mainly concentrated in New York State with bases in Buffalo, Rochester and Albany. This assignment I particularly enjoyed because of the people I was working with.

And once again Don worked himself out of a job! This time I was assigned to manage the Kitchener lab as Regional Manager at a time when the company was going through its "simplification" or restructuring process. There would be much downsizing. The challenge was that the staff had been there forever and this region had operated autonomously and in relative isolation, if not insulation, under its previous Regional Manager. They were a tough sell and totally resistant to the type of change that was going to be expected of them. I didn't yet know the business well enough to be able to effectively introduce and implement the required changes with these seasoned and resistant veterans.

I had been up against some challenging situations before but this one really got to me. I was so extremely stressed out that I collapsed in a meeting while addressing the troops! I ended up in hospital briefly after the doctor from the urgent care clinic upstairs had been called down to attend. That was it! I didn't need the stress anymore and told my manager that I was "stepping away" from this assignment. In retrospect MDS management and I both felt that I had in this case been placed in an untenable position, a no-win situation for me.

My boss told me to take a few days off and so I headed to that one place in my life that I could always count on for peace and tranquility— the cottage. A few beautiful fall days there, a 36" Muskie, and I regained some perspective. I shopped myself around MDS and landed a six month assignment, this time to develop a marketing plan for a new business for the Vice-President of New Business Development. But, the writing was now on the wall at that point and, after five years (1988-1993), I left the employ of MDS Health Group. While I had never really got to do what I was originally brought in to do, I did gain tremendous business and management experience in analyzing, deconstructing and finding solutions to a wide variety of either troubled or orphan businesses. Since I left Upjohn eight years before, I had now worked for two of the three firms that I had wanted to! And that ain't bad!

"Love on the Rocks"
Neil Diamond, 1980

There is this expression I once heard, "The grass doesn't grow any greener on the other side of the hill; it's just that the brown spots are in different places." How true is that! The implication is that relationships are all about "fit". They are about complementing each other, embracing positive attributes and accepting one another for who they are, rather than expressing dissatisfaction about what someone is not. They are all about finding a mate—a soul mate, if you are lucky—with whom you are compatible in most ways, not just some ways. You may indeed love someone, but sometimes love just isn't enough by itself. Love is not logical. I was coming to realize that life was about choices, and their ramifications. And I hadn't made the right one! I'm not saying that Pam and I didn't have good times; we did. And, out of our relationship came two wonderful children, and four precious grandchildren! So, while I perhaps didn't marry for all of the right reasons, there is no question there have been lasting blessings.

The second worst day of my life came in late April, 1989. Our relationship had deteriorated to the point that, sadly, there was no love left between us. On my part I had tried my best to change some behaviours that Pam felt needed changing, but it never seemed to be good enough. Or, perhaps it was too little too late; but, I felt that Pam was never satisfied. We were supposedly trying to work things out, but Pam was seeing someone else. I was being ripped apart emotionally dealing with suspicion and wondering about the unknown. I finally couldn't stand it any longer and called Pam out. We made the final break and we separated.

Our home had now just become a house, and that house which I had come to love dearly would now have to be sold. We would all be uprooted from the community we loved and the lifestyle we enjoyed. Good Lord, here comes the change thing again! Traumatic didn't begin to cover it. I really was at a loss as to what to do on the night Pam and I made the final split, so I showed up on the doorstep of my dear friends, Craig and Nancy Truscott, the most steadying influence I know, and poured my heart out to them. Their support bolstered my spirits. I then went to my mother's apartment to crash; feeling totally drained both physically and emotionally.

I was eaten up with jealous thoughts of Pam being with someone else, and the possibility of another man acting as father to my children. And, the fact that I had failed at marriage was a huge burden and certainly was at that time a social stigma. Failing at first year university was bad enough, but this took the concept of personal failure to a new level, particularly for a "hearth and home" kind of guy. In actuality, I entered a period of mourning for the death of my marriage. There was no question that I was grief stricken.

What had kept me hanging in for so long was very simple—the children. While Pam and I agreed on joint custody with the children living with their mother, I did seriously consider challenging for custody; however, in those days the custody courts most often found in favour of the mother. It seemed that she had to be either abusive, or on drugs, or preferably both, in order for a father to be granted custody.

I remember the day I had to tell Kate and Matt that when they got home from a visit to Barrie, there would be a "For Sale" sign on the only home they had ever known. Matt's questions and responses triggered a tidal wave of emotion and I went down into an abyss of depression. I honestly didn't know whether I would come out of that. Matt asked me, "Are we selling the house because it's too old? If you and Mommy are each going to have your own house, we've only got one fridge and one stove …" Ah, the logic of small children! Matt and Kate were everything to me. I held on tightly to the knowledge that they loved me and that no one else could replace their dad. I grasped for sanity amid chaos!

I felt more alone at that period of my life than at any other time. It seems the world revolves around partners, and suddenly I was without one. I faced the scary prospect of living on my own, something I had never done, and didn't feel at all confident that I would be good at doing. Friends, relatives, co-workers—everyone became my support group. That was a tremendous help. Nevertheless, whenever you say "so long" to friends at the end of an evening, you do still ultimately have to go home alone…and that is where you have to survive, to wrestle with your own personal demons, to make it on your own. And the silence can be deafening!

I knew that I would at some point again like a relationship with a woman—someone who would accept and love me for who I am. This whole experience matured me and I could see things differently. I felt light years ahead in awareness and relationship building. I am aware that there are two sides to every story and that the truth is usually somewhere in the middle! From day one of our relationship I thought that I could make Pam happy; but, that was misguided logic! Actually, I'm not sure that was logic at all! I tried hard to make Pam happy. Many, many years later I finally realized that only you can make yourself happy.

But, what really tore my heart out was that, while I might find another partner, I would never have my children living with me on a day-to-day basis. Matt and Kate lived with Pam, who had more time for them with school breaks and summers off. A custody battle would only incur great bitterness that would hurt the kids even more and probably irreparably kill any chance we had of ultimately co-operating amicably in our parenting responsibilities.

Regardless of my feelings, I had to put Matt and Kate first—no question! And so I sucked it up, and didn't fight for custody, although I desperately wanted to try! Maybe I was wrong not to fight. I do know it was an extremely tough decision and the greatest personal sacrifice I will ever make. But isn't that what any parent would do for their kids—make sacrifices? To give the kids the best chance for a relatively happy childhood after their parents screwed up. For them to (hopefully) not feel too torn between two parents is a better alternative than having the parents pitted against one another. What would have been gained by having Pam and me at each other's throats forever? Perhaps much would have been lost.

Donald Gordon Ross

"Back On My Feet Again"
Michael Bolton, 1990

After Pam and I separated, I lived in a state of pervasive unhappiness
and a feeling of complete isolation for months. How could it have
come to this? Everything was chaos! I couldn't sleep. I couldn't
concentrate. Being on your own is one thing; being alone is quite
another. Knowing I wouldn't see Matt and Kate on a day-to-day basis
was killing me. I stayed at my Mom's apartment, coincidently the next
building over from my mother-in-law. I visited the kids and sometimes
stayed with them overnight at Claremont during the week while Pam
stayed at her boyfriend's. I spent most weekends with the kids, either
at the cottage or in Claremont.

But, how did I cope? How did I survive this emotional turmoil? One
thing that I remembered was what my Uncle Al said to me once,
"Nothing happens unless you make it happen!" How true! I needed to
deal with the circumstances and take initiative. I was in this situation
(never mind that I was a least part of the cause) so I had a choice to
make—continue to feel sorry for myself, or decide to exert some
direction and control over the outcome. It was a matter of attitude,
and attitude is what it's all about. Despite being beaten up
emotionally, I desperately needed my usual positive attitude to prevail!
I needed to rebuild my life. I still had my career, my friends and my
family. The kids were the best thing to ever happen to me. I thought,
"Let's start with that."

As I just wanted to be with my family as they grew up, I easily
committed to devoting most weekends to Matt and Kate. My life
revolved around the kids, and I cherished every minute. The kids—
both my salvation and my Achilles heel emotionally! I sat and watched
them when they were asleep. I hoped they knew how much their dad
loved them.

After a couple of months I was at least having the occasional good day,
making adjustments, and not as severely depressed as I had been. I
was definitely still unhappy, but starting to adjust my attitude. I felt
that if I could just get the right perspective that I would be able to start

enjoying life again. I'm told that you will survive a marital break-up; but, I wanted to live, not just survive. How could I have ever imagined then, in 1989, that twenty-three years later I would be called upon to face an even greater personal challenge and many important choices— this time for the physical as well as the emotional survival of my life?!

Over to Mom's for dinner, Father's Day at Sherry and Sean's, going to the cottage every weekend—a great source of tranquility amidst the personal turmoil! The cottage was a therapeutic retreat, a safe haven, the one constant all my life—a place that was like a friend! I had a visit from my childhood cottage friend, Dave Beardslee, now of Los Angeles, and his fiancée, Becky, whom I was meeting for the first time. They seemed well paired and indeed I was subsequently honoured to be included in their wedding party in Florida.

I also came to revel in the freedom of being on my own. I had never lived on my own. I would often have *Phantom of the Opera* blasting over the stereo at midnight as I prepared for guests to come for dinner the next evening. I kept busy with friends and family and began to carve out a new life by myself, for myself. I came to enjoy my own company. The silence became less deafening. I may have still been "emotionally unavailable" but I was getting back on my feet again.

After a year or so passed by, Matt and Kate were still spending most weekends with me, usually at my apartment at 2350 Bridletowne Circle in Scarborough. This was a great condo that I had rented—terrific layout, including a family room. My focus was to spend as much dedicated time as possible with them to ensure their Dad was an integral part of their lives, especially because their family unit had been torn apart. I would take care of business, errands, shopping and socializing as much as possible during the week so the deck was cleared for the weekends.

We all loved going to the show and there were many good movies for children that were always coming out during that time: Aladdin, Ghostbusters, The Lion King, Home Alone and Teenage Mutant Ninja Turtles come to mind as some of the more popular ones. We were, of course, no strangers to popcorn and candy while watching the show. The kids, I think, viewed visiting Dad on weekends as more of an adventure than the routine of home and school. Of course, their mother was more of a disciplinarian than I ever was, so there was that.

Sometimes we would play mini golf, visit with relatives, go tobogganing or go to Chuckie Cheese for pizza and games. I think there is still a roll of tickets around which Matt won and which has never been redeemed. Occasionally their Nana, my mom, would accompany us. She certainly enjoyed seeing her grandchildren. We would sit on the living room floor playing Quicksand, Life, Fish or Tornado Rex. I usually had a special dinner for the kids on Saturday night. The beef macaroni casserole and my spaghetti with a special meat sauce were favourites. Of course there would always be a dessert treat. Sunday nights we would often have my mother for dinner, or go to her place. During the week I scouted the TV listings for entertaining "age appropriate" movies to tape. Perhaps I should assume some responsibility here for being an early contributor to foster in my children, particularly Matt, a tendency to favour horror, science fiction and over the top action films.

I hated to have to take the kids home Sunday evening. That was always a downer. Occasionally I would go out to Claremont for the weekend while Pam was away. This had the added benefit to me of keeping in touch with our neighbour friends, the Watsons, the Watts and the Marshalls. Sadly, the Watts and the Watsons shortly thereafter each split up (there must have been something in the Claremont water) and the Marshalls moved to Edmonton. I, and latterly Allison and I, have kept in touch with Don and Lynn Marshall. Their son, Matthew, was one of my son's best friends. I used to call Matthew Marshall the "Double M", and later started calling Matthew Marshall's mom the "Triple M". But I didn't stop there, as I called Mathew Marshall's mother's mom the "Quadruple M"!

The two Matts would always be playing together. I would always call Matthew Marshall by both his first name and his surname so that he would know I was speaking to him. We originally met at a children's hour reading at the tiny Claremont library where we also discovered that both Matts shared the same birth date of July 6. At about six years of age we started letting them walk back and forth to each other's homes which was the equivalent of 2 or 3 blocks away. As parents, we would be phoning back and forth on their progress, as they were inclined to get sidetracked into snowdrifts or backyards. In their case, the shortest distance between two points was definitely not a straight line!

Once when he was nine, we sent our Matt to Edmonton to visit his good friend, Matthew Marshall. He flew unaccompanied, but Air Canada took good care of him. Quite an adventure at that age! While we parents have kept in touch over the years, the two Matts have not, partially because of the distance factor, and partly because they have become two different people going in different directions. In 2006 Allison and I, along with Matt and Kate, took a trip out West and visited with the Marshalls on the way. That was the last time we were all together.

Of course, going to the cottage with the kids was great, and we went together most weekends. We might stop at Hy Hope Farm to pick up some butter tarts, cookies, or bread pudding (a favourite of mine). We might hit Dave's Hamburgers in Minden for dinner, if we were early enough. My mom would still be staying at the cottage all summer, so weekends brought together the abridged family unit.

Matt, Mom, Kate, and me at the cottage

Matt and Kate loved the cottage, and as they grew older would often bring a friend along. Matt might bring Matt, or often Erik Reid, or Jay.

146

Kate might bring Christine Upton and later Kaitlyn Wild. Swimming, fishing off the dock, tubing, playing in the sand, mini golf and treats at the Donald Dairy Bar, and going to Head Lake Park or the Kinmount Fall Fair, were all activities they enjoyed.

Matt had a propensity for fire and knives—not exactly a parent's preference of occupation! He would smuggle up some caps or little firecrackers and blow up frogs or devise some other incendiary device. I remember years after he was grown up finding a 10" carving knife in the woods by the shore. I had always wondered where that knife had gone!

Just like for me, the cottage became the one constant, in terms of a home, in my children's lives. Matt and Kate have come to the cottage every year of their lives, and now their children are beginning to do the same.

Donald Gordon Ross

"The Twist"
Chubby Checker, 1960

In the summer of 1994 my good friend, wild life artist Glen Loates, his wife, Sally, and children Michael and Christopher, visited us at our cottage. I had originally met Glen in 1975 as a neighbour who had come knocking on our townhouse door wondering if we had lost our cat. As we talked, I found out Glen was a painter, which I took to mean as in "decorator", painting walls in homes. Little did I realize that he was already a renowned wild life artist taking the art scene and industry by storm! We had remained good friends over the years and socialized as couples, often with Ann and Paul Gibson.

Glen's wife, Sally, had been managing Glen's career and business in recent years but had returned to teaching. As I was consulting at the time, they asked me if I would be interested in preparing a marketing plan, as a consultant. Now here's the thing, if I had one wish, the one thing I would always like to have been able to do was to be an artist. If the truth be known, I should probably have taken some art classes in school to see if that interest was genuine and to determine whether, in fact, I might possess any natural talent. Glen certainly did and he was largely self-taught. At this point I could only draw stick people, and not very well!

I had always loved and appreciated art so it was never hard to be enthusiastic about Glen's work. I had, as his friend, the frequent opportunity to watch him draw and paint and I greatly admired his inspiring talent. His renderings positively leapt to life! I thought that the next best thing to being an artist was, in my case, working with one. I could see me tapping into my own creative side here. So, I easily accepted their offer. I was in seventh heaven! And so began what I didn't realize at that time would be a career changer!

Glen's work had been at the forefront of a booming interest in wildlife art in the 1970s and 1980s and he was certainly one of Canada's pre-eminent wildlife artists during this period. Glen was the first Canadian artist to be represented in The White House when, in 1982, he presented his painting of The Bald Eagle to President Ronald Reagan on behalf of the Canadian people. As the 1990s progressed though, interest in wildlife art had begun to wane in the marketplace. The wave had crested. We were on the down slope. That made it a tough go when Glen's images had already been mass produced as prints and published as limited editions. Glen had also enjoyed license agreements which had brought in royalties on many gift products from coasters and place mats to plates and calendars.

My consulting role soon turned into a permanent one as I began working out of the MGL Fine Art offices on Edward Avenue in Richmond Hill. (Still can't escape those three or four letter corporate abbreviations—this one stood for Martin Glen Loates!) Glen and I had many good times together and frequently went out to lunch or a movie together. Often I ended up at Glen and Sally's home to discuss strategy and spending Friday nights watching Mulder and Scully in *The X-Files* was a weekly must!

Working with Glen and Sally was never boring and I think they would unequivocally agree. Working with friends may or may not be the best idea but our friendship was never tested to an extreme. I did, however, often find myself in the middle of spirited discussions between Glen and Sally as they were frequently at odds over different directions to take. There were never any grey areas between them; points of view were always black or white, whereas I could often see both sides of a discussion. I'm so about being diplomatic.

I was fascinated by Glen's avid collection of Disney cartoon collectibles, as well as Star Wars and movie memorabilia which he had meticulously and strikingly showcased in the lower level of their lovely home in Maple. His keen interest and scientific knowledge, not just in the North American birds and animals for which he was renowned for painting, but also in the portrayal of all living things from the unplumbed depths of the sea to the creation of creatures of horror and the stuff of science fiction was truly incredible! I admire Glen's creative genius. It was truly astounding to me that he could, for example, sit down and play the piano. Nothing unusual in that, you might say. However, not only had Glen never had a piano lesson in his life; he was creating the music as he played!

I worked with Glen to set up exhibits and shows of his artwork and we relaunched his prints with new framing treatments. Various corporate deals were struck. Some original artwork was sold. I loved working with Glen's art and thoroughly enjoyed the creative aspects which ranged from the selection of framing treatments to the provision of advice on image choices.

Glen Loates sketching on our Florida trip

It was reinforced to me that skill sets are transferable. If you have developed the requisite fundamental business skills such as organization, operations, budgeting, sales and marketing coupled with sound common sense, rational thinking and relational abilities, these are applicable to any business. If you have these then you just have to gain product knowledge. I loved art, had a creative side and greatly admired Glen's talent in bringing nature and wildlife alive on paper. Moving from health care to art, then, was not so big a leap as you would at first think! But, it certainly was a twist in my career direction!

I worked with Glen and Sally for about four years and in the last couple of years was holding many travelling art shows of Glen's framed prints. But they both were getting frustrated that we couldn't generate more sales of Glen's artwork. Wild life art sales were continuing to soften. They wanted to consider new directions for the business so I now faced an important career choice. I phased out of my working relationship with Glen and Sally. I decided to venture out completely on my own in the business world of art. In 1998, I set up my own sole proprietorship called Canadian Brush Strokes. And, with my continuing history of abbreviations in companies I associated with, I privately thought of my company as CBS!

By then I had realized that I had an untapped creative side. I chose a new career path direction, forever leaving behind traditional employment in the corporate world. I encourage everyone to seek out their natural interests. Many of us "fall into" a career path. Do some self-analysis to discover your natural interests and aptitudes. Determine how to mould them into a vocation or career path. If you haven't always followed a dream you have had you may just need to uncover what's in your heart as well as what's in your head!

"I Left My Heart In San Francisco"
Tony Bennet, 1962

Mom was stoic after my Dad passed away. But that was her nature. Whatever had to be done, she sucked it up and did it. It doesn't mean she wasn't hurting or that she wasn't afraid or that she wasn't feeling bereft. She was. She just didn't show it, or talk about it, at least to us.

Because Mom was a social person and had many friends, she began to carve out a new life for herself and I admired her for being able to do that. She was always on the go with bridge, bowling, church, going to the movies, a play, reading, or lunch or dinner out with a friend. She kept busy. Both she and I were fortunate that my brother, Al, did not return to his job out west in Jasper after my father died, but rather stayed home to live with Mom in this most difficult time. I will always admire his sense of family obligation. That he was a great support and comfort to her, I have no doubt. After a year or so, Al headed out to California to visit friends. He never returned to live back here; he only returned for an occasional visit. He couldn't put his wanderlust and life on hold forever.

In 1983 after declining health, my mom's father, my Poppa, passed away. It was one of the saddest days of my life! Another blow, but at least without the unexpectedness and shock that my father's passing had caused. Also, in 1983, my first child, and my mother's first grandchild, Matt, was born, and then my daughter, Kate, came along two years later.

Having the regrets which I've already noted about time missed with my father in later years, I was bound and determined not to make the same mistake with my mother. I made a conscious effort not only to be supportive but to make sure that we kept Mom involved in family activities. Pam and I included Mom as much as possible with the kids' upbringing, birthdays, Christmas and the like. She adored her grandchildren and loved to visit or have us over. Mom would play games with Matt and Kate and read them stories and make her special brownies. I used to jokingly complain that when Al or Matt was around the brownies were always iced, whereas, if it was just me...well, let's just say there was something missing for this chocoholic.

Mom began to go to Naples, Florida each winter for about three months and stayed in my Aunt Marge and Uncle Al's condo which they had originally purchased for my grandfather's use. Mom still stayed at the cottage for July and August each summer. She would have her friends up to stay for a week and still found bridge partners, especially with our old Rykert neighbours, Betty and Max Strang or Glenna Beckham. Pam and I would visit on the weekends with the occasional full week of vacation.

In 1977 Pam and I had bought our own fixer-upper cottage on Monrock Lake in Haliburton east of Tory Hill. "Fixer-upper" was the operative word and gave new meaning to that phrase. The roof line had a decided sag to it and the cement block pillars underneath lurched at what I could only describe as jaunty angles, somehow collectively supporting the structure. And don't lean on the deck railing! The place came with the requisite outhouse, on a hill no less, and there was no running water. Or, at least like at Chateau Woodland, I provided the running! The precipitous 300 ' Monrock Lake driveway made the steep hill on the driveway of my parents' cottage on Peninsula Drive look like a straight stretch on Hwy 401!

Actually, I loved the "project" that our little retreat became. I loved the work and I loved the quiet isolation on the motor-free lake. And autumn walks on old logging trails were an experience where you could both revel in the beauty of the pre-Cambrian shield and experience the sheer joy of solitude at the same time! Once I remember my friend, Glen Loates, sitting in our living room one rainy afternoon drawing this incredibly huge deep sea creature lunging up out of our tiny calm lake. What a juxtaposition of opposites!

In 1980 though, Pam and I decided to give up our own cottage and just go to The Trossachs. With Dad gone, I couldn't keep up both places. Our own fixer-upper still needed a lot of fixin' up and there was just no way that my parents' cottage could be maintained by my mom.

Mom and her grandchildren, Matt and Kate

Over time, Mom had two heart attacks, one at the cottage, but recovered well from both. I remember the second one because I was living with her at the time after my separation from Pam. I came back to her apartment one day to find a note she left on the hall mirror indicating that she had gone to the hospital with a suspected heart attack. Typical Norma—just go and deal with it!

For Mom's 75th birthday we had a big party at the Granite Club attended by many friends and relatives. Mom enjoyed pretty good health until she was 78. The doctors had been monitoring a stomach aneurysm and were concerned because it was growing. Should it rupture, she would almost certainly not make it to a hospital in time and would die! So, surgery seemed a reasonable course. It was deemed relatively routine. The night before the surgery we were at Heather and Mike Weaver's for dinner. We all had a great time, but I wondered, just like I had with Dad, whether it would be the last dinner we would have together. In a way, it was.

Mom told me on the way to the Toronto General Hospital that she had a bad feeling about the surgery and told me that she had left her will on her dresser. But, Mom sailed through the surgery! Great! I phoned everyone to tell them the good news. Whoa, boy, hold on! A few hours later, while in the step down unit, she suffered a debilitating stroke! Her last words to me were "I just want to go." And with that she lapsed into a coma.

Here we go again. Even though one is always nervous before an operation, I was certainly not expecting this! Seventeen years after my father's death I had seen a lot more of life and could handle this in a less personally devastating way, but I was still terribly upset. I had to start phoning people with this drastic turn of events, just after calling them a few hours before with news of how successful the surgery had been—déjà vu.

After two weeks in a coma, Mom was not improving. The prognosis was not good. The doctors counselled us on the option of discontinuing the feeding tube, in which case she would die peacefully in a few days. I had the Power of Attorney for Personal Care. Now here's a moral and practical dilemma, an agonizing decision. It's a terribly stressful position to be put in to decide whether "to pull the plug" on your mother's life. Ultimately, I believed that her wishes would be for us to let her slide peacefully away when there was so little chance of recovery. And so , after consultation with family members, I authorized the discontinuation of my mother's feeding tube, and in so doing, made a decision to end my one remaining parent's life. It was a most burdensome choice to have to make! It was tearing me up!

Two days after we discontinued the feeding tube, I brought 11 year old Kate and 13 year old Matt, her grandchildren, to see her probably for the last time. Kate was speaking to her Nana, as we all did when we visited, in the off chance that she was trapped in her brain, unable to communicate or move, but possibly able to hear us. As Kate spoke with Mom, she woke up briefly and responded. We were stunned. OMG, what to do now?

"What we do", I said, "is start the feeding tube again." I could not bring myself to pull the plug if there was any kind of sign of possible recovery. Not sure I had full family support on this point, but it was my decision to live with either way. Tough choice! Let's see what happened. What happened was that my mother came out of the coma and started on the road to recovery.

Now "recovery" is a relative term. Mom was conscious and could understand us. Her ability to speak was severely impaired. A yes or no response initially was all. The occasional two or three word sentence followed later. She could haltingly read parts of get well cards. She could not move her legs. She did learn to feed herself. Mom transferred to a nursing home close to where I lived and I visited her frequently. I would call up her friends on the phone from her bedside and have them speak with Mom so that she had some connection with the outside world—with her former world. She smiled and laughed when I made jokes. Little did I know that—fast forwarding 15 years—I would be in a similar state as my mother in many ways!

Her friends came to visit. Later I arranged for Wheel Trans to bring her to and from the nursing home to my apartment on many Sundays when the kids were there so that she could join us for dinner. I got rid of my dining room suite, replacing it with hers, in hopes she would feel more at home. I still wonder if I did her a disservice keeping her alive with such a frustratingly restrictive recovery. I wondered whether the pity and sadness that her friends and relatives must have felt for her would be so evident to her as to make what was a miserable life even more miserable. I wondered if I had been selfish in my decision to keep her alive.

I asked her on several different occasions, "Mom is it worth it? Are you getting enough out of this restrictive existence to make being alive worth it?" Her answer each time was an emphatic, "Yes!" The will to live is an amazing thing! I worked even harder and more consciously to try to maximize what she could get out of her radically altered life, one in which she now didn't even remember that she had a cottage or even remember being married to my father.

Mom lived for two years after we had disconnected the feeding tube and passed away at last in 1998 in her 80th year. My last words to her were, "I love you, Mom." Her last three words to me were, "I love you." We had a memorial service 10 days later. Al and I put together the service in conjunction with the minister at Northlea United Church. We both spoke and we had some of her favourite songs played, including *I Left My Heart in San Francisco*, *Chances Are* and *This Guy's In Love*. The church was packed. It was a real tribute of respect, support and friendship. Norma Ellen was well loved. Her ashes were spread over Grass Lake, Haliburton, in the same spot as my father's—a fitting resting place near the cottage they loved!

Mom and me at Al and Gail's wedding

1999 – 2011   A Man in Love!

"Take A Chance On Me"
Abba, 1978

For many years after my break up with Pam, I considered myself "emotionally unavailable". I knew deep down that I would like another relationship but I was afraid of being badly hurt again. Those scars seemed to be taking a long time to heal. My focus had been on my kids for several years and I certainly didn't regret that at all. I knew one thing for sure and that was that I did not want to get married again!

Some people look for love for years and never come close to finding it. And sometimes love sneaks up on you when you least expect it. I had been on a few dates, and even dated someone for a few months, but nothing had clicked. One day in late June of 1999, my friends, Blair and Sandy Forsythe, invited me to dinner at their Huron Street century home in downtown Toronto, and mentioned a friend of Sandy's would be joining us for dinner. (Actually Blair and Sandy were very good friends of my brother's and that's how I had come to know them.)

I certainly had no suspicion at the time that they were setting me up, arranging an introduction, as it were, with a friend of theirs, Allison Elliot. Apparently Sandy had been telling Allison for some time that she knew of a guy she should meet. Finally Allison told her to "get on with it then", and hence a plot was hatched for this dinner meeting. It was a particularly busy time for me in my life with a number of things going on so I wasn't really looking for anyone at that point. However, Allison and I hit it off from the opening hellos. We shared the same sense of humour and it felt, like it does on some occasions when you meet someone, that we had known each other for years. We were very comfortable with each other and had a fantastic evening. As we bid our goodbyes to Blair and Sandy, I escorted Allison to her car and bestowed a chaste kiss on her cheek. Little did I know that gesture virtually sealed the deal in her mind!

I thought about asking Allison out; but, as I mentioned, it was a particularly hectic time in my business. I was also facing an imminent move, and I was going to the cottage on weekends, so I didn't. Should have, but I didn't. Choices! But, Allison too made a choice—to call *me*. Chicken that *she* was though, Allison called me up on a weekend, when she knew I wouldn't be home, and left a message. One of the best decisions she ever made! Choices—what if she hadn't called? Our first official date was going to the Toronto Outdoor Art Show at Nathan Philips Square with a bite to eat afterwards at Le Marche. We had a fun time together and started seeing each other. And the rest, as they say, is history!

Allison and me

A big test for me was bringing Allison up to the cottage for a weekend. It was absolutely wonderful! I felt like I was 16 again, only with 50 years of seasoning! I remember one weekend in August turning to her in the cottage kitchen, as she was washing up some dinner dishes, and telling her, "I think I'm falling in love with you." An even bigger test was introducing her to my children, Matt and Kate. They were 14 and 16 at the time, certainly a very impressionable age, so we wanted to orchestrate this meeting very carefully. We decided to have Allison drive to the cottage for the day only, no sleepover, on the day of our annual Thanksgiving party for our cottage neighbours. We wanted to do this in a crowd with the kids having home ice advantage.

I would not risk jeopardizing my relationship with my children no matter what the cost. A lot was riding on this meeting. The neighbours all received Allison very well and one in particular kept insisting that she should stay over; however, we stuck to our original plan and were reluctantly adamant that she had to leave for another commitment. As I came down our driveway after escorting Allison to her car the kids said, with big smiles on their faces, "Gee, Dad, you were a long time at the top of the hill." Allison had passed the test. Our strategy had worked!

So who took a chance on whom? Did Allison take a chance on me, as I am inferring...or, did I take a chance on myself?

"(You're My) Soul and Inspiration"
The Righteous Brothers, 1966

Allison and I were so immediately well connected in mind and spirit, so complementing to one another, so instantly "joined at the hip", that I knew I had found my true soul mate. "We are a unit," as Allison likes to say. I now knew that relationships were all about "fit", and Allison "fit like a glove". We loved each other unconditionally and passionately. Although past experience held me back a bit, I now knew I did want to marry Allison; it was a natural progression of our relationship, and I nervously contemplated how to propose. I thought that the most fitting location would be on our upcoming trip to France. Allison loved France, so it seemed apropos. Having never been there myself though I wasn't sure where exactly might be the most fitting place to make a declaration. However, I knew that when I saw it, I would know.

On May 29, 2003 we headed across the big pond to Paris and spent three fabulous days visiting the fabled city, staying in the charming Hotel du Rond—Pointe de Longchamp—just down the street from the Eiffel Tower. We toured Paris on top of a double-decker bus. Amid throngs of tourists, we visited Trocadero, Notre Dame Cathedral, the Arc de Triomphe, the Champs Elysses and the Grand Palais. Using Le Metro, we toured Versailles, bowled over by the chateau's opulence, the majestic setting of lawns, gardens and fountains, and the treasure trove of art!

And what would a trip to Paris be without visiting the Louvre! And so we did. Magnifique! We reveled in history seen through the fabulous exhibit of paintings, statues and murals. As I had been using a wheelchair (la chaise roulante) on some outings to ease the pain of heel spurs, I found myself having to climb a seemingly never-ending staircase, if I wanted to view the famed *Mona Lisa*. Well, I wasn't coming all this way not to! I pretended to struggle up out of my wheelchair to stand. As I self-consciously did so with all around watching expectantly, I raised my arms skyward, and in mock exaltation, exclaimed to everyone around, "It's a miracle!" And to everyone's amazement, I began to walk up the stairs and down the incredibly long marble corridor. All this to wait forever in line to see that the world's most famous painting was disappointingly less than two feet square and protected behind a glass shield! Never mind, I now had my own Mona Lisa in Allison!

Renting a cute little Twingo, and with Allison driving and me navigating (as was to become our custom in France) we headed for the autoroute and our destination of Lausanne, Switzerland. With posted speed limits of 130 km/h driving in France seemed to be well suited to Allison's particular abilities! The numerous roundabouts stressed me out completely, but Allison thrived on them! Fast speeds, following close, crazy French drivers, driving an automobile like a standard— France is a perfect fit for my lady! She had my complete support and respect for it. So she did all the driving, and I was quite happy to let her.

However, our pleasant motoring experience through delightful villages and picture-postcard valleys was interrupted, as Allison seemed to have attracted the attention of "les gendarmes". In hot pursuit they pulled us over and we played ignorant maintaining, "Nous ne parlons pas le francais." At a stalemate because of the professed language barrier, the three young gendarmes eventually left in frustration. We knew it was something about crossing a pedestrian crosswalk which unfortunately happened to have a pedestrian on it at the time. Heaven knows what we promised the exasperated policemen.

On our way to Zermatt, Switzerland, we motored through terraced vineyards and gorgeous scenery dotted by villages nestled on the mountainsides. Parking our conveyance in Tasch, we boarded the train to reach (no cars allowed) Zermatt up in the mountains. The towering mountain scenery was spectacular! After breakfast at the Primavera looking out at the Matterhorn, we boarded another train to take us to the top of the Gornergast. At 10,000 feet above sea level we gawked at the mountain peaks, as we were, oh so close to the clouds. Words were totally inadequate to describe the beauty and majesty of the scene. An emotional experience, we were in awe and humbled by nature's incredible arena. We stood in wonder. In recovery mode, we later dined at the Derby Hotel on the best saddle of lamb we had ever had! What a way to finish a day we will both treasure for the rest of our lives!

Saying "auf wiedersehn" to Zermatt, we pushed towards Monaco in the south of France, taking in the breathtaking panoramic coastal vistas and spectacular gorges as we approached the Mediterranean Sea— including hairpin turns, tunnels carved through mountains, steep canyons. And suddenly we burst out of one world into another equally memorable one, gazing upon tier after tier of cliff-side homes encircling the coastal undulations. We headed towards Monaco with Allison at the helm—full speed ahead!

We found our Hotel, the Westminister, perched on a tiny street just east of Monaco overlooking the blue azure Mediterranean. The view was worth millions. We had to pinch ourselves. After partaking of dinner, at an *Italian* bistro of all things, we took a bottle of wine out to the garden terrace overlooking the ocean. It was nighttime; it was the Mediterranean; it was Monaco! Romance was in the air! Earlier in our trip we had said we would talk about what we wanted to do with the rest of our lives. I was wondering if this was the right moment to pop the question. I realized that I probably wouldn't find a better moment, or place.

When a guy is thinking about popping the question, he doesn't expect to get upstaged before he can get the words out of his mouth, particularly by his intended! One glass of wine and Allison went from first to fourth gear—something like her driving—and floated the idea that maybe we should get married! That's it...pull the rug out from under me...steal my thunder! I think her exact words were something like, "I'm just going to throw this idea out on the table." Admittedly this opening sally caught me off guard and I started to chuckle. This, of course, was not quite the response that Allison was looking for. Realizing this, I quickly told Allison that I too had recently been giving considerable thought to the idea of marriage, and was, in fact, just looking for the right moment to propose to her on our trip! Now we both laughed!

The timing was right. It felt right. And, not to be one-upped, I came back with the suggestion that we get married right there in France! It's not often that Allison is at a loss for words but, after she stopped sputtering on her wine, she (shall we say) warmed to the idea. After some discussion on how, when, where and if, we tabled this line of thought for the evening. We retired for the night with excitement and much on our minds. And, how co-incidental was this, we made the decision to get married on the 4th anniversary of the night we met?!

Allison and me on our honeymoon in France

Allison and I toured Monaco and Aix-en-Provence, visiting medieval towns that were quaint, charming and entrancing. We experienced breathtaking vistas and hair-raising drives on every excursion. We were finally able to determine in Aix-en-Province that there is a 30 day inhabitancy period that couples must have before being able to get married in France, so that finished our thought about getting married on our trip. But, we felt that this special and most wonderful trip was our honeymoon. My intended and I were having a fabulous time together experiencing new wonders every day, soaking up the atmosphere from another time and place.

We stumbled upon an enchanting woodland lane trying to find a hotel called Domaine de Tournon. We emerged into what I can only describe as paradise in the blistering heat we had been experiencing. Ahead of us sprawled a 17th century stone chateau with fabulous grassed grounds, walkways, restaurant and swimming pool. We stayed for three days, basing day trips out of our new oasis.

With Allison's stellar driving and my intrepid navigational guidance, we threaded our way across lovely country back roads on day trips.

Trying to get around Aix-en-Provence was merely prep work for our assault on Marseilles. This was the big league of mazes, jumbled in every direction. We went round and round in circles, but getting downtown was impervious to vehicular assault, largely because of a massive demonstration of civil workers in the Ville Centre. From the huge flags that the citizens were waving, I thought we were reliving The Storming of the Bastille! Everything was gridlocked, and with impatient Frenchies breathing down our backs we didn't stand a chance. Allison, bless her heart, continued to drive in a state of "du calme" but we made a decision to cut our losses, get out of Dodge and make a run for Les Baux, a 15th century village and chateau, steeped in history and with yet another commanding panoramic view of Provence!

We were captivated by the ochre cliffs and village of Rousillon and were thrilled to meet artist Philippe Janin in his Bonnieux gallery. On one excursion we found ourselves in Arles standing in front of the café scene that Vincent Van Gogh made famous in his painting, Café Arles. A highlight of our Montpelier stop was the discovery of an art gallery in la Rue de l'Ancien Courier which carried original works by a Parisienne artist named Jean Pierson. We fell in love with his work and bought several high quality posters for my business. He had one original that I regret to this day not buying.

We had experienced a 16 day non-stop incredible journey—a feast for the visual senses and an emotional high—two soul mates in love, inspired by the trip of a lifetime together! And why not do the honeymoon first!

"Unforgettable"
Natalie Cole and Nat King Cole, 1994

Although we couldn't pull a fast one on all of our friends and relatives
by getting married in France, we still decided at our mature age that we
didn't have time to waste, so we set a wedding date for September 6,
2003, only eleven weeks after our return from France! We'll show
those young folk that you don't need two years to plan a wedding! It
was, admittedly, a busy eleven weeks putting together a wedding that
suited us both, as it was, after all, Allison's first marriage, while I had
been through this elaborate undertaking before

A wedding for two people in their fifties is quite a different vibe than
for two people in their twenties. It was more like a big party with all of
the people we would want to attend. One of Allison's key
requirements was that the wedding take place outdoors and by water,
and Allison's sister-in-law, Wendy Elliot, and her partner, Bob Burt,
graciously and enthusiastically agreed to host the occasion at their
lakeside home on Lake Couchiching. They threw themselves into the
wedding preparations; getting their lovely home ready and helping us
organize the grand event.

No decision had ever been easier for me than the one I was making to
spend the rest of my life with my lovely lady. No decision had ever felt
more right! I had found love when and where I least expected it. I
never thought that I would find my soul mate, and that is something
special. Our parents, Norma and Gord, and Dorothy and Douglas,
would have been delighted with the match! We knew we would have
had their blessings. Nonetheless, the groom was nervous on the big
day. I was up at sunrise at the Sundial Motel because I couldn't sleep.
The weather was perfect…24°C, bright sunshine, blue skies…as we
knew it would be, since for 26 of the last 27 years the weekend after
Labour Day had perfect weather!

We had a harpist playing soft accompaniment music as friends and
family gathered lakeside in the early afternoon. Wendy Tibbles, a good
friend of Allison's, was the official greeter. Allison's brother, John,
stood up for her along with her first friend, Judy Ross, as matron of

honour. And, what a wonderful experience it was for me to have my son, Matt, as my best man, along with my daughter, Kate, both standing beside me on the happiest day of my life. They are my pride and joy.

I acknowledged Bob, Sherry, Carolyn and Craig who were in the wedding party for my first marriage but who were not included in my wedding party this time. In my speech I told the audience that I felt I needed a fresh line-up—with the exception of my brother, Al, of course, whom we dusted off and reinvented for the occasion! Yes, we played a little joke on the 80 or so friends and relatives in attendance. We had my brother, Al, officiate!

Our wedding, September 6, 2003

No one except us knew that my brother, who had been living in the San Diego area for years now, was qualified to perform marriage ceremonies. There was astonishment as Al took his unannounced place at the front of the wedding party to perform the ceremony, not just because he was acting as the officiant, but as much because they considered him the most unlikely candidate to be performing this function at all! We did have to have a local minister co-officiate, as Al was not allowed by Ontario law to pronounce us husband and wife. It was really neat to have my brother co-officiate at our wedding and it added a very personal touch to the proceedings. We got the audience good on that one!

Allison had selected a traditional white wedding dress. After all she hadn't taken this leap before. She looked radiant! Her girlfriends had held showers for her and she had a blast! The guys all wore white silk shirts with Nehru collars and black dress pants. No jackets, no ties! Ye-s-s-s!! It was a blend of the formal and informal, which is what we were trying to achieve. It was a joyous occasion with a party atmosphere in a beautiful outdoor setting! Everyone attending had known us individually for most of our lives. The wedding took place a little after 2:00 p.m. with all of the guests seated facing the lake. The vows were customized. Everyone was so happy that Allison and I had found each other. I was thrilled that I had found true love and Allison kept repeating that it was worth the wait!

Wedding Party members Al, Matt, Allison, me and Kate

While the happy couple posed for photographs, guests enjoyed a cocktail reception. Round tables were grouped on a section of the lawn close to the lake and, as a nod to our honeymoon in France, decorated in the vibrant Provence colours of blue and yellow with table bouquets of yellow sunflowers. A wonderful buffet was served with a porchetta featured as a main dish. I had prepared a special honeymoon photo album of our trip to France all laid out in the style of old photo albums.

After the delicious feast of a dinner, there followed the requisite toasts. Allison's dear friend, Susan Tuck, proposed a toast to the bride.

Refraining from a roast of the bride, she spoke sincerely from the heart. Allison's brother John spoke, referring to how "twitterpated" his sister had been when she telephoned him upon our return from France, and how stunned he was when I asked him, as the senior family member, for Allison's hand in marriage. This was the only time I had seen John at a loss for words!

My childhood friend from Leaside, Heather Weaver (Moore), read a poem she had written for the event. My son, Matt, made a speech, despite severe stage fright, that brought tears to the eyes of several guests. And I, too, spoke on behalf of Allison and myself with a mix of humorous anecdotes and heartfelt appreciation for what we had found in each other. As the sun began to set, Allison and I cut the wedding cake and took centre stage for our first dance. It was "*Unforgettable*"!

Allison and me looking to the future

"In My Life"
The Beatles, 1965

So who is this special lady who captured my heart? What is her story? Well, AME—Allison McFaul Elliot—was born on June 3, 1947 in Toronto. Conceived out of wedlock to parents unknown, Allison was adopted six months after her birth by her most loving parents, Douglas and Dorothy Elliot. Douglas and Dorothy had already adopted one son, John, and had sadly lost three girls in childbirth or early infancy. Although they also had a child who survived, David, they desperately wanted a little girl and Allison was perfect! They had to wait to welcome her home, as she spent the first six months of her life in hospital to correct a wry neck.

Allison grew up in Weston, at the time a desirable family-oriented middle-class community in the west end of Toronto. Her father was a pharmacist, ending his career as Ontario Sales Manager for what was then Wyeth Pharmaceuticals. Allison always jokingly refers to her father as "the resident drug peddler". Her mother was a talented commercial artist for such major retail chains as Eaton's, Simpson's and Holt Renfrew.

After graduating from Weston Collegiate Institute in 1965, Allison continued to live at home with her parents. She worked for several businesses, before securing a position with AGF Management, a prominent mutual fund company in Toronto's financial district, where her adventurous spirit began to emerge. After a few years there, she was offered a position with AGF in Calgary as an administrator in their sales department when she was twenty-two. It didn't take her long to jump into her 1962 Anglia and head west. But, as much as she enjoyed spreading her wings, she returned home within the year to be at her parents' side when malignant tumors were discovered in her father's thyroid during a routine check-up. They were successfully removed, fortunately, and there was no recurrence.

Being so far from home when something goes wrong made her realize Toronto was the better place to be—but in her own place. She answered a shared accommodation ad in the newspaper (something one would never do today) and so began a lifelong friendship with

Susan Polly (Tuck) in Forest Hill. They soon became fast friends and the two toured France, Italy, England and Germany for a month the next year, knapsacks on their backs.

Leaving AGF, where she again had secured employment after returning to Toronto, Allison joined the Investment Dealers Association, advancing to the position of Assistant Secretary. She had fallen into a pattern of changing employers about every five years, and indeed after this requisite term moved to Junior Achievement of Canada where she launched Project Business across Canada, an in-school program that matches a business person with a grade 8 or 9 class. Continuing on her five year pattern of changing employers, she was invited to join Midland Doherty Limited as Corporate Secretary when it went public. She returned to her King and Bay haunts. It was while she was at Midland that her mother passed away.

Five years later, and with a variety of solid experience under her belt, Allison set up her own business called The Canadian Corporate Secretary Inc. In this capacity, she performed outsourcing work for companies that did not have a corporate secretariat, and found some fertile ground with junior mining companies, in particular. However, shortly after launching this endeavor, her father developed congestive heart failure and died within the year at 87 years of age.

The loss of her father hit her hard, but what really rocked her world only fourteen months later, was the sudden death of her brother, David, with whom she was so close. David was only 45 and had recently married. He was diagnosed with pancreatic cancer and quickly succumbed three months later on Christmas Eve. Two close family deaths falling so fast on the heels of one another emotionally devastated Allison.

**Back Row: Allison's brothers, John and David
Front Row: Allison's father, Douglas and Allison**

Adding to the emotional turmoil, Allison's start-up business just was not making it financially and within a year she had decided to give it up. She had also bought a house in Weston close to David and his wife, Wendy, after her father died. That placed added financial pressure on her situation. It was easily the most stressful time of her life. Little did she know then that 20 years later another life-threatening pancreatic illness to a loved one would cause her to shoulder another traumatic and heartfelt emotional journey!

But, back to her story…fortunately, at least from a work standpoint, Allison always seemed to land on her feet and find a job. After the venture into self-employment, she accepted the position as manager of the membership department at the Toronto Real Estate Board (TREB). Part way through her usual five year stint, Allison suffered a massive heart attack at 48 and almost died. Emergency bypass surgery was required and the doctors cracked open her chest cavity! A 3½ month recuperation followed the surgery and she has never had a problem with her heart since!

When her position at TREB became redundant in 1996, Allison took a crack at starting her own business again, this time calling it The Practical Paralegal. The focus was on incorporations, uncontested divorces and small claims court matters. She picked up a new gig working at the Real Estate Institute of Canada and continued to develop her own paralegal business. Finding it tough to make The Practical Paralegal lucrative enough for her requirements, Allison became Assistant Corporate Secretary at Foresters, but after 18 months she was laid off due to a restructuring. Now Allison looks forward to retirement in 2014 after 10 years in the corporate secretariat at Professional Engineers Ontario (PEO)—her longest term of employment at any one company—rounding out her full and active career!

TREB and AGF were probably the most enjoyable places that she worked, perhaps because the camaraderie and the environment jived so beautifully with her own fun-loving spirit and irreverent sense of humour. Interestingly, she maintains that despite a challenging working environment, her last position at PEO was where she learned the most!

Allison always thrived on an active social life, particularly capitalizing on her adventurous travel spirit, with ski trips to Aspen, Lake Louise, Banff, Whistler, Switzerland and Austria. While also a one-time avid squash player, her real passion was sailing Georgian Bay out of Midland in her CS22, a 22 foot red-hulled sailboat which she had christened "In The Red"! As she laughingly likes to boast, "It was 'in the red' and so was I!" Allison seemed to make friends everywhere she went, socializing with a wide circle of good buddies she had met through the years from childhood, business and recreational activities.

A true Gemini, Allison is gregarious, loves to talk and shares herself with her friends. A mixture of the Ying and Yang, a Gemini is well represented by the twins. Allison can see both sides of an issue, sometimes to a fault, as it can occasionally be challenging for her to make up her mind. Blessed with a congenial, flexible, "go with the flow" personality, Allison is never boring, and always irreverent.

Curiously, there are a number of coincidences in our respective backgrounds. Listen up. Allison's father, Douglas, worked for a pharmaceutical company; so did I for eleven years. Allison briefly worked at MDS Health Group where I had worked for five years. She also worked at Foresters where my father-in-law, Harold Gould, had spent his entire career. Allison's mother was a commercial artist, and I, too, have a creative side, having worked in the art business. Allison worked at King and Bay in Toronto for many years, as did I in more recent years. Allison's brother, David was a JUNO nominee at a time when my family was so dominant in the music business! Allison's other brother, John, moved to the U.S. as a young adult and continued living there until his death in 2011. My brother, Al, did the same; only he continues to live to tell the tale. Coincidence, fate, or were the stars aligned?

Allison lived on her own for years, independently, and thrived on it. She never married until she met me, although she had opportunities and "had fun waiting". We both agree though, that had we met much earlier in life, it would never have worked between us. I was a homebody, and Allison had "things to do, places to go, and people to meet!" We weren't "ready for each other" until much later in life. Our respective personalities, experiences and outlooks modified and shaped over the years, remarkably coming together in an ideal complement to each other. Both in our early fifties when we met, we fit like a glove! We now suffer separation anxiety when we are apart. We cannot imagine ourselves *not* in each other's life!

Donald Gordon Ross

"Mr. Businessman"
Ray Stevens, 1968

In 1998 I was, for the first time, really venturing out in business on my own. Since leaving my corporate career in the private health care field, I had been self-employed. I was working with artist Glen Loates but I hadn't, in the true sense of the word, been operating my own business because I worked exclusively for Glen. But, I was now "an entrepreneur"! I was a small business owner by choice, although I didn't really have a business yet. Here I was with change thrust upon me once again. What was becoming clear to me was that the one constant thing in life appeared to be change. Hmmmm!

I had fallen into a business that I felt I really had an affinity for—art. My creative side, as it were, was really coming out and I found this aspect immensely enjoyable and that there were aspects that I was good at—naturally. That word "naturally" was key as I didn't recall that I had ever been particularly good at anything "naturally" in my life! But I had a natural flare for colour and decor, for image composition, for framing choices and treatments, for furnishings, for exhibiting artwork and for the placement of artwork in office and home environments. This was a big plus if I was to build a business in the field of art when I was certainly not an artist myself.

I wanted to work for myself and stay in a business that I loved so I had to determine how exactly to approach this new challenge. One business strategy that had been working well for the sale of Glen's work had been exhibitions of Glen Loates' Wildlife Art in the lobbies of major downtown Toronto business locations, such as First Canadian Place, The Toronto Dominion Centre, the Sun Life Centre and One Financial Place, to name a few. I had even taken the show to Ottawa and tried shows in Cleveland and Buffalo, although not with great success in the U.S. But, there were occasions in downtown Toronto when people were actually lined up at my sales desk at noon hour to place orders!

I thought there was potential to make a business of this approach and began looking for a product line to market. It didn't take me long to find one. I attended The National Home Show at Exhibition Place in

Toronto and met Paul Bremner of Northland Art—and so began a long association and friendship. Paul had recognized the increasing popularity of the work of iconic Canadian artists Tom Thomson and the Group of Seven. You can't get more Canadian than that! As a staunch patriot, and as someone who still had memories of U.S. business people who viewed Canada as a fiefdom, this product line held great appeal.

And so, I fell in love again, this time with the works of this groundbreaking and influential group of artists. I just loved the idea of bringing their images to market as beautifully framed prints. I initially started collaborating in an operating partnership, so to speak, with Paul at Northland Art to put on shows of Group of Seven works at the downtown locations I was coming to know so well. They were wildly successful. We were ecstatic! I was the front man, Northland was my supplier. I expanded the business building list to the North American Centre, the Atria, the ManuLife Centre and Commerce Court to mention a few more. I added consumer home and cottage shows in the GTA and took the show to London, Hamilton and Ottawa.

After a while, it seemed to make sense that I simply develop the retail side, as Paul wanted to develop the wholesale side, so our relationship became effectively one of dealer and supplier. But, I was never an art retailer in the traditional sense of just having a bricks and mortar gallery location that relied heavily on framing. Under my company name of ManorHill Fine Art, I carved out a niche as a travelling art show for many years. At one point I took over retail space at College Park for a two week stint, and ended up staying two plus years! That was my first foray into a fixed site location and I continued to hold my art shows around the downtown to try to drive follow-up business to my gallery.

I developed a website primarily as a sales aid initially, so that became a virtual gallery. I began renting a small storage facility in Thornhill to store my exhibits, art and other props, which I continue with to this day. I employed young men to help with the set-ups and tear-downs, such as my young friend, Scott Maple, who had an artistic flare himself and later went on to develop his own business in the creation of characters and creatures for sci-fi movies, events and movie theatres.

When Paul and I decided to separate the retail and wholesale functions, part of the deal was that I "inherit" Dave Nancekivell, an employee of Paul's. Now there was a character! Everybody on life's journey meets up with and knows a character, a rascal, a one of a kind, an individual that is a little "over the top" in many ways. Well, that was Dave in spades! This was an individual so diametrically opposite to me in character, temperament and personality, that had we not been thrown together through business, we surely would never have had much common ground for working together, let alone forming a friendship. Yet, over the years a friendship did develop, and I considered Dave to be one of my best friends. To know him was to (eventually) love him. He kind of grew on you!

Dave and I worked closely together for twelve years. Dave was always positive, and when it came to selling, he was the consummate optimist! Now, Dave had a way with women that defied all laws. Rascal that he was, Dave seemed to know "what women want". I've never met anyone who could get away with how Dave operated. I'm not even sure to this day how he did operate, other than to say that he exuded a charm and smile that was deadly for a 64 year old bald man with no teeth!

Dave loved to laugh and he loved to joke, and he loved the camaraderie of his friends. As the song says, "You're here for a good time, not a long time." My world was rocked when I received another middle of the night phone call to tell me that Dave had suddenly died that evening after watching his favourite Monday Night Football. So, Dave and I came to respect each other's differences and learned that we complemented and influenced each other in many positive ways. Dave was a big part of ManorHill Fine Art. I would never have envisioned this 15 years ago, but I still today very much miss Dave as a good friend and dedicated colleague. But Dave left a legacy behind— his zest for life.

Dave Nancekivell and me at one of our art exhibits

In 2005 - 2006, I was holding Tom Thomson and the Group of Seven art road shows in Sam's Clubs around southern Ontario. As luck would have it (good luck that is) the president of Costco saw this road show and decided she would like to have it at Costco. Well, that was a "no brainer". Costco had 25 established stores in Ontario to Sam's six new ones! From 2007 - 2009, that's all I did—Costco road shows with Tom Thomson and The Group of Seven art. That's all I could do! Highest art sales I ever had. Sadly, though, all good things must come to an end. Costco never retains one road show product line for too long as part of their strategy is to change things up. They sure run an efficient operation though and hold your feet to the fire as far as sales and service expectations. That's okay; I was up to the challenge.

If I have enjoyed any success in the retail art business, it is partially because I have been able to reinvent the way that I did business, responding to changing economic times—curiously, *responding to change*! From September 2009 - January, 2012, my focus was the operation of an art gallery in the underground PATH under the Toronto Dominion Centre in downtown Toronto. This was complemented by a framing service, home and office consultations and occasional consumer and business building shows. Our space was beautiful and well lighted. It was a showcase for the artwork. By now I offered a wide array of subject images—landscape, floral, figurative and abstract—both prints and originals. Canvas presentations were rapidly becoming the décor fashion over the traditional prints under glass presentation.

I also employed several key people (we were all in our sixties or older) to assist me in the gallery. I met my good friend, Rick Brooker, when I worked for Glen and Sally Loates in the 1990s. Rick, who worked for the Canadian Federation of Independent Business at the time, used to lunch every day at The Edward Avenue Eatery. Every day Rick would have an eggs, sausage, home fries and coffee breakfast at 11:30 a.m. And, if I was working out of the office, I usually went there for a bite of lunch. We all kibitzed around with the owners, Jimmy and Christine. And that's where I originally met Rick, a class gentleman, schmoozer extraordinaire and a staunch race car fanatic.

We kept in touch and Rick provided stellar service on behalf of ManorHill Fine Art for several years; first, when I landed the road show contract with Costco, and later at the TD Gallery downtown. Along the way, I was able to help him as he published canvas prints of his grandfather's art. His grandfather was renowned Canadian artist Bertram Brooker, who was a contemporary of The Group of Seven, and associated with them, particularly Lawren Harris. How coincidental was that!

"I Get Around"
The Beach Boys, 1964

I wouldn't exactly call myself well travelled, and I haven't seen as much of the world as I would like to, but I have got around from time to time. The first big trip I experienced was when the whole family took a spring vacation to Florida. My parents had, since the mid-1950s, gone to Florida for two weeks every winter—their little getaway from us kids, no doubt. In later years they took vacations to Jamaica, Hawaii and Europe; but, in 1964, when I was 16 and my brother 12, we all went on this amazing outing to Florida. Boy, were we excited! First up was Ft. Lauderdale for a few days and then our family motored over to Treasure Island near Tampa on the gulf side. As a seafood aficionado from an early age, I was in my element, and that's what I ordered just about every meal I could.

Sadly, what stands out the most for me on that trip was how I discovered that I was susceptible to sun poisoning. The very first day we arrived in Fort Lauderdale, we immediately went to lie on the beautiful sand beach, obviously a novel experience for my brother and me. It was quite overcast, so we didn't bother to put on any sunscreen, if they even had such a thing 50 years ago. Wrong decision. That evening I was covered in an incredibly itchy rash that was driving me insane. My skin was extremely sensitive to the intense rays of the Florida sun. You might almost say that I was allergic to the Florida sun.

As soon as I stepped out into the sun the next day, my skin immediately began intense itching and burning. I could not go outside and had to remain inside for three agonizing and frustratingly long days, trying to get relief, or at least minimize the effects of my condition, and only venturing outside after dark to go to a restaurant! For the rest of my life I have had to be careful about being in any sun, and have protected myself according. Unfortunately, both of my children inherited this same predisposition!

You might think that I would not want to return to Florida, or any southern clime, because of my propensity for sun poisoning. I have always been very uncomfortable in heat, particularly humidity, even at home.   For that reason I've never sought southern vacations; however, it was sometimes inevitable and there were some occasions where I just couldn't turn down opportunities.

In the 1990s I took Matt and Kate to Naples, Florida on spring break for several years running. My Aunt Marge and Uncle Al had a condominium there that they kept first for my Poppa's use, and later for my parents or friends to use. After my father passed away, my mother spent three months there each winter and I began to visit for ten days each spring break with the kids. We were clearly very aware of the sun poisoning issue, and the kids did, despite all precautions, occasionally get some, but we managed. Matt and Kate really looked forward to these trips and I really looked forward to spending concentrated time with them. These were some of the happiest of times for the kids and me with Mom, and we were appreciative of the opportunity to get together and enjoy the Naples experience.

Through business at Upjohn HealthCare Services I saw much of our great country over the years. I visited all provinces except Prince Edward Island. I stared at it from the New Brunswick shore, but, sadly, didn't have enough time to cross before my flight left Halifax. I have had the privilege of seeing all of Canada's major cities. I was fortunate to also visit on business some major U.S. spots like Chicago, New York, Phoenix, Washington and Los Angeles. I tried to sightsee a bit when time permitted so I have skied down Blackcomb at Whistler, visited Peggy's Cove in Nova Scotia, toured The White House and dined on the 95th floor of the John Hancock Centre in Chicago.

Dave Beardslee and me in California, 1989

In 1985 my mother and I made the trip to San Diego for Al and Gail's wedding. Aunt Marge and Uncle Al also attended the festivities. As we stayed with my brother, we partook in all of the lead up preparation activities, thoroughly enjoying ourselves in the process. I also returned to Florida—this time to Cocoa Beach to be a groomsman for my good friend Dave Beardslee at his and Becky's wedding.

And one year I took the kids to California to visit their Uncle Al and Aunt Gail near San Diego. We all had a great time touring around from the beach caves at La Jolla to the San Diego Zoo to Disneyland and Sea World. Of course Matt and Kate adored their Uncle Al, the perennial kid himself! In the middle of our visit, Al and Gail moved from one house to another, packing only the night before, after hosting the American Thanksgiving dinner, if you can believe it! We left the old house in the morning and returned to the new house in the evening. Somehow the move had been completed!

There have been several trips that Allison and I have made that are significant enough to mention—California in 2001, France in 2003, Western Canada in 2006, Nova Scotia in 2009 and British Columbia in 2013. Then, of course there are Matt and Kate's destination weddings in 2008 and 2011 respectively, both in Punta Cana, Dominican Republic, but I will relate more on those stories in another chapter.

By the London Bridge, 1995

"No Surrender"

Bruce Springsteen, 1985

Considering that only three generations back it was not uncommon to have 10 children, as my family so ably demonstrated, it seems that I got rather shortchanged in having only one sibling! My one and only brother, Allan Bruce, was named after my mother's brother, our Uncle Al, and Bruce, our grandfather on our father's side. My mother had a name picked out, Mary Ellen, taken from her mother's and grandmother's names, in case she had a daughter. But the millionaire's family was not to be!

Al is four years younger than I, so I have always been the "big brother", the older sibling, for whatever that is worth as far as sibling theories and dynamics go. I have to own up to being a terrible tease as a youngster which I came by honestly from my father and I recall at times being the bane of my brother's existence; but, there wasn't much Al could do being physically always much smaller than his older brother.

My brother and I look nothing alike. My brother favours my father in looks, while I resemble my mother's side. I always felt that Al got the better deal; no offence to my mother. You see, Al has the handsome chiseled features of our dad, while I favour the more rounded features of my mother. Al tans; I burn. Al has a wave to his hair, while I have fine straight hair and could never train it even to this day. In fact, I would be happy just to have hair today! Al was always quite slim and I, while not being heavy, never considered myself in the slim category. Al has always seemed to make friends easily and has that outgoing personality of our dad. He loves a party!

Four years age difference at a young age is huge though! When I was eight, Al was only four. When I was twelve, my brother was eight and when I was sixteen, Al was not yet a teenager. While we were, of course, playmates at home, and often each other's *only* playmates at rented cottages in the summer, our age difference meant that we were four school grades apart with a wide gap in our growth and development. Therefore, as time went on, we each developed our own circle of friends.

Al as a young boy with Dad

It is usually the role of the older sibling to pave the way for the younger sibling with respect to pushing the boundaries with parents who naturally are initially more hesitant to give reign to their first child. It is the unrecognized role of that first child to soften up the parents so that requests by the second in line can be more quickly acceded to, or permission to do certain things can be obtained at an earlier age, or at least with less resistance. And that was the case with my brother and me although we certainly didn't recognize it as such as we were growing up.

As was the case in 1950s' family life, Mom and Dad were reasonably strict parents. And, as my brother and I both reached our teen years in the 1960s, it took much persuasion and perseverance on our part just to be allowed to let our hair grow longer than our childhood brush cuts when the advent of The Beatles revolutionized North American culture, fashion and mores. And who would guess that my younger brother, the fussy eater who seemed to only like to eat hamburgers, bacon and steak as a child would, at 21, become a vegetarian for the rest of his life!

When our parents decided to make the move from Leaside to Bayview Village in 1966, Al finished up public school at Northlea. The next year a move to a new school was in the offing for Al when he started Grade 9 at Bayview Junior High in Willowdale, while I continued to commute back to Leaside High.

The year 1967 was remarkable for Al on two counts. First, he had a kidney operation. This was quite a serious matter, as it turned out. Al had for several years complained of his "pain". He would often say, "I've got my pain." We always thought that he was faking this complaint just to stay home from school. I thought the only pain was Al! So, we were all surprised when the doctor indicated that he had a kink in his artery and it was a serious situation. They opened him up, leaving a huge sweeping scar, and he recuperated at home for several months with teachers actually bringing him homework. Nice gig! The operation did correct the problem though and there has been no recurrence.

The second occurrence of note during our centennial year was a European trip that Al took through the Ship's School. He visited England, Scotland, Portugal, Spain, Norway, Sweden and Russia. And this adventure opened Al's eyes wide to the world of travel and other lands. He was bitten with the travel bug thereafter! It was also on this trip that he met Tom MacCormack with whom he became fast friends and was subsequently introduced to the Gibson family who became an important part of his life.

Al's secondary education, such as it was, took place at Earl Haig High School in Willowdale, while I began university at U of T. I say "such as it was" because Al was not one to favour classroom attendance if there were more social options. Hanging out with his new friends at Meisterschaft School suited his purposes infinitely better and Al also travelled to Burlington and Honey Harbour for visits with his new comrades.

Our circle of friends really did diverge at this point and we didn't even have schools in common. We both were based out of 12 King Maple Place but very much had our own lives, with overlapping family activities. By our teen years it was clear to me that my brother and I were quite different in personality, but we always got along with each other. I was definitely a hearth and home type of person while Al had a more adventurous spirit than I.

Al at 22

This further distancing of our respective social networks, along with the difference in school bodies and our age difference, solidified the development of our own separate lives and worlds.

Al graduated from high school and got a job right away test driving for Shell Research blasting through their giant banner sign in their advertisements. Al didn't remain in one job for very long but he always had the knack of landing on his feet with some gainful employment, often through a friend—often using the old "it's not what you know, but who you know" principle. At 20 Al attended the Lewis School of Hotel Management and landed a front desk job at the reputed Inn on the Park adjoining the Leaside area. This was actually the hotel where Pam and I had held our wedding reception.

But, the lure of a trip to California with his friends, the Gibsons, proved too much of an enticement, and off he went. Al's road trip across America was another life-altering travel experience, and one in which he forged a lifelong friendship with Tom Gibson. Al knew upon his arrival in California that he would live there for the rest of his life. He was offered an open-ended invitation to stay, and that was irresistible for my brother.

Subsequent to his stay in California, Al spent time on Vancouver Island where he worked in a hotel, then moved back to Toronto where he drove for George Jeffrey's Meat Market (the Jeffreys were Rykert neighbours). Earning enough scratch to fund a return trip to Europe, Al was off again on a European junket, this time travelling and working for six months in 1973-74. When Al took off on his travels to Europe at age 21, I was embarking on a corporate career. I jokingly told friends that my brother retired at 21 to travel. Actually, I'm not sure that Al really didn't have it right!

When Al left on his travels, part of us went too. The world was his home. We were now all adults and the age difference was no longer a factor as we grew into our twenties.

More travels back to California followed and then, in the late 1970s, Al landed at Jasper Park Lodge in Alberta for several seasons—which for Al was an *extended* term of employment. But, in 1979, our father's sudden death called him back to Toronto and he ended up staying with our mother for a year, never returning to his job at the lodge.

Tragedy struck Al again when his good friend, George Manson, died in a mountain climbing accident in Alaska in 1980. Shortly afterwards, Al enrolled in a psychology program at the University of California, San Diego; but, after a year, my brother started travelling again, this time around the western United States. He performed various odd jobs to sustain his travelling exploits through the early 1980s. Al's first legal job in the U.S. was as a bread man in 1985! That's okay—our great-grandfather was a fruit peddler.

Al was now based out of California with his Canadian friends, the Gibsons, whom he had originally met through his school travels.

While these folks were very welcoming to my brother, their family cast of characters seemed to read like a reality TV show. I affectionately coined the moniker "The Gibsonian" in reference to their home and family, a phrase which remains fondly used to this day. We wondered whether Al would be the type to ever settle down and get married, so he surprised us when he told us about Gail who had come into his life. They married on September 14, 1985 when Al was 33. Mom and I flew down for the wedding near San Diego. Gail came with a package, two children from a previous marriage, so Al was quickly catapulted into fatherhood not long after I was. On the marriage side I had a 13 year head start on him. Today Gail's two children are married and have several children themselves, so Al is a Grandpappy!

Al and Gail on their wedding day, September 14, 1985

Then we knew for sure that my brother would never return to Canada to live, and indeed he has not; he became an American citizen while retaining his Canadian citizenship. He loves the San Diego climate and the laid back California lifestyle just too much. And I know Gail cringes at the word "snow". But, Al remains staunchly Canadian, following the Toronto Maple Leafs and continuing to celebrate the Canadian Thanksgiving.

Al periodically returns to Toronto to visit. We're not sure whether it's more for Canadian beer and Swiss Chalet than to see us, but we'll take it. Sadly, though, we don't see enough of him. I am closer to my brother now than I was for many years. We enjoy our time together. The deaths of our parents helped to bring us closer, as we are now the only immediate family that we have left from our childhood. Clearly our expanded families would spend much time together both at each other's homes and at the cottage (which my brother loves) if we were geographically living in the same city. I certainly miss that opportunity.

And, for reasons of economic necessity, Al did come out of retirement to become gainfully employed. He ran his own package delivery business, RPS, for many years in the late 1980s and through the '90s until 2005, and at one point operated five trucks. RPS was ultimately bought out by FedEx operations (those three letter company abbreviations seem to run in the family) and Al continued under the rebranded FedEx Ground as an independent operator for several more years. But, the big company slowly ground his business into the ground, as they really didn't want independent operators. At the same time, schlepping boxes and packages for many years took its toll on the body. Al finally gave in and quit the business.

His independent spirit prevailed and, despite suffering a severe heart attack in 2005, he undertook the daunting challenge of buying, setting up and operating a Taco del Mar fast food franchise. Unfortunately the timing sucked. By the time the franchise was finally up and running, the country was into its worst recession since The Great Depression. Hindsight is 20/20, but in retrospect, the business didn't stand a chance, as Southern California turned out to be one of the areas hit hardest by the devastating economic downturn.

Al subsequently lost the business, and what followed was an extremely dark, depressing period as he and Gail fought for survival and a way to extricate themselves from their financial obligations. Gail continued her newspaper career at the San Diego Union-Tribune where she had been employed for the past 15 years. (She was a seasoned veteran having previously worked for a similar length of time at the L.A. Times prior to the San Diego posting.) Al took a job driving for a health care company that did clinical trials, and they moved from the Escondido area to Elsinore. That put them close to their daughter Shantala and her twin boys, but meant an insufferable 1½ hour commute each way to work.

They were not in a good place literally or figuratively, as they coped with trying to get out from under their financial burden. Then, to add to the conundrum, Gail's job became a victim of budget cuts. I have great admiration for how they worked through the crippling problems, and kept their marriage together. It was hard but they found a way. One might say that this kind of experience builds character, but there must be easier ways!

Al and Gail with their grandchildren, Tyler, Nathan and James

It is a great testament to Al and Gail's family values that they credit their twin grandsons, Tyler and Nathan, along with their son Rick's boy, James, as a key part of the reason that they pulled through their dark period "whole". Despite the myriad of financial problems and stresses that they were overwhelmed with in recent years, it was the grandchildren who were instrumental in sustaining their spirits. Their love for their "awesome" Grandma and Grandpa was continuously uplifting, as, with delight, Al and Gail watched them grow from toddlers to teens.

As I write today, Al and Gail are thrilled to have moved back to Escondido and both are now gainfully employed. At long last, the arrows are starting to point upwards again. Al has persevered through tremendous personal challenge and his indomitable spirit continues. "No retreat, no surrender", as Bruce Springsteen says, and that could be Al's theme song. Through the years, Al and Gail have enthusiastically attended over 30 Bruce Springsteen concerts all over the U.S. Al somehow found a way to come up twice to Toronto in 2012 and visit his older brother while I was so seriously ill in hospital. His visits meant a lot to me personally. They also gave Matt and Kate some Uncle Al time. They unfortunately don't get to see him as often as they would like, but they love their Uncle Al. Everyone should have an Uncle Al! My brother may no longer be "forever young" but his thinking continues to be.

Al and me at the cottage, Thanksgiving 2013

"The Kids Are Alright"
The Who, 1965

After Pam and I split up, Pam and the kids moved from Claremont to Oakville to Green River and finally settled in Stouffville which is where they finished public school and attended high school. Always one to enjoy the outdoors, Matt enthusiastically participated in Cubs and then Scouts where he met one of his best friends, Evan Barker. His mother's partner introduced Matt to casting competition and Matt was proud to be the Canadian Junior Plug Accuracy Casting Champion in 1995, 1996 and 1997. To cap off this illustrious career, he also took honours as North American Junior Plug Accuracy Casting Champion in 1995 and 1996!

Matt played baseball which ultimately led to a part-time job as a senior umpire for Softball Ontario, not always an easy test for a 15 year old dealing with occasionally emotional parents in the stands. Matt also worked in the butcher department of the local Stouffville A & P grocery store while he went to high school and later Seneca College. This actually became a rather handy future skill to have when it comes to the knowledge and selection of meats. After graduating from Stouffville District Secondary School in 2002, Matt successfully undertook the new Electronics Engineering Technician (Broad Band Cable) diploma course offered at Seneca College, graduating in 2005. He was following right in his techie father's footsteps. Not!

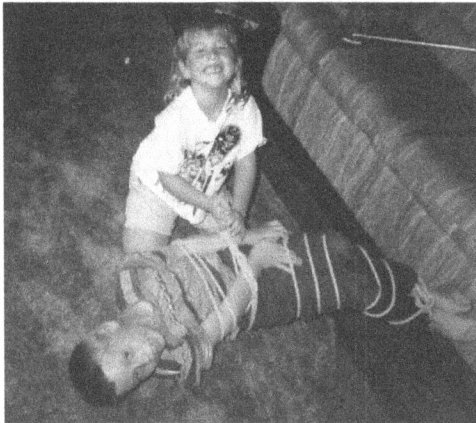

Kate has her older brother hogtied!

199

Matt, a somewhat quieter type like his dad, is friendly and congenial, and loves a good party. He is respectful and helpful towards others, and is focused and hardworking in business and home projects. He responsibly does what he has to do. He built his mother's basement into a self-contained apartment, and more recently has been hard at work renovating the home that he and Natasha purchased a couple of years ago.

But, like his father, Matt does have a creative side; it just evidences itself in different ways. For example, his woodworking abilities emerged in high school to creatively shine far beyond my struggling efforts in Shop at his age. Like a sponge, Matt has (over time) soaked up the skills for electrical wiring, drywalling, construction, plumbing, renovations and installations, clearly becoming the "go to" guy in the family for all such projects. I, on the other hand, have to humbly, but unabashedly, call Matt when I can't get the DVD working, or when I have screwed up the satellite dish!

Now Matt does come by one of his mother's family traits honestly. Just like his Uncle Bob Gould, if Matt mentions that he is thinking about buying something, or considering doing something in the future, one thing is for sure, the timeline will not just compress, but will in fact rapidly kaleidoscope to a "fait accompli" whether it be a truck or house purchase, or the acquisition of a pet!

Matt was most fortunate to find work in his chosen field immediately after graduating from Seneca College. He joined Automated Entertainment Inc. in Markham where he now programs and installs all things connected to home theatre systems and electronics for this high end specialty company. A chip off the old block!

Matt and Kate grown up

Matt took a bride, as they say, and was married in a destination wedding in Punta Cana, Dominican Republic in 2011. The Reverend Al, my brother, officiated of course, as Matt and Natasha became husband and wife in an afternoon ceremony on the shores of the Caribbean. That was a very busy year for the happy couple. They sold their first house, were homeless for a period of time as a result, launched an extensive renovation of the new home they finally bought in Queensville, and acquired a husky. Oh, and did I mention that Natasha was pregnant throughout, delivering our first grandson, Lukas Kerry Donald Ross on March 7, 2012! They don't seem to do things in half measures! And Lukas was born one year to the day of his cousin Kylie! As brother and sister, Matt and Kate are close, but really!

**Matt and Natasha's Punta Cana wedding,
October 25, 2011**

Kate, two years younger than her big brother, has a wonderfully warm and easy-going personality and the patience of Job with her two young children. As a youngster, Kate was an active participant into her teens on Stouffville hockey and baseball teams. I very much looked forward to attending both Matt's and Kate's league and tournament games, and watching with pride as they developed their skills and reveled in the camaraderie of team sports. Through her high school years Kate attended McDonald's University as she worked part time at the local fast food outlet for several years—always a great training ground for young people! Following her brother to Seneca College, she elected to study accounting and business, successfully completing her diploma in 2006.

And Kate, too, was able to find employment in her chosen field fairly soon after her graduation. She joined the staff of State Farm Insurance at their head office in Aurora and, again like her brother, continues today to work for the same company. Working in customer service and agent support is right up Kate's alley, as she is naturally a thoughtful, considerate and supportive individual. And, she hands down wins the title for being the most well-organized and punctual family member!

Now Kate may be two years younger than her brother, but she got married two years sooner than Matt. Kate and Kevin had been attached since their teens in high school; Kevin originally being a good friend of Matt's. They set the standard for destination weddings with their selection of the Paradisus Resort in Punta Cana, Dominican Republic in 2010. An afternoon wedding on the beach was always Kate's dream, so it was truly a dream come true. And, I was bursting with love and pride as I walked my daughter "down the aisle" which was in this instance "across the sandy beach". Kate's Uncle Al was, as usual, in attendance to perform in his repurposed official capacity, as Kate Ross became Kate Cinnamon! Back home a couple of weeks later, we held a wedding party/reception at the Angus Glen Golf Club celebrating the recent nuptials in grand style, and staging the event to recreate the Caribbean ambiance.

Kevin and Kate's Punta Cana wedding, October 20, 2008

Kate always knew she wanted to have children. The timing was just a little quicker than she might have preferred. Our granddaughter, Kylie, popped out on March 7, 2011, and then eighteen months later along came a grandson, Kody. Kate and Kevin have their hands full for sure these days; but those days are joyful!

Matt and Kate have developed into well-grounded responsible adults. They have both found their complements in their choice of mates. And, both have found careers in the sectors that they trained for. Each has remained employed at the first firms they joined after graduation and both couples are raising families. What more could one ask for! They have strong family values. Both own their own homes. These are not easy economic times for young folk to do and accomplish what they already have by the time they were 30! I couldn't be prouder of them!! They have made many good choices on their life's journey.

"Drive"

The Cars, 1983

I am not a gearhead. I'm the complete opposite, in fact. I had
absolutely no aptitude when it came to the sciences in school, for
example, or the rapidly advancing technology of the computer age. No
affinity at all and no interest! And as far as how cars operate, the
engine size and statistics or watching car racing…forget it, no interest
and no aptitude! If it has four wheels and operates, that's fine for me.
A car is a conveyance that will get me from point A to point B. If the
car won't start and it's not out of gas, and doesn't have a dead battery, I
don't have a clue! I couldn't care less, just fix it!

However, when it comes to an appreciation of car design, my artistic
side emerges. I admire vintage automobiles with the best of them. The
sleek sculpted lines of anything pre-1970 catches my eye. It does occur
to me, too, that there has been a fair family history of car ownership
which should perhaps be acknowledged. My son, Matt, and
particularly my son-in-law, Kevin and his father, are quite keen on cars
and car racing, and good old Uncle Bob Gould, Pam's brother, and
now his son, Adam, my nephew, sell cars for a living at Georgian
Pontiac in Barrie. It's been from Bob that most of us in the family
have bought cars for many years. He's our go-to guy for expert advice.

So, as a nod to those interests, and to my interest in the 1960s in
general, start your engines! I also think it would be fun to see if I can
write a chapter on a subject about which I know absolutely nothing and
care little about! Why not, it's my book! And, as I love the song,
"*Drive*", by The Cars, I just had to use that song as a chapter title
somewhere!

I got my driver's license shortly after I turned sixteen, so I have been
driving for almost half a century! By now, the reader will be familiar
with the vehicle that I described as a "chick magnet" in my Chateau
Woodland summer fun of 1965. That was, of course, my dad's sea
green 1964 Ford Galaxy XL 500 convertible with four on the floor and
bucket seats. Anyone who knows me will be extremely impressed that
I know it had a 427 cubic inch 7.0 litre engine! Not to dash your
hopes that I may have finally seen the technological light, it is amazing
what you can find on the internet these days! For any of the cars I am

going to mention, just Google their description and you will get photos and details. (You think I'm going to do all the work for you?)

The "chick magnet!"

Ford built some special models of the Galaxie XL 500 to enter in drag racing and designed for performance on the racetrack. This XL 500 was "the car" that epitomized my teen years. I borrowed that wonderful conveyance every chance I could get. I got high marks socially when I drove to high school in that baby! Girls loved it. Guys were envious!

So far this chapter is reading like a Jerry Seinfeld episode, 30 minutes about nothing, so let's get on with it then. My father's cars were the most interesting. The first car that Dad owned was a 1939 Ford with a rumble seat. Now that was a hoot! The rumble seat concept was an upholstered exterior bench seat which hinged from the rear deck of pre-World War II automobiles. It offered no protection from the elements for its guests, and was often referred to as "the mother-in-law seat".

I never saw the '39 Ford, of course. The first car of Dad's that I do recall was a 1957 green Ford Meteor. He started to ratchet up the racy factor with his next vehicle, a 1959 Mercury Monarch. This beauty was the first in a line of two tone colours that were all the rage in those times. Sadly, today's predominant colours of silver, black and white are incredibly boring, as are the designs. There are no big fins, no curves and no sex appeal! The Monarch was a fabulous red and white—as stunning in its own way as Rita Hayworth!

Dad always seemed to have a new car every two or three years. We used to joke that "the ashtrays are full…time to trade in this car for a new one!" No one in our family smoked although every car came with ashtrays in the front and back seats. We had to roll down the windows by hand. Seatbelts weren't introduced until several years later, and I remember presenting a news feature in school about these new fangled straps called seatbelts that would buckle up across the waist and were about to become the law.

A 1962 Dodge Dart Polara convertible followed the Monarch. It was white with a snappy red interior. If you wanted to put down the canvas roof, you would have to manually help it fold down to fit properly in its recessed hideaway and then affix the cover with metal snaps much like you still have to cover a boat with a tarp today. There were many sudden showers which would cause you to have to stop the car to put up the roof, and that took a lot more than the few seconds that today's fully automated convertibles need. We were sometimes a little damp after that "hurry-up offense" exercise.

Dad briefly had a honking big four door 1965 Chrysler New Yorker. It was an imposing black beast with a 375 hp engine. No trouble passing with that one! A 1967 Oldsmobile Cutless Supreme entered the mix. It boasted a "330 cu. in. ultra high compression Jetfire Rocket V8 with a four barrel carburetor"—whatever the hell that all meant. Remember, I only went for the looks. A Pontiac Parisienne and an Oldsmobile 98 followed in there somewhere too.

I recall in the mid '60s when the Don Valley Parkway opened in Toronto. For the first time four highways formed a box to allow you to travel unimpeded by traffic lights in a square around Toronto by taking the DVP, the Gardiner, Hwy #427 and Hwy #401. We drove that route at night for the first time, top down, screaming at the top of our lungs. Today, if you take that route, you once again will be screaming at the top of your lungs, but for an entirely different reason!

I like antiques and collectibles. Whether it is a vintage car or a period piece of furniture, an early edition children's book or old coins, a century home or a cigar boat, the sense of history and attractive designs are what captures my interest. So, by the time I could afford my own car, the designs were sorely flagging in terms of sex appeal! The eye candy of the '60s was disappearing. The first car I owned, or rather Pam owned when we got married, was her rather boring looking 1963 black Volvo, and it was a standard. For someone who admires design but not substance, I held no affection for driving this baby with a clutch!

I recalled my first ever time driving a standard. When I was working at the Driftwood Restaurant in Haliburton a customer asked me to move his car after I filled it with gas. He was going in for something to eat. I had no idea that it was a standard! I had no idea how to drive a standard! I generated hoots of laughter as the car lurched, stalled and jumped across the parking lot. It's a wonder I didn't strip the gears. So, Pam's Volvo was definitely not a guy magnet for this guy!

Pam and I did graduate to a brand new 1972 metallic blue Volkswagen Beetle. We upgraded to magnesium wheels—pretty snazzy for the time—and it cost $2,695! The VW Bugs were remarkable little cars with a tiny trunk in front and the engine in the back. Now for everyone who knows my total lack of mechanical aptitude and technological expertise, and non-existent interest in the operation of cars, do I have a story! I, Donald Ross, successfully changed the fuel pump on our VW all by myself. "How could this be?" you ask. Well, on the Friday night of a long weekend our car quit. As we were planning to go to the cottage, the only way we could get there was if we repaired the car ourselves. The service station was about to close. They "thought" it might be the fuel pump, but weren't sure. They offered to sell us the fuel pump, assuring me that "anyone" could replace the old one. Clearly they didn't know whom they were dealing with!

So, there I was squatting on the driveway of 36 Millgate at 6:30 p.m. trying to figure out how the knee bone connected to the thigh bone, so to speak, in the little engine. At least the little VW engine was quite accessible to work on at ground level. However, with me in charge, perhaps that should be termed Ground Zero! I was not brimming with confidence about whether I could connect the tubes and hoses properly without any guidance. But, isn't it wonderful what motivation can do! I did not want to miss a long weekend at the cottage! There I was doing a happy dance in the driveway, as Pam, her mother and our neighbours gaped in astonishment at my orchestration of this minor miracle when the car started as though there had never been a problem! So there, to my naysayers…take that, stick it in your tailpipe and smoke it!

In 1978 we became a two car family when I received my first ever company car—a burgundy Pontiac Station Wagon. Ever practical, I selected a station wagon for trips to the cottage, foregoing the zippier models that were available to us. I think it was 1983 when we acquired a new blue Dodge Jeep Grand Cherokee though. Now that car I did like tooling around in, as I did the 1988 black Buick Bonneville I got a few years later. Great styling! Sadly, after just three days, some bozo rear ended me on the Gardiner Expressway—in rush hour! I was not amused. Nor were thousands of motorists!

A 1993 white Chevrolet Lumina with a spoiler was also a favourite. Boy, was I ever living on the edge in car land! Then came one of my all-time favourites—the 1999 sea green Chrysler Intrepid. It came with a V6 225 hp engine. Very stylish—a classic for all time—and with a trunk size so large that I referred to it as the in-law suite! Shades of my dad's rumble seat, although advancements had moved the in-law accommodation indoors, so to speak! I finally had to trade the Intrepid in, well before its time, to lease what was to be one of a series of Montana vans over the ensuing years which I very much needed in order to accommodate my growing art business.

So, alas, just when I was enjoying some excellent automobile selections, I had to defer to the practical again, for all of the schlepping of artwork product that I was now doing. I am now in a black 2010 Dodge Caravan, although it does boast some creature comforts such as U-Connect, Sirius Satellite Radio, power driver seats, a CD player and tons of room for cottage trips—none of which the VW Beetle had! Of course, it isn't the sea green 1964 Ford Galaxy XL 500 (chick magnet) Convertible with bucket seats either, and that ran on 35¢/gallon gasoline!

"Spookie"
Classics IV, 1967

My first pet was named Doc, and my brother's was named Sleepy.
They were hamsters, which our parents graciously allowed us to have
when I was nine. We cared for them, watching intently as they built
their nests out of cardboard Kleenex boxes, tissues, toilet paper rolls
and cedar chips. We fed them their seed mixture and filled their water
bottles; but, of course the most fun was watching them run around
spinning on their exercise wheel in an almost frenzied fashion.

Once, almost 30 years later, when I was home alone on kid duty trying
to capture my son Matt's pet hamster, the damned thing bit me. As I
couldn't remember when I had last had a tetanus shot, I decided
prevention was the best course, so I bundled Matt and Kate into the
car and headed to the Uxbridge Cottage Hospital. We were living in
Claremont at the time.

While I was getting my shot, I asked the attending doctor to take a
quick look at Matt's back, as he seemed to have a rash. You can
imagine my surprise when, after a quick look, he informed me that my
six year old son had shingles! This was extremely rare for someone so
young to have this painful and itchy affliction—a disease that normally
afflicts adults. The rash looked like a condominium of blisters and
kept Matt home from school until they dried up. Poor little guy!

My parents weren't big on pets and viewed them as an inconvenience,
so it wasn't until about 1964 that (by default) we acquired another pet.
One day while we were living on Rykert Crescent in Leaside a dog just
curled up on our driveway and went to sleep. He seemed to adopt us.
He was black and sort of a mixed breed, but had some spaniel in him.
We endeavoured to find his owner, but to no avail, and prevailing upon
our parents to let us keep him, my brother and I gave him the terribly
original name of Blackie.

Blackie got walked every night by my dad and travelled back and forth
to the cottage with us every weekend. I remember once when Blackie
met up with a porcupine and Frank Chisolm and my dad had to use
pliers to pull out the quills from his face. It was very sad for all of us

when, after we had been moved up to Bayview Village for a while, Blackie just disappeared one day much in the same way that he had mysteriously appeared at our home in Leaside. Everyone, even my parents, was quite upset, as we all loved Blackie; but, unfortunately, despite extensive searching, we never saw a trace of our much loved pet again!

That was the end of pets for our family other than a budgie named CHUM, named after my Uncle Al's Toronto radio station—that's assuming you call a bird a pet! However, that was definitely not the end of pets for me—oh no, not by a long shot. When Pam and I got married, we got a cat right away, which was fine. I had never had a cat but Pam had grown up with one, Whiskers, who we were all very fond of. Whiskers jumped for playing cards as we threw them in the air to him, much like a dog will run and leap after a Frisbee.

Hallie was our first cat and was a tortoiseshell. Somewhere along the way, we did acquire a chinchilla; but, Pam was very passionate about cats, particularly ones who were homeless. Soon, Janine, Mike, Charles, Mr. Gibson, T.S. and many others followed. We topped out at nine cats! Our home was the "Ross' cat house". Can you imagine 36 little paws, 9 upright little tails and 18 perky ears all stampeding down the stairs in the morning almost trampling me in the process, as I flung out food to keep them at bay, all while being raucously serenaded by a meowing chorus echoing throughout the kitchen. It was a Steven King nightmare!

I will forever remember somehow herding several felines into our Volkswagen Beetle and travelling back and forth to the cottage with them perched and meowing on laps, headrests, seats and dash board. And then climbing up a ladder and scrambling to grab them by the scruff of the neck from the cottage rafters and then stuffing them into the VW Bug to make the trip home. Don't ask! Clearly I was not in my right mind! When Pam and I separated many years later, I couldn't agree fast enough to let her have custody of the cats. She maintained that I didn't like cats; but, the issue was never my affection for the feline species, but rather who in their right mind would ever want nine cats living with them! Clearly I wasn't—in my right mind that is!

Many years later, when I first met Allison, she tentatively brought up the subject of her "package" which she brought to our relationship. I asked her what that would be. She replied that she had a cat. I replied, "Only one!" "Yes", she said. I responded, "No problem!" I mean, really, with all my experience! And besides, my "package" was two children!

So…back to Allison's "package". Yes, there were three of us in this marriage! There's no question that Spookie was a fur person and a full family member with rights. She was 18 years young at the time that she went to that great big litter box in the sky. Allison had her devoted companionship for 14 years and developed an unusually close bond with her during her convalescence following her heart attack in 1994.

I had the pleasure of Spookie's company for 7 years. Little did I know what I was getting into with Allison's "package"! Although in my former life I had numerous associations with cats as pets (no kidding!), I can honestly say that the closest relationship I have ever had with one of the feline species was with the Spookmeister. Yes, I was indeed very fond of Her Highness. In fact I grew to love her very much and am proud to say that my love was reciprocated. Spookie was friendly, loyal and loving. She loved to get up on my shoulder and would start her motor running. Often, when I would sit down for a moment, suddenly out of nowhere, there was Spook at my feet waiting for an invite to my shoulder. And, it was always my left shoulder! I guess that was consistent with our belief that she was left-pawed!

Spook always waited until both Allison and I were in bed before she would jump on the bed. Then she would parade around the bed, walking all over us, as we were trying to read, until finally she would settle into a far corner of the bed for much of the night. In the morning when she thought that we should be getting up to get her breakfast, Spook would give one or the other of us an "oh so gentle cuff" with her left paw—always her left paw. Definitely a southpaw!

Allison named her pussycat Spookie because she was forever startled by any loud noise. In fact she would head for the hills! In particular, our Spook was not a fan of the vacuum. She would hide under a chair or the bed whenever the vacuum came on, and would make a beeline for the opposite end of the apartment when the vacuum was too close for her liking. And thunderstorms! Poor Spook! At the first distant rumble of thunder, Spook would hop down from whatever perch she was on and head very low to the ground to the darkest reaches of the apartment or cottage. She clearly was spooked!

Spookie (the Spook Meister)

Spook's title of Miss Snark was well earned. No one could give a snarky meow like Spookie when she wanted something like her treats, or if she felt that you weren't attending to her dinner requirements quickly enough. Her sharp meow always got our attention and our laughter. She had cat-titude!

Spookie loved the cottage. However, she wasn't particularly fond of the ride to get there. She always parked herself sitting on the lap of the driver, regardless of who was driving, and she never moved. She just leaned into the driver's stomach and stayed there the whole trip; occasionally taking on the airs of Miss Snark to be sure we knew that she was not pleased with the travelling arrangements, or perhaps the necessity of traveling at all!

But once at the cottage, she relaxed and had her favourite perches depending on the time of the year and the temperature. On a hot day, it would be the pine floor, the dining room table, or perhaps the old dining room chair beside the buffet. In cooler weather, the Spookmeister loved to be a "lump". She would burrow up under the bedspread, curl up and sleep for hours. It was the first place we would often check for Spook—to see if she was a "lump".

It tore us up to make the decision to let Spookie go. Right to the end, even in considerable discomfort, if not pain, she responded with a purr to gentle stroking. On her last night with us, Allison lifted Spook onto the bed, and she snuggled down between us, as if she knew that it was her last night and this was a final goodbye. Spookie—the endearing personality loved even by those who were not disposed towards feline creatures. She will forever remain in our thoughts and hearts.

I knew that when the Spookmeister went to the great litter box in the sky, that it wouldn't take long for us to acquire another pet. Notice that I didn't say replace our dear departed Spookie, as she could not be replaced. I certainly never thought that I could become so attached to a cat, as I did to Spookie. But, then again, I hadn't yet found Mr. Dickens!

Our latest acquisition came to us courtesy of a recommendation by our dear friend Susan Tuck who had eyeballed a pair of fraternal kittens at her vet. We were a soft touch for the champagne and white Domestic Short Hair. As I had been a long time admirer of Charles Dickens's novels, and as we were always wondering, "Where the dickens is that cat and what the dickens is he up to now?" it seemed natural to name him Mr. Dickens!

Our track record of finding skittish cats remained intact, as Mr. Dickens is most loving to us, but immediately runs for cover from just about everyone and everything else. He is now pushing 20 pounds so could benefit from more exercise. However, instead of stalking and chasing the chipmunks and other rodent life at the cottage, Mr. Dickens stands and watches the world go by, which does absolutely nothing to move him towards a more ideal and trimmer summer weight.

Mr. D. is no picnic when it comes to going to the cottage. Just like Spookie, he does not in any way, shape or form like to travel. He will lie in your suitcase when you are packing the night before, but his sixth sense seems to kick in when our departure is imminent, as he immediately dives for cover. Locating and then rousting him out of his hiding place usually requires both Allison and me to be lying on the floor on either side of the bed, one of us with a broom nudging him towards the other.

While these acrobatics are indeed challenging enough for two senior citizens, the real challenge is having our prayers answered that at least one of us is able to get up off the floor to assist the other one up! And this little exercise is only exceeded by our Keystone Cops act , as we scramble to push, shove and cajole our beloved Mr. Dickens, paws flailing, fur flying, and cat squawking into his travelling cage, the whole scenario of which tends to resemble the reverse order of a mare giving birth to a colt!

Mr. Dickens (the Golden Boy)

"Memories"

Barbara Streisand, 1981

"The Cottage" has meant so much to me for over 50 years that it is difficult to describe its impact on me. It has been primarily people and experiences that have been major influences on my life. The cottage is bricks and mortar; it's a thing, not a person. However, it's the only thing, or possession, or inanimate object that is dear to me in this world, as I am certainly not a materialistic person.

The cottage is much more than a building to me—the cottage is a way of life. Each time I arrive, I shed life's pressures and step into another world—another life! The cottage has been the meeting place where almost every single friend and relative who has been a part of my life has passed through—the Times Square of my life! It has continuously and steadfastly been a place of fun times, joyous occasions and growing up. And, it has been a place of sanctuary in difficult times. It is the family homestead. It is the one constant through many changes. The cottage has always been there for me. It is the one "thing" in life that I love dearly.

Me barbequing

Opening up the cottage in early May is accompanied by great fanfare—
at least by me. Originally as a kid, I helped open the cottage and
learned the ropes from my dad, but for the last 34 years the opening,
and closing, of the cottage has been my responsibility. I do it most
willingly and enthusiastically—after all, it is my parents' legacy, and a
damn fine one, to our family. My nephews Adam and Mike Gould
often helped me for many years with the opening and closing
"ceremonies" for which I am forever grateful. But, then again, they
had a blast spending weekends at the cottage with their Uncle Don.
And I certainly loved being with them! Once Matt and Kate got into
their teens they too were "taught the ropes" to the point where, Matt in
particular, now just does everything that needs to be done, and that I
can't do anymore.

Every year I revel in the outdoor and indoor environment of our
cottage retreat. It is at the same time both my hobby and my passion.
Whether casting a line by a submerged log, silently gliding through the
marsh in my canoe, or powering our boat down through our five lake
chain on a sunny, blue sky forever afternoon—it is both a privilege and
a wonder at the same time! A walk on the cottage road is also a simple
pleasure that Allison and I thoroughly enjoy.

I gain immense personal satisfaction from puttering around tweaking
(not twerking) the surrounding landscape, sculpting the small balsam
trees to rein them in as attractive shrubbery, trimming down the
driveway weeds that proliferate after a rain, or raking a few wayward
leaves that have prematurely fallen from the maples and birches. With
the solid experience I gained when living in the Claremont house, I
have personally sanded and refinished the pine floors throughout the
cottage. There is always a list of projects designed to help maintain the
property and maintain its original look and feel, whether a new dock or
sand beach, or a bathroom renovation or new window coverings.

Cottaging is also very much about deck time, which includes everything
from reading and serious discussions to wine and *hors* d'oeuvres before
dinner…from socializing with friends and family…to breakfast, lunch
and dinner…to birthday celebrations. Not to forget star gazing at
night to view the spectacularly clear Milky Way and Big Dipper, or

watch in awe as a full moon rises over the hill on the far shore, casting glowing reflections across the glass surface of Grass Lake. The deck *is* the outdoor summer living room! It is in its second incarnation, having been rebuilt once in the late 1990's since my father first built it in 1966. We replicated my father's design, as we couldn't figure out how to improve on it, expanding the dimensions slightly. I directed operations; Uncle Bob Gould was the carpenter. My son, Matt, and nephews Adam and Steven Gould added able assistance.

Barbequing is a must for virtually every dinner, if I am at the cottage. And that would be rain or shine! The umbrella is well employed, as The Hollies said. Steak, chops, chicken, ribs, and fish—it's all been done. And I'm no stranger to the rotisserie for making porchetta, chickens and even a turkey in the distant past. Love to BBQ!

My cousin Sherry, Aunt Marge (Sherry's Mom), Amy (Sherry's daughter), me Kate, Matt, Mom, Darren (Sherry's son) and my Uncle Al

My secret breakfast recipe for pancakes (made from scratch and started the night before) is legendary and always in demand. We have most folks converted to banana or blueberry pancakes now, topped, of course, with strawberries and maple syrup. And, it is a tradition for Allison and me to start the new season off with a big breakfast at the Kozy Korner in Haliburton. And, for special occasions, such as our anniversary, or a birthday, we usually go to Sir Sam's Inn on Eagle Lake and Bonnie View Inn on Lake Kashagawigamog for a fine dining experience.

Since Haliburton's Molou Theatre has closed down, on a rare occasion some of us drive the 35 minutes to Kinmount to take in a first run new release at the Highland Cinemas—an absolutely unique assembly of homemade theatres cobbled together by a dedicated hobbyist in his home. The complex is a rabbit's warren of passageways housing a vast collection of movie posters, equipment and props that has to be seen to be believed. Definitely worth the price of admission! But, more often than not, we settle back into the comfort of our living room couches and chairs to watch a Bell ExpressVu featured movie, a Maple Leafs hockey game or a DVD on our new flat screen. Yes, once again I have been dragged kicking and screaming into the 21st century! And the younger folk seem to be quite capable of viewing a movie while multitasking with iPads, iPhones and iPods.

My children kid me about chatting up the neighbours but I really do enjoy socializing with them. We are so fortunate to have such a friendly, helpful and caring group who all get along. Gary and Lynda Williams, our next door neighbours who bought the Pearces' cottage after they passed on, considerately paid homage to our good friends by naming their cottage, which they have turned into a permanent home, Pearce's Point. They scored big points with me on that one, as Cy and Isobel Pearce were such a close part of my family life. Gary and Lynda host a Canada Day celebration for the shore every July 1. This annual social event fosters a wonderful spirit of fellowship on Peninsula Road with a mini golf tournament, BBQ and fireworks display. Kudos for them!

I enjoy the shoulder season of spring at the cottage before the heat and humidity of summer. Buds are bursting and crisp fresh air abounds. Our lake's pair of loons return (they mate for life) and the sound of the red-winged blackbird is music to my ears. But, my favourite time of the year at the cottage is definitely fall! Hands down winner! I love the crisp autumn air…blue, blue sky…and explosion of glorious colour as the leaves turn. The incredible reds, oranges and yellows of the maples, the stunning majesty of the blazing hills, and their mirror-like reflections on the lake skyrockets me to an emotional high. They launch me into a state of jaw-dropping awe and wonder of our natural environment!

Thanksgiving weekend has always been a highlight of the cottage season. From my time as a young boy when my parents took our family up north every year to celebrate Thanksgiving with our good friends the Pearces and Browns at lodges such as Birch Point, the Golden Pheasant and Blue Spruce Inn…and continued the holiday tradition when my parents and Cy and Isobel built neighbouring cottages…through when my mother and I forged a new family unit with my children, Matt and Kate…to today when Allison and I gather with the children and grandchildren to continue old traditions, create new ones and celebrate our family being together. It's all about creating memories for the family!

One of our Thanksgiving traditions is to have a pumpkin on display. The challenge is that we want a big pumpkin, and it is not always an easy task to find one, so I start looking two weeks ahead. Haven't been stymied yet! I have searched as far as Oakville and Kitchener to find them! Originally I carved the pumpkin when Matt and Kate were small; but, Matt's creative side emerged, and he is now a carver extraordinaire, researching intricate designs and creating what amounts to a work of art on the Saturday morning of Thanksgiving weekend. At night with the pumpkin candle lit, Matt's penchant for the macabre, sci-fi and horror films is effectively reflected in the latest demon faces or dark creature that he has expertly sculpted.

What has become a Thanksgiving weekend cottage tradition is the season ending Open House which we host on Saturday afternoons. With the exception of 2012's "brief hiccup" the party has been held 21 of the last 22 years. It started out as a small affair in 1992, as my mother and I invited a few neighbours in a nod to the party times of our family in the 1960s and 1970s. I remember wondering the first time whether anyone was going to show up, as the clock kept ticking away. Then eight to ten folks arrived. These days we regularly have 40 plus people in attendance (once we had 52) and the closing out event is much looked forward to by everyone along the shore.

This event initially facilitated an introduction of many of the neighbours to one another and has since helped to foster a strong sense of community. The cottagers are all friends now, and many, such as the Magees, the Langdons, the Smiths, the Devolins and we have been on Peninsula Road for 50 years. Some, like the Miles and Plummers, have been around for 25 years, so I guess that makes all of the rest relative newbies! We decorate the cottage with leaves, put on a roaring fire and move around some furniture. Everyone brings a pot luck appetizer. There is much laughter and camaraderie, and Gord's Bar looks like a retro flashback to the 1960s. If my parents are looking down from above, they would be smiling with approval.

Of course, a turkey dinner has been the centerpiece of the weekend-long celebration for years. Allison and I jointly prepare the dinner. There is much talk and fanfare surrounding the size of the bird to be chosen, and whether fresh or frozen, pre-stuffed or a homemade dressing. Over the years we have tried all combinations, and they are all good. There's no such thing as a bad turkey; some are just a little better than others! The requisite accompaniments are mashed potatoes, sweet potato casserole, Nana's (my mother) famous broccoli casserole, lots of gravy and cranberry sauce.

Our dear friends Ernie and Marion Magee who cottage down the road, and were friends of my parents, join us for dinner. They always bring pumpkin pie and whipped cream, which my son-in-law Kevin can almost single handedly demolish. Now in their mid-80s, Ernie and Marion are like a part of the family and add a lively conversational air to the festivities. And, even after 50 years, there continues to be a race for the couch after dinner, where the winner can recline in stuffed comfort.

2012 A Fighting Man!

"Against All Odds"
Phil Collins, 1984

Life is all about the journey, and these past two years have certainly been an unexpected chapter in my life. Saturday, March 31, 2012 was a most significant day for sure! A completely unexpected turning point in my life! I had, for years after my father's passing, been deathly afraid of dying at the age of 60, just like my father did…just like his father before him at age 61…and just like my great-grandfather did at 63! All from massive heart attacks, or at least heart related problems!

I progressed through my fifties with great trepidation. At age 58, I suffered a mild heart attack and had two stents inserted. At age 54, and just a few months before my own heart attack, my brother, Allan, had suffered a very serious heart attack himself. I didn't need a specialist to tell me the writing was on the wall. There was no party planned for my 60th birthday. I didn't want one. I did not feel celebratory. I waited.

However, much to my pleasant surprise, the years passed without any further cardiac events. I gained growing confidence in my ability to outlive my ancestral predisposition to early demise. What was astonishing was the "out of left field" life-threatening health event that flattened me on that Saturday in March. One day I felt as healthy as I ever had, the next day I was rushed to Sunnybrook Health Sciences Centre by ambulance. I had no idea that I would be hospitalized for 9½ months—291 days! I had no idea that I would become someone who had one of the most severe and lengthiest cases of pancreatitis that my doctors had ever seen!

The week previous, on Friday, March 23 to be exact, I had been taken to Sunnybrook by ambulance with chest discomfort. Although it didn't feel like a heart attack to me, you don't fool around with these things given my heart and family history. I stayed two nights in hospital but all of the tests came back negative and my symptoms had disappeared.

Six days later, after being out early in the morning to a client's home and feeling fine, I suddenly developed very severe chest pain and was violently sick to my stomach. I collapsed to the bathroom floor in agony. My wife, Allison, didn't hesitate to call the ambulance again. Rushed back to Sunnybrook, I was diagnosed within about 5 ½ hours of my arrival as having pancreatitis—caused by a gall stone which had lodged in my pancreatic duct. This immediately gave Allison fits, for her brother, David, had died of pancreatic cancer, and her sister-in-law's son had died of pancreatitis. And now her husband also had pancreatitis?

I was initially isolated in Sunnybrook's ER and moved to the 6th floor of C Wing around two in the morning. When I had great difficulty breathing later that morning, I was moved to the Critical Care Unit (CCU). I continued to be in excruciating pain and was now being dosed up with morphine to alleviate my suffering and intubated to help me breathe. Initially I didn't know *what* was happening to me. When I was conscious, I was scared shitless of what *was* happening to me.

I had no control over anything. With a tube down my throat, I couldn't speak. I motioned for paper and pen. Always a neat writer, I now had almost indecipherable writing, as I frantically wrote out phrases and questions, trying to get answers. What was wrong with me? Could they fix the problem? My frustration at the complete loss of verbal communication was sky high! I was way out of my comfort zone. Always calm Don was freaking! The doctors, nurses, Allison, Matt and Kate all tried to interpret my scribbles. Communicating was like playing charades. I thought that I was going to die! I wrote last thoughts to my children and asked them to take care of Allison, if I didn't make it.

I don't remember a lot of the initial part of this protracted ordeal, but I do remember distinctly being so desperately out of my mind with thirst for anything to drink that I begged and pleaded with the nurses. But initially they wouldn't budge an inch! Finally though, they eventually took pity and swabbed my mouth, but only on a strict schedule of every 30 minutes which was like having one potato chip—almost worse than having none. This went on for two agonizing days. At one point, my arms and legs had to be put in restraints as I desperately tried to pull the tube out of my throat and leave the hospital. That really freaked out Allison and the kids! I remember nothing of this behaviour!

I ended up being intubated a total of three times. I was in CCU for a week and then moved to the Step Down Unit in preparation for being transferred to the floor. My condition deteriorated and I was transferred back to CCU, then back to Step Down, then finally to the floor. Crashing again, I found myself back in CCU one more time!

My condition had now developed into acute necrotizing pancreatitis, which is as bad as it sounds. The acute part means that the condition appeared quite suddenly. The pancreas is an important organ in the process of digestion and the production of insulin, producing very powerful enzymes whose job it is to help in the digestion of food. The pancreas becomes inflamed with pancreatitis and can in severe cases progress to necrotizing pancreatitis—a potentially fatal condition in which the tissue begins to die. The organ begins to digest itself!

Symptoms include intense pain, respiratory problems, nausea, vomiting and low blood pressure and can lead to possible kidney, respiratory and heart failure. These symptoms become a cascade of impairments in which one deteriorating situation leads to others. The annual incidence of pancreatitis is 17 out of every 100,000 people and about 20% of the people with pancreatitis develop necrotizing pancreatitis. About 200 patients a year die in Canada from these complications. What are the odds!!

I was a classic case! I quickly developed severe respiratory complications. My lungs had collapsed. I was on oxygen for months to allow me to breathe. The pancreatic enzymes were prematurely dying. I was "out of it" much of the time… sleeping much of the time…conscious occasionally…fighting infection after infection with antibiotics. For weeks I had so many medications running through my two Pic lines that bags of antibiotics were lined up on the stand beside me. As soon as one was finished, the nurse would hang another one up to drip into me.

There were x-rays, ultrasounds, EKGs and MRIs too numerous to tally. By my estimate there were well over six hundred injections and needles—all this for someone who throughout his life has had a tendency to faint at the sight of blood and needles! And no, this didn't cure me of this predisposition in the males of my family!

A feeding tube was inserted through my nose and down my throat which resulted in extensive gagging each of the three times it had to be replaced. As some medications had to be delivered by being crushed and injected through the feeding tube, often the result was clogging. After six months a G tube was inserted through my abdomen to replace the feeding tube down my throat. I thought that would be a blessing. Boy, was I wrong! Agony...constant irritation...the feeding tube was the only way that I got nutrition, the only way to keep me alive, as I was unable to even stomach (pun intended) the thought of food. Any attempt to eat resulted in immediate vomiting.

Now I had tubes invading my emaciated body and protruding out of both my left and right sides, and out of my stomach. These three tubes drained ugly, brown, stinking, liquid infection from throughout my abdomen. Numerous procedures were conducted to reposition the drainage tubes to siphon infection from different pockets they discovered. I couldn't turn, even if I had been able to. I lay always on my back with no relief from discomfort. I looked like Frankenstein!

Time passed inexorably. I stared at the wall clock that passes as adornment in each patient's room. Tick tock. Tick tock. I watched the seconds tick away, feeling too wretchedly sick to do anything but blindly stare and watch the passage of time, the passage of my life. Tick tock. Tick tock. Minute after minute. Hour after hour. Day after day. I thought I would go insane!

I was fortunate to be isolated in a private room for much of my stay because of my condition, although one time it was because I had contracted the dreaded and highly contagious C-Difficile which causes infectious diarrhea! In the early going, some patient rooms that I was in were so hot, or at least I felt so hot, that I constantly wore a cold, soaking face cloth on my head for days on end to give me relief. In other rooms, I could never get warm enough and pulled blankets up to my neck. Once, when I had a fever, I was so cold the nurses wrapped me in seven blankets, and I was still shaking! Two hours later they were putting cold, wet towels on me, as well as ice, to cool down my spiking temperature.

I would take one step forward and two steps back, as infection after infection kept rearing its ugly head. It was like the *Whack-A-Mole* game where the mole keeps popping up only to be banged on the head each time he does. You have a little bit of hope, and then you are whacked on the head and thrown back. It was almost impossible to believe that, as a once vibrant and energetic man, 63 years young, I could experience such a life-altering and life-threatening change. I was literally in a fight for my life.

The worst thing of all was constantly feeling sick to my stomach and vomiting for 8 ½ months! I could not even look at food, let alone ingest it, or I would immediately throw up. One of the things that I hated the most was the unfortunate tendency to vomit without warning. This may be TMI for the reader, but, I was a very sick puppy. It was not pretty and I'm not going to sugarcoat the truth or spare you the details for the sake of nicety. When I say "without warning" I mean exactly that. I would often be in the middle of a sentence and I would suddenly just throw up! It wasn't quite like projectile vomiting by Linda Blair in *The Exorcist*, but it was close.

So by my side at all times for months was what I called my barf bucket, a paper mache-like disposal bowl which, if it was not within easy reach, would cause me to freak and frantically ring the call bell for someone to put it close by. The barf bucket and my ice bucket were my constant companions each time I was wheeled down for another test or procedure. If I couldn't keep my mouth moist with ice chips, I would likely throw up. I remember one time that I jokingly inverted my barf bucket, placing it on my head for a photo to be sent out to friends and relatives in an email update of my condition that Allison came to periodically send out. An email blast came to be the only way she could manage to keep up with the inquiries about my status. The photo was a communication from me to let everyone know that at least my sense of humour was still relatively intact!

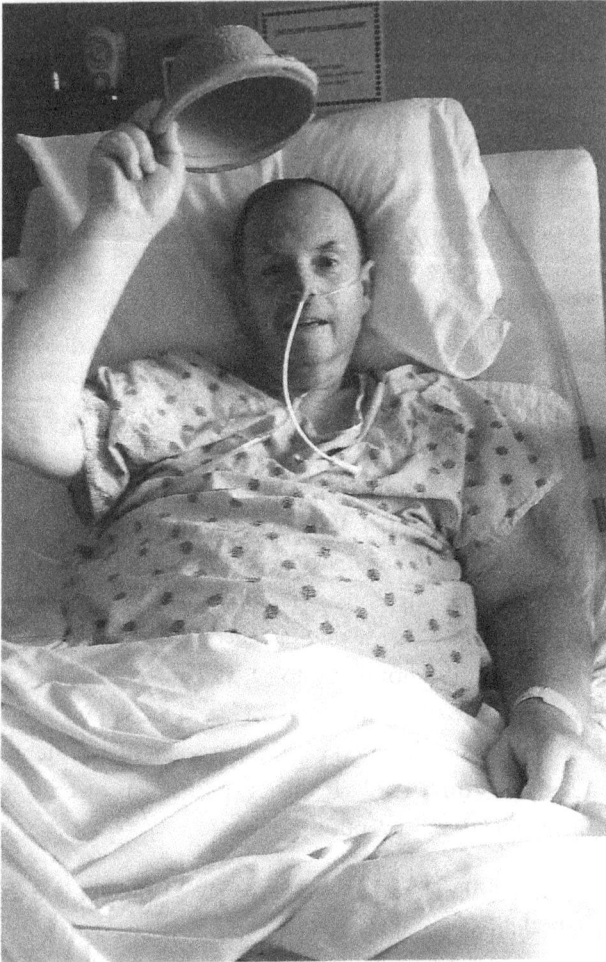

In Hospital doffing my barf bucket hat

When you are as ill as I was, you cannot be your own advocate. You need someone to act for you, the patient. My wife, Allison, was that advocate. She was always searching for a nurse to get me a shot of morphine, or a doctor to explain to us in layman's terms the nature of the latest infection that I had developed. Freshening my ice water, repositioning my pillows, grabbing an extra blanket, clipping my nails, scratching my back, bringing me a juice, finding my Lypsyl, straightening my table, emptying my urinal, reaching my call bell—the never-ending little things that I could not frustratingly do for myself. I required almost as much care as my newborn grandson!

"White Rabbit"
Jefferson Airplane, 1967

At one point I was so dehydrated, suffering from such a lack of nutrition and on so many medications trying to rid me of multiple infections, that I started to have what I came to call, "my imaginings". I was so weak that I would nod off to sleep in the middle of a visit from Allison, and while she patiently waited or read, I would imagine that I was reaching for a pen, or a drink, or a Lypsyl, or whatever, and it would drop out of my grasp, and instantly and mysteriously vanish, never to be found again. It was very scary because my "imaginings" seemed so real. What was happening was that I was hallucinating. I thought I was "losing it". And I was. This scared the shit out of me! (Pun intended.)

But, worse than this were the hallucinations that I got from sleeping pills when I was in the CCU. One night I was convinced the CCU was under attack from terrorists with bombs assaulting the unit with their AK 47s. I desperately wanted to warn the staff and help victims. There was also an episodic dream sequence that I experienced night after night where I had an evil twin brother who plotted and murdered to undermine the business and family that I worked hard to build and hold on to.

I also experienced a recurring dream that made me feel as if I was in my own reality series. I was part of an underground colony of a subterranean culture of little people which existed near the hospital and underneath a garden centre. They were stealing supplies, medications and food in order to exist, and planning for an eventual escape to establish a legitimate colony. And I was trapped between the real world and a secret life as part of this subterranean culture, helping them to attain their goals, but guilt-ridden with betrayal of my own people. It continued and progressed night after night, episode after episode! (Hey, maybe I should sell the movie rights to this one, it is so unbelievable!)

At one point I was also absolutely convinced that I could get up and walk when no one could see me, leave the hospital, drive home and tidy up our condo which Allison had said was a disaster area, as she did not have time to keep it up. This dream was so real that on my first trip home in eight months, the first thing I did was look around to see if the stack of magazines was still piled on the coffee table where I was so sure that I had carefully stacked them on one of these secret trips home! Now that was really weird!

But all of the foregoing dreams and hallucinations were kindergarten compared to the frightening nightmares that I experienced about my family! I was absolutely convinced that my son Matt had been in a horrible industrial accident blinded by chemicals and with extreme physical damage to his legs. I was apoplectic! I was so freaked out at 4:00 in the morning that I started to phone people to confirm what I was convinced to be true and find out about Matt's condition. I was in extreme distress! (I was almost ready to call his mother, but that would have been an extreme step!) Another night I had a similar nightmare about my daughter, Kate. I have never in my whole life experienced such real nightmares. I woke up, tried to convince the hospital staff that they had happened, and tried to take action on these beliefs. I was absolutely convinced that this was reality!

I couldn't get to sleep at night in the hospital. I know...most people have trouble sleeping, or sleeping well in hospital. However, I was taking this to a new level. Usually I could get to sleep by four or five o'clock in the morning which, of course, meant that I was awakened by doctors rounds at 7:00 a.m. Then back to sleep again, playing havoc with any type of scheduled therapy or tests. But, there were many nights when I could not get to sleep at all. No exaggeration! Hour after hour, with lights out or lights on, I just could not get to sleep. On those nights when I was wide awake, much to the consternation of the night nurses who regularly checked in on me, they were greeted with a cheerful, "Hello, this is *your* wake up call!"

I am a pretty "up" kind of guy. It takes a lot to really get me down, and I always see the bottle as being half full, not half empty. However, the constant one step forward and two steps back progress, or lack thereof, month after month wore me down. I was emotionally beaten up after this relentless series of infections and never-ending litany of drainage tubes and constant "sick to my stomach" feeling. And I was depressed—I hated being so totally dependent on others for my care with no end in sight, no solution to my dilemma being found.

As I stated, the team of doctors, who religiously made their rounds at 7:00 a.m. each day, usually had to wake me up after I had finally gotten to sleep only two hours before. As they knew my condition was getting me down, they had asked me a couple of times if I would like to speak with someone professionally about my feelings. They meant a psychiatrist. I groggily kept saying no, as I knew myself well enough to know that I don't feel that way for too long before my true positive nature emerges again. I hadn't given up, but I was getting close. In a weak moment on one such occasion, I said, "Alright, I will see someone. What harm can it do? Maybe it will help." Well, it did help, but not at all like you or I could ever have imagined!

You could not have scripted the stereotypical psychiatrist for a movie any more accurately than the doctor who walked into my room. He was young (of course, these days at my age almost everyone seems young!), in his early thirties at most. He was tall, skinny and gangly. He had a long scraggly beard, wore glasses, was dressed in civvies and carried a clipboard. After briefly introducing himself the first words out of his mouth were, "When did you first have thoughts of suicide?" "What did you say?" I exclaimed. "Okay. That's it. You're out of here. We're done!" Where he got that notion, I had no idea. I never had thoughts of suicide, no matter how bad I felt! This served as a wake-up call for me and I immediately shook off whatever depressing emotions I was feeling. The session improved my outlook immensely! Seeing the psychiatrist had made me feel a lot better. The methodology was just a lot different than I had expected!

Donald Gordon Ross

"That's What Friends Are For"
Dionne and Friends, 1985

For the first few months I didn't feel like seeing anyone other than my immediate family, mainly Allison, Matt and Kate. The three most important people in the world to me were my only lifeline to the world I once knew and from which I had been so drastically cut off. I felt so bloody alone, and I desperately wanted contact with them, particularly as I didn't know how long I would live!

I was out of it much of the first few weeks. I couldn't even have visitors. Allison, of course, visited me virtually every one of the 291 days that I was in hospital! Could I ask for more! Matt and Kate, obviously very worried about their dad, and thinking more than once that I would not make it, visited as often as they could, initially every other day. We had honest heartfelt discussions. I hugged them closely. I told them I loved them. There were times when one visit to the next, I honestly did not know whether this was the last time I would see them.

As the weeks rolled along, I couldn't ask them to visit as often. They lived north of the city, had small children, held down jobs and had lives of their own. They couldn't keep up the initial frequency of visits forever, although I had no doubt that when I really needed them to come down they would. I felt I had to give them permission to not feel guilty about not getting in as often as they would like. I know it bothered them that they couldn't do more. And it certainly tore me up not being able to see them more often or my grandchildren hardly at all. But a hospital is no place for babies.

One Saturday in late September while I was at Sunnybrook the doctors unexpectedly told me that they would have to do some serious emergency surgery—likely in a couple of hours—even though the risk of me not surviving was significant. I was in rough shape. It appeared that some infection had leaked into my gut when a drainage tube was inserted and that was something that could not be left unattended. We, of course, had to advise the kids immediately.

Matt and Natasha were at the cottage! They packed up right away and headed down to the hospital, a three hour drive. Kate got her mother to drive her and the kids to the hospital. Kate had just given birth to Kody 12 days earlier and I had not yet seen him. If anything happened to me during the surgery, she at least wanted me to have seen my new grandson before I died! The nurses were very kind. Where they would normally have prohibited a 12 day old baby from coming into the hospital, they were sympathetic to my situation and simply turned a blind eye.

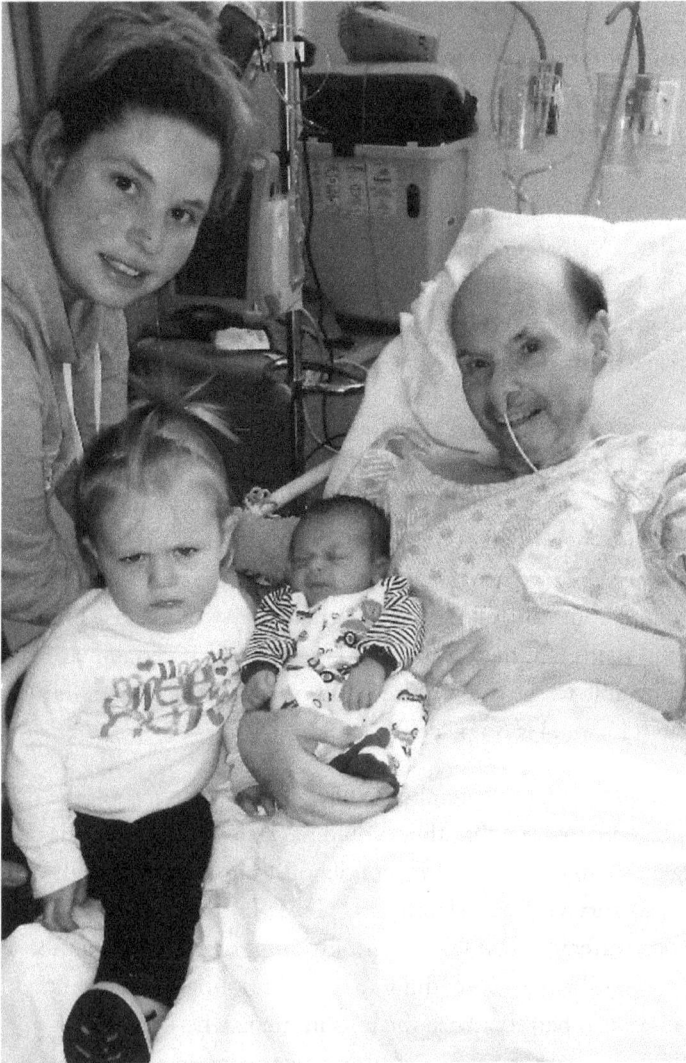

Kate, Kylie and me holding my newborn grandson, Kody

The doctors kept delaying. Allison and I held each other. We were very stressed. More tests. More delays. Everyone had now arrived and the evening hours ticked away. I was trying to hold it together, as was Allison. Emotions were running high. Eventually the doctors decided not to do the surgery. There was palpable relief. I was pretty upset that we had all been put through this high stress for nothing; but, we made the most of it and, in the end, it turned out to be a memorable family gathering.

From the outset of my hospitalization, cards and well wishes poured in from everywhere. Allison was deluged with emails of concern. She was hard-pressed to keep up with the phone calls and messages. After two or three months Allison thought I should start to see visitors, as it would do me good. I, on the other hand, felt so crappy that I didn't want to. This was certainly at odds with the social type of person that I was normally. Eventually, I reluctantly agreed, even though my voice was terribly raspy, and at times even non-existent. At one point I was seeing a speech therapist, as the tubes down my throat took away my ability to do anything more than whisper, so even talking on the phone was not possible.

But, when I could, I did start to use my cell phone. Boy, did it become well used as time went on. More than once it got a soaking when a water glass got knocked over, but it kept working. Then I began to initiate calls. This was extremely important to my mental state of well-being. I had been totally cut off from friends, relatives and business associates. By calling *them*, I established a connection to the outside world, the world I *used to* belong to. Then they began to call me. They would take their lead from me. They would respond according to how I acted and sounded. I tried to be positive about my situation, although I rarely had any good news to deliver. They were always supportive; but, no one could believe that my condition was going on for months, and getting worse. The prognosis remained grim! The doctors had tried everything they could.

I remember speaking with my good childhood friend from the cottage, Dave Beardslee. He and his wife, Becky, now lived in Colorado. They had just lost their home and all possessions in the out-of-control wildfires that raged in the Denver area. Dave and Becky had nothing left but each other, but they at least had that. I admired his composure, and he called me frequently to see how I was doing. On one occasion, when I was at a particularly low point, Dave was speaking to me in a way that he had never spoken to me before. It was then I realized that he felt that this very well might be the last time that he would speak with me. Dave thought I was going to die! And he was not alone!

Almost all of our friends and relatives came at one time or another, and often several times, to visit me. It became a matter of strategizing and scheduling visits in order to offload the visitation burden that Allison valiantly bore. After a time I looked forward to visits, even though many were temporarily thwarted by unscheduled tests and procedures, and on occasion I was just too sick to see anyone. But, as the months slipped by, the visits were a great help to keep me connected to our circle of family and friends.

My visitors included Craig and Nancy Truscott, Glen and Sally Loates, Rick Brooker, my cousins Bev, Dianne, Brian, Ross and Carlies, Allison's family members Heather, Judy, Jim, Susan and Wilf Tuck, Ginny, Judi, Susan, and the list went on. My good friend and business associate, Paul Bremner, found the time to leave his terminally ill wife, Georgie, to come down to the hospital. He first saw me six months into my hospitalization. He walked into my room and walked right out again. I looked so emaciated and thin that he didn't recognize me. Paul thought he was in the wrong room! That gave me a jolt!

My cousin, Sherry and her mom, my Aunt Marge, separately dropped by to see me on several occasions. Their unwavering support was so much appreciated. I could feel *their* pain for *me*. My Aunt Marge, who was 91 at the time, was in better shape than I was! On one of her visits she expressed great surprise that I didn't have an iPad. She said that she "couldn't do without hers!" My 91 year old aunt was healthier and more tech savvy than her bedridden nephew 27 years her junior! She told me to get Matt to search out an iPad for me and to send her the bill! Once again I was dragged kicking and screaming into the 21st century!

It's usually only when people die that you hear at their funeral what wonderful individuals they were. The accolades come pouring in.

They only speak in positives. While I lay in hospital, I had the rather unique opportunity to find out who my true friends were. Their unflagging support for both Allison and me, their heartfelt expressions of concern and admiration for my fight, and their continuous encouragement over this 9 ½ month ordeal went far beyond being gratifying and being appreciated.

Good friends aren't just for good times. When the going gets tough, you need to be able to lean on them and count on them for support. I didn't ask for it; they just gave it, unconditionally, to both Allison and me. At some point in our life we stand alone in a dark hole. You need a foundation of friends and family to help pull you out of that bad place to keep moving you forward. I had the opportunity to see and hear what people thought of me while I was alive. It certainly made me feel good and was a crucial plank in the foundation of my recovery!

Donald Gordon Ross

"It's My Life"
Bon Jovi, 1993

I have often been asked, "What did I fear the most about being so severely ill in hospital?" When I throw the question back at people and ask them what they think I feared the most, they most often answer that it was likely that I was afraid of dying. But, that wasn't it. Quite the opposite, in fact! For what I feared most was *living*! No, I didn't misspeak...I said that what I feared most about my life-threatening situation was that I would live. And my response to that question is not at all what people expect. Let me explain.

I was petrified that I would survive my illness, but remain in a perpetual state of bedridden ill-health. I was terribly afraid that I would not improve, that I would not get any better than I was. For me, surviving would not be living! I was afraid that I would feel like crap, constantly vomiting, being totally dependent on others to take care of me. I thought I would have drainage tubes invading my body, be lying inert in diapers, existing on a feeding tube for the rest of my life, constantly medicated, unable to have the strength to get out of bed (never mind walk) and unable to even feel like reading or watching TV, or having visitors.

That was not the kind of life that I would wish to lead, and what kind of life would that be for Allison? A living death of a once vibrant, active husband! Sure, Allison unquestionably loved me and was so devoted to me that she would continue to stand by me to whatever degrading and pathetic end I might eventually reach. But that is going far beyond "in sickness and in health" and not what I would want to put her through for goodness knows how long. I had watched my mother waste away in illness totally dependent on others. I knew what that was like, and I wanted none of it!

It comes down to that age old discussion of "quality of life". Assuming some degree of recovery, I could certainly accept some physical limitations. But, the quality of life question is as personal as it gets. I believe that it is up to each individual and his or her personal circumstances as to what constitutes an acceptable quality of life for him or her. It should be his/her decision. The twin ideals of today are "autonomy" and "choice", and should, I believe, also apply to death. A "peaceful passage should trump playing out some cosmic script".

After the events of last year, I can now better understand the rationale for physician-assisted suicide for the "un"coerced terminally ill, and I strongly endorse it. Political, religious and legal issues aside, in the last decade the time was right for the acceptance of gay marriage. Now, with a rapidly aging population, the time is right to generate greater discussion on the terms of ending life with dignity!

Let's be clear. *At no time did I want to die*; however, I reached a point where I decided I did not want to live the rest of my life in the condition I was in, so I was prepared to make high risk surgical decisions, if there was a chance that they might help improve my condition. Having come to this place in my mind after much contemplation and a great internal struggle, one of the toughest things I then had to do was to tell Allison that this was my wish, knowing it would stress her out even more.

Then I told my doctors that, if my condition did not show some signs of improvement in the next two to three weeks, we should look at their recommended surgery options, in spite of the high risks. The next step was to get Matt and Kate down to tell them of my decision. I had no compunction in telling them. For months now they had seen what I had been going through—what we had all been going through! Allison and the kids understood and supported me. Not sure if they *entirely* agreed with me; but, as they say, "Until you walk in a man's shoes ..."

That decision was a turning point. Up until this point I had had no control over my situation. I was at the mercy of doctors telling me what to do, and they now had exhausted all normal treatment options. There were no more options! No one could tell me what lay in store for my future. Now for the first time I could take a stand. For the first time in all of these months of being hospitalized, I finally had the option to exert control and make a choice. I made a decision. This, I believe, was a defining moment.

I had reached a place in my mind—a place where my decision rested comfortably. I was confident that this decision was right for me. I was no longer scared of the unknown. I was facing my fears. I had a plan; I had a strategy.

Over the next two to three weeks I began to see minuscule improvements—a part day here and there where I didn't feel sick to my stomach; I wasn't throwing up as often, occasionally for a few hours I felt like conversing, or reading, or perhaps even having a visitor. Brief moments of *almost* feeling half human gave me renewed hope. The therapy of the mind—the mental game, the psychology of regaining some control over my life—was now influencing the physical body.

I didn't realize it at the time, but I believe that this was also the first indication that it was not "my time". I'm not a religious person by any means, but I will be the first to acknowledge that there must have been some form of divine intervention at work on my behalf! Some greater power determined that I had suffered enough, that I had gone through enough to serve the purpose that this ordeal was meant to have.

I get asked frequently what the toughest thing was that I had to do in hospital. Well, it wasn't the 600 injections or the humbling experience of going through 1500 diapers and being dependent on others to change me; nor was it the 8½ months of vomiting, or the drainage tube procedures to insert or reposition them. No, it was none of these. The toughest thing for me to do was this: for every one of the 291 days that Allison visited me in hospital, I had to suck it up, screw up the courage to kiss her goodbye, lie to her that I would be fine, and then smile and say goodnight to her. She had to go home alone...and I was left alone...the emotional distress of each parting was gut-wrenching! On more than one occasion I broke down after she left my room.

And, there were times after Allison had left to go home that I would have yet another vomiting episode, or suddenly have tremendous pain. Setback on top of setback, month after month, beat me up emotionally to the point where sometimes I felt I just couldn't take it anymore. I hated to call Allison at 11 p.m. when she had left only a couple of hours before, and had to be up at 7 a.m.; but, sometimes my level of emotional distress was so sky high that I had to turn to my "rock". On those rare occasions when I did succumb when I really needed her, I called Allison and her response every time was, "I'll be right over!" And back she drove at midnight. We would hold each other tightly and cry together, each in our own agony, sharing emotion with each other like we had never shared it before.

These were the thoughts going through my head: How did I get so sick? How could I be so sick? How can this go on and on? I have always been such a healthy person! Why can't they successfully treat my pancreatitis? I don't know how much more of this I can take! And how much more can Allison take?

I was so worried that Allison would suffer a collapse, and indeed she ultimately had to take a leave from work to deal with my situation for the sake of her own health. She was frightened, strung out and feeling helpless, watching me waste away day after day.

When two people love each other as we do, and circumstances prevent them from being together, it is agonizing for both. I can only imagine how Allison felt watching me suffer, close to death more than once, and wasting away before her eyes. My lady visited me every day while holding down a demanding full-time job, keeping the household together, fielding the hundreds of calls and emails from concerned friends and relatives inquiring after my health status, and trying to keep the shreds of my torpedoed business together. We didn't think we could love each other more than we already did; but, this ordeal brought us even closer together. Our love and devotion for one another was taken to a new level of intimacy and caring. Without Allison's love and devotion, I could not have survived.

"Walk Like A Man"
The Four Seasons, 1963

I must give a gigantic thank you and "group hug" to all of the Sunnybrook staff for their outstanding care, compassion and dedication. Over the 6 ½ months that I spent in Sunnybrook there was a huge and diversified cast of health care professionals and specialists who played a critical role in first saving my life, and then stabilizing my condition and ultimately exhausting all options to get my necrotizing pancreatitis under control. I extend a nod of appreciation to the many doctors, including Dr. Frances Wright, Dr. Natalie Coburn and Dr. Homer Tien and the many specialists and residents who worked on my case.

There were numerous x-ray, ultrasound and MRI technicians and doctors, who collaborated on the many tests and procedures which I underwent. Although I will mention a few individuals by name— Jeanie, Angie, Tiny, Christine, Amanda, John, Elizabeth, Tammy, Pearl, B.J., Anastasia—there were nurses and personal support workers too numerous to list and even remember. They all unfailingly attended to my every need while being under a demanding workload that stretched human staffing resources to the limit! Both individually and collectively, they make an impactful difference every day in their patients' lives.

Melissa and Brenda were the rehab team assigned to work with me at Sunnybrook. They had the daunting task of trying to get me out of bed and learning to walk again. The hospital schedule only allocated them about three half hour sessions a week with me. It was a woefully inadequate amount of time to dedicate to my extensive requirements, if I was to have any chance of some recovery. Compounding the problem of learning to walk again was my completely depleted strength, and the fact that I felt so horribly sick that I had extreme difficulty motivating myself to even attempt to get out of bed. Sometimes, after forcing myself to stand, the exertion made me vomit!

But, both Melissa and Brenda had the patience of Job! Melissa was the size of a minute, but with the strength and determination of Mighty

Mouse. I affectionately referred to the much taller Brenda as Herr Brenda since, with my best interests at heart, she showed me no mercy in relentlessly pushing me to keep trying. They gave no quarter, and I will forever be grateful for that.

A Hoyer Lift was used to hoist me in and out of my hospital bed just to sit in a wheel chair, as I was simply too weak to do so myself. Picture a crane using a giant net to lift wooden crates from a dock to a ship. This I found to be most humiliating—all strapped up and swinging in mid-air! It was a feeling of total helplessness! Total dependency! And, it was absolutely agonizing to sit for 30 - 60 minutes in a wheelchair, which they insisted I do, particularly during the period when I was so excessively bloated. Because of the bloating I was also on a strong diuretic which meant I would have to pee every 15 minutes over several hours. This went on for days to reduce my bloating which had become a serious problem. My hands and feet had swollen to twice their normal size. At one point I resembled the Pillsbury Dough Boy!

Suffering from complete muscle atrophy, it took me many attempts just to be able, with two people assisting, to stand up from the bed to the high walker. This was complicated by a mental battle, as I was petrified of falling after I had slipped out of my wheelchair once before, crashing to the floor. I had absolutely no strength to break my fall! Initially I could take only a couple of halting shuffles before needing to collapse back on the bed. But, persist I did. I didn't give up. I couldn't give up! It had been ingrained in my life experiences to not give up. Those words were *not in my vocabulary*!

Finally, after many months of fighting the relentless series of infections, at long last I started to see slow improvement. Finally, the medical issues were being wrestled under control, and I found myself facing a new battle—the road to recovery.

I was deemed to be a suitable candidate to move out of Sunnybrook (an acute care hospital) to be placed in a rehab facility to receive much more intensive rehab therapy. This would begin what would undoubtedly be a long journey of rehabilitation to get me to a point of getting back home and being able to perform normal "activities of daily living", as they put it. I still felt it to be too soon. I didn't feel I was yet ready for the move. And, to be truthful, I was very nervous of leaving the security of what had now become my home for the last 6 ½ months.

Nevertheless, on October 19, 2012, after 6 ½ months at Sunnybrook, I came through the doors of Providence Healthcare to begin my rehab. I knew absolutely nothing about Providence, but had been reassured by our good friend, Nancy Truscott, who had worked there for CCAC (Community Care Access Centre), that it was a top notch rehab hospital. Little did I know that it would be providence that I ended up at Providence.

The care team that greeted me had a very difficult task ahead of them for I had lost 83 pounds and had no muscles left after months of being bedridden. Both the physical and emotional toll on me had been devastating. I had become so weak that my body was reduced to skin and bones. It hadn't been long since that Hoyer Lift was used to get me out of the hospital bed just to be able to sit in a wheelchair! Only on a good day could I strenuously drag myself to the edge of the bed, and with great exertion haul myself into a standing position to the walker and take a few halting steps.

On the ambulance ride over from Sunnybrook, I gazed in wonder at being outside for the first time in 204 days! But my joy at briefly being outdoors quickly evaporated as, during the hospital transfer, my tubes had been jostled and I was in excruciating pain. Torn from the safety of my Sunnybrook "home", I was deposited in a totally new environment and I was starting over. I knew no one, and no one knew me. When I arrived at Providence, I was afraid of what lay ahead. Curled up in pain in the fetal position, I was being attended to by staff who knew nothing about my complicated condition.

I had a decision to quickly make. I knew my condition much better than they did, but they were the experts. I had learned how to work together effectively with the Sunnybrook team. I banked on that approach working at Providence. And it did! I comprehensively briefed each staff member on my complicated situation. To the extent that was appropriate, I was specific and directional, while at the same time asking questions and seeking their recommendations. They were the experts. The goal at Providence was much different than the goal at Sunnybrook. I needed to exert some control. I was feeling well enough to do so, and the staff was professional enough and experienced enough to recognize and acknowledge my opinions.

I have to admit that, even from that very first day, and even in as much pain as I was in, I had a reassuring feeling from the Providence staff. They were so warm and welcoming, and couldn't do enough to help me. I felt safe. Every member of the Providence staff exuded a positive and encouraging attitude—nothing was ever too much trouble; no task was too difficult to undertake. It was all about getting me comfortable and back on my feet again, ready for my journey home.

When I first arrived at Providence I was quite sick and in a great deal of pain, as I mentioned. A big problem early on was regulating my feeds. My nutritional supplement was the only nourishment I was receiving. If I tried eating, I would vomit! At Sunnybrook, it had taken careful and tedious experimentation to identify the best make of supplement and then the dosage level that I could tolerate. The doctors slowly increased the dosage to up the desired caloric intake to keep me alive, but only after much unfortunate trial and error. Providence didn't have access to the same supplement. When they started on a new feed and fairly high dosage, I started vomiting. Doctor Papadopoulos, the dietician and the nurses went out of their way to work with me to get the right make and dosage of supplement so that I could begin to actually gain weight.

I knew right away that I was going to get along with my primary day nurse, Jannette, when she walked into my room and announced, "Well, Mr. Ross ..." You see I liked being respectfully addressed as Mr. Ross. No, only kidding. I don't stand on formality. I much preferred to be addressed as Don. Anyway, Jannette's opening salvo, delivered in a most serious tone, was "Well, Mr. Ross, we have to do some negotiatin' about your medications." To me that was just an invitation to begin a friendship!

I got so that I could push Jannette's buttons. Near the end of my stay at Providence, I knowingly baited her and said, "You know, Jannette, there are a lot of positives that have come out of my illness." She looked at me skeptically while raising her eyebrow, "Like what?" she retorted. "Like, if I had never gotten sick, I would never have had the opportunity to meet *you*!" Jannette positively beamed!

I was fortunate to come under the care of some extraordinary human beings—first at Sunnybrook and then at Providence, my new home. Whether it was Jannette or Denise, or Victor or Arnell or any of the other nursing staff…whether it was Joyce, or Jennifer or Samantha, my rehab team… whether it was the dietician or Dr. Papadopoulos… everybody was on the same page. All of the staff members were always informed and up-to-date on my condition—a turn for the worse, or a turn for the better. If I was feeling particularly sick one day, my rehab team usually knew it when they came to get me going on my regimen. If I had gained a pound or two, there was wild celebration.

The way I saw it, everyone had a clearly defined role. Every staff member acknowledged and respected the other team members and their respective disciplines; yet, everyone had the same goal. Everyone did everything they could to support me and prepare me as well as possible for discharge to home where I could continue my recovery and resume my activities of daily living. I could appreciate, as a business person, that there must have been a vision, goals and an organizational philosophy created at a senior management level, because that vision had been effectively implemented through to the front line. I could see that the staff was striving to establish a partnership between the health care providers and the patient in a collaborative approach to shared decision making.

One thing, among many that I learned through this whole ordeal, was that, as a patient, you have to take ownership for your own health and well-being; you have to be your own advocate. The health care staff members are the professionals with the expertise; but, better decisions can be made if the patient can properly articulate his condition and his problems. After 6 months, and by the time I got to Providence, I knew my condition, I knew my symptoms and I knew my health problems almost as well as the doctors and nurses. The staff at both Sunnybrook and Providence all respected my opinions and consulted with me on all treatments and rehab programmes. They listened to me. They were considerate, respectful and collaborative; and we established a relationship of trust.

I am inclusive here when I speak on a broader scale of how supportive the health care team of professionals was at Providence. My inclusiveness extends to all staff in the facility, not just the health care professionals by title. I include everyone from Donna, the Unit Admin. Assistant on B4 …to the custodial staff who kept my 12' x 15' world clean and were often good enough to hand me a book or a drink that I frustratingly couldn't reach…to Tracey, the Recreation Coordinator, who scrounged a radio so that I could listen to Christmas music…to George the wonderful piano player who came in twice a week to entertain the patients and provide some much needed diversion…and even to Mabel, the basset hound, who made visits on Wednesday nights. Getting me *literally* back on my feet was a united effort.

Shortly after my arrival at Providence, I made a request that proved to be significant—another turning point! Watching the weather forecast, I saw that on Thursday, October 25 it was to be 22°C and sunny. That summer in Toronto had been about the hottest and sunniest on record. I missed it all, and the entire season at the cottage, not that I felt well enough to really miss it. But, I really wanted to get outside at least once before winter, after almost seven months cooped up indoors.

My rehab team included Samantha (Sam), a physiotherapist, Jennifer, a rehabilitation assistant and Joyce, an occupational therapist. That beautiful sunny day I persuaded them to forego my exercises, get me into a wheelchair, and wheel me out into glorious sunshine. I soaked up the sun's rays and welled up with emotion. The tears ran down my face. For months I had wondered if I would ever again feel the warmth of the sun's rays, or even have to squint again! I knew that the experience of getting outside into fresh air and sunshine would give me the lift I so desperately needed to help me carry on. If you think about it, and know yourself well enough, sometimes you can create your own motivation and inspiration!

The dedication and compassion from the staff were empowering for me. My rehab was tough and it was grueling, and it was, at times, frustrating. Sam, Jennifer, Joyce and Jannette pushed when I needed pushing, and at times I did need pushing, particularly in the early going when I was always feeling sick; but, they knew my limits. The rehabilitation exercises were difficult—but I did them. I had to dig deep to accomplish the goals I set for myself; but, I found a will and determination I never knew I had. I am so grateful to all of the Providence staff. *If Sunnybrook had saved my life, Providence gave me back my life.*

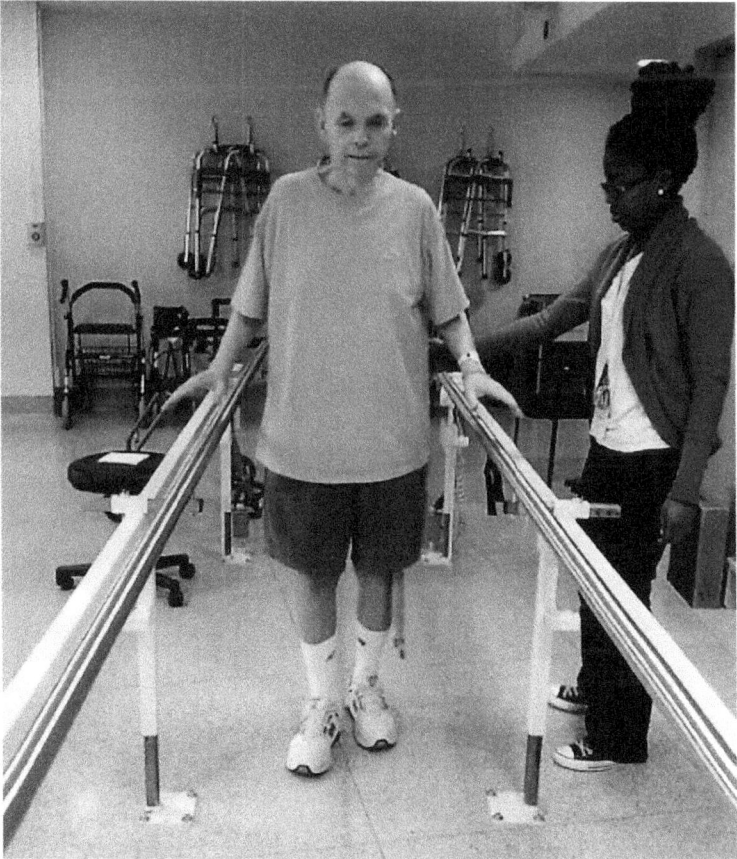

Learning to walk again at Providence, Jennifer coaching me on.

"Laughter In The Rain"
Neil Sedaka, 1974

Two hundred and ninety-one days…women conceive and go through to a full-term pregnancy in a shorter time than the length of my hospital stay! You always have choices. I often chose to have a sense of humour about my situation, although I will admit that at times it was put to the test!

Filling the hours of the interminable sleepless nights was one challenge. I don't think that there's a reality TV show that I didn't try watching, except *Duck Dynasty*. I could never bring myself to watch that one. However, I am almost embarrassed to say that I became a fan of *Mantracker, Canadian Pickers, American Restoration, Shipping Wars, Ice Road Truckers, Pawn Stars* and *Storage Wars*. Hey, desperate times call for desperate measures! However, I will say thank goodness for TCM (Turner Classic Movies)! Those old black and white films from the 1930s, 40s and 50s were a godsend and helped to save me from complete boredom. I love those weekly features on such favourite screen idols as Katherine Hepburn, Barbara Stanwyck, James Dean and Humphrey Bogart.

At Sunnybrook, one night after midnight, when I was, as usual, lying awake, there was great commotion as a new patient was being transported into a bed in my room. I could hear him coming long before he arrived. I couldn't see my new roommate because of the curtain between us; but, I knew he was an elderly man. I figured out that he was going to be operated on the next day, so he was still in good spirits. So good, in fact, that he was singing to all of the nurses. They were all laughing uncontrollably, not at him, but rather at what he was singing. I happened to know the song and thought it would be great sport if I sang along—a duet, so to speak. And, as I was having one of my better feeling moments, I joined in his singing, as we serenaded the nurses together with great animation and exaggeration as follows...

"I'm just a gigolo, everywhere I go,
People know the part I'm playing.

Paid for every dance
Selling each romance
Every night some heart betraying.

There will come a day
Youth will pass away
Then what will they say about me?

When the end comes I know
They'll say just a gigolo
As life goes on without me."

I remember one day when my occupational therapist, Samantha, came
for my walking session. Each day I would drag myself to the side of
the bed, pull myself up into a standing position at my walker and
mentally ready myself for my walking exercise. First, of course, we had
to put a second hospital gown over my back to cover the gaping
opening of the first gown. Each time I said to Sam, with exaggerated
flare, "Please put my James Brown cloak over my shoulders, Sam."
And, with great fanfare and flourish, she complied. "Do we have my
barf bucket available?" was my next question.

And so I would begin my arduous trek…out the door and down the
hall…one foot ahead of the other…one step after another. Sam
would follow closely behind me pulling my wheelchair for the time,
when at the end of my strength I had to sit down to rest before getting
up again and returning back down the hall to my room. It was a
grueling exercise. Each day I tried to go a little farther, setting a goal
to reach a particular door or line on the floor.

One day, I suddenly stopped up well short of my normal distance, and
in the most serious voice I could muster, I said, "Sam, I can't go any
further." A little quizzical, she said, "Okay, I'll bring up the
wheelchair." I replied, "No, you don't understand. My bloody diaper
has fallen down around my ankles and I can't move." I was hogtied!
With that I broke into hysterical laughter, and Sam joined in. One has
choices to make on how to react to situations; it would have been easy
to be embarrassed and flustered at this predicament. I found that
laughter was the healthiest reaction I could have! Laughter can truly

be the best medicine! I told that story to everyone and got hoots of laughter back!

The only good thing about not having solid food for 8 ½ months was that I felt so sick to my stomach all of the time that I didn't even feel like eating! The very thought of food was abhorrent to me for all of those months. Finally, in my ninth month, I caught myself drooling over *Eat Street* on the Food Channel! Ah ha! Was this a sign that the thought of food might be gaining appeal—at least with my visual senses? While I could never bring myself to eat hospital food, I did venture to try a bit of Tim Hortons chicken noodle soup which Allison would pick up for me—in December, my ninth month in hospital. Isn't there a book called, "Chicken Soup For The Soul"? How apropos!

The doctors and nurses asked me every day if I had eaten even a little Jell-O or a spoonful of pudding, or if I'd managed to drink any Ensure, which I was never able to do. There was wild celebration when a few spoonfuls of soup stayed down; so we tried a little more the next day. There were a couple of missteps, but it seemed I was now at last on my way to recovering my appetite. This was absolutely critical because, if I could not eat, I would never begin to gain weight. I was now down to a dangerously low 122 pounds and dropping! And, if I could not gain weight, then I could not start to redevelop my atrophied muscles. And if I could not build up some muscles, then I faced the scary prospect of never walking again. I would remain bedridden for the rest of my life!

Up until now I had been seriously worried about facing that scenario; but, this turn of events gave me renewed hope. I asked Allison to make up some spaghetti with basic tomato sauce. This I actually quite enjoyed and it led us to be cautiously optimistic that my eating abilities were on the upswing. Most of the infection had now been drained out of my body, and the vomiting appeared to have finally run its course, so I continued to eat modestly. I had no taste buds to speak of, as they had completely disappeared. During one of many sleepless nights that drove me crazy with nothing to do, I had the brilliant idea of composing a list of food dishes that I would like to have, assuming that my eating ability continued to progress and I actually got out of hospital. What I made up was a *food* bucket list!

My food bucket list consisted of about 35 selections which included a hamburger, bacon and eggs, smoked salmon, pizza, steak, shrimps, a PEP chocolate bar, a chocolate Dairy Queen milkshake, bruschetta, linguini marinara, back ribs, french fries from a chip truck, and a sausage from a BBQ cart. Of course, I would be happy to have a few fundamentals like a toasted BLT, an Egg McMuffin, an all day breakfast at the Kozy Korner in Haliburton, a chocolate double dip donut from Tim Hortons, my own special pancakes made from scratch and a ham and pickle sandwich. Two of my favourites, that I found myself almost salivating over, were sushi from Yang's Kitchen in Unionville and a quarter chicken dinner with fries and extra sauce from Swiss Chalet. But, truth be known, I would have been quite happy to be able to just eat a plain tuna sandwich!

In the months after my release from hospital, I enjoyed, to an inordinate degree, checking off every item on my food bucket list, as I munched my way slowly through each selection, savouring every single morsel, always waiting for the blow back that fortunately never came. After two months, my taste buds were just about back to normal and a Swiss Chalet fry didn't taste like cardboard anymore, as it did when I tried one on Boxing Day.

"Ac-Cent-Tchu-Ate the Positive"
Bing Crosby and The Andrew Sisters, 1944

Life is about making a difference; but, it is also about making choices. We all face them. For me, it was a choice to carry on, to persevere and to try to get better, to keep going in spite of pain and setback, not to have my life dictated by it. To do whatever it took to survive. It is said that 10% of life is what happens to you and 90% is how you react! One of my strategies was based on self-knowledge. I hate change; many of us do. But I had learned through life experience that I was fairly good at adapting to change.

I thought back to my initial struggle at Big Doe Camp, when I was surreptitiously dropped off for two weeks, and, a few years later, when I was dumped into the Grade 8 "brain class". I remembered how I had to find ways to deal with my father's death and survive a marital break-up. Remembering the strategies which I employed to deal with these circumstances, I consciously set to work, drawing on these life experiences. I had been torn from my world, my career, my friends, and my loved ones. I was confined not only to a 12' x 15' room for 291 days, but I couldn't even get out of bed for most of that time! Prison cell or opportunity? Adapt or die. Choices.

I repeated at Providence what I had done at Sunnybrook, and what I had done more than once in my life. I carved out a new world for myself. It wasn't perfect, of course, but it provided me with some of the fundamental tenets to be able to survive socially, and eventually, in later times, to actually thrive on certain aspects. I had the opportunity to make friends with the staff and to create a new social network. Yes, they were health care professionals and there to do a job. They had signed on for the sometimes thankless work knowing there would at times be frustration and heartbreak; but, they never complained about the crap (literally and figuratively) that they had to put up with. You see, most importantly they were first and foremost human beings— warm, caring human beings. They chose their career path out of a desire to take care of their fellow human beings. They have a tough job, but it can be a gratifying one. I find that if you treat people the way you yourself wish to be treated then you will reap what you sow—

sounds like The Golden Rule.

I developed good working relationships with all of the staff at both
Sunnybrook and Providence, and over time they really became friends.
We joked and laughed, and I looked forward to seeing them each day.
I had developed a new world of friends to live in and with whom I still
feel connected to this day. In my final weeks at Providence when I
was feeling fine once again and getting around, up and down the hall
and around the complex in my wheelchair, I started making friends
with fellow patients, expanding my new world. That process gave me
joy, laughter and a sense of connection and social stability.

I struck up a friendship with one of my hospital neighbours who
resided in an adjoining room. We shared the same bathroom
although, in the early going, the shared part was "in name only", as I
couldn't even get out of bed to use the facilities until well into my time
at Providence. There was wild celebration on my part, and by the
nurses, when one day in December, after eight months of being in
diapers, I was actually able to get up out of bed and, albeit with
assistance, slowly wheel into the bathroom and use the toilet! A major
hurdle on my road to recovery!

There were several patients for whom I developed a great deal of
respect and admiration for how they handled adversity. I was
astounded at the grace with which they handled their disadvantages.
Many had serious health challenges and some were wheelchair bound.
I gravitated to those who had no negativity about their lot and who
weren't mad at the world. I visited with those who had a positive
attitude and just kept persevering at their recovery, even very limited as
it was in some cases. We talked about football, hockey, family and life.
Why did I take to these patients? I liked their positivity and I admired
their choices. They played the hand they were dealt extremely well.
We related to each other. I gained a perspective from others who faced
perhaps even greater challenges than I had. Our discussions helped all
of us in our respective recoveries to keep a PMA—Positive Mental
Attitude.

"Alone"

Heart, 1987

There are vastly different versions of aloneness, being alone and feeling lonely. In the past I have often revelled in the opportunity to be by myself, where I very much can enjoy my own company. When partnered with someone 24/7, despite how much I may treasure their company and companionship, sometimes, just on rare occasions, I relish the chance for a day, an overnight, or even a weekend by myself. Especially at the cottage, it is a brief getaway that I savour. It is that little bit of independence, that short burst of freedom to be totally on your own for a short while, to do whatever you want to do, unfettered by time restrictions or responsibility; but, at the same time, I feel totally safe, secure and grounded in the loving and all-encompassing relationship with my life partner. And I know that I could not be able to truly enjoy being alone unless I was.

I have also been in a partnership, however, where I have never felt so alone and lonely in my life! This is one of the worst kinds of loneliness that I have ever experienced. There I was, partnered and supposedly in a loving relationship, yet it was a relationship in legal name only. The two of us were leading separate lives. There was no "us". There was no relationship, no security, no companionship and no love. Technically we were together, but relationally, we were miles apart. In many ways it was excruciatingly painful, if not crippling, emotionally. I was both alone and lonely. I felt like I was in a daze, a surreal state. I felt detached and seemed to watch the world carry on while I observed. I did not feel connected or involved. I felt trapped and helpless. The silence was deafening. I wanted to scream!

When I was in the hospital, I experienced a different version of aloneness, unlike either of the foregoing. First, I had been, by virtue of my illness, surreptitiously cut off from my entire world. Not by my choice, I had absolutely no control over what happened to me, or what was happening to me. I was thrust into a situation where I was totally dependent on strangers for my every move and care. In an instant, I was suddenly catapulted into a new unfamiliar world; cut off from friends, family, business and home—the entire outside world that I lived in! I was on my own and very alone. And, I was scared!

Friends and family came to visit, but I began to feel, after many months, that I was on display, like I was in a zoo, as everyone briefly passed in front of my enclosure. In my life so momentarily, so fleetingly, so tantalizingly close to providing me with a brief sense of normalcy—and almost being part of my old world again, but just for a flash. And then, poof, gone, they vanished like magic. Like one potato chip. Back to their world of normalcy, while each time I was left feeling almost bereft, psychologically gasping for air where just a moment before I'd had a glimpse of my normal world.

Yes, I was, in fact, surrounded by many people—good care-giving people—but, figuratively, at the end of the day I was still left on my own. The most important people in my life had to leave me after seemingly ever so brief visits. I had never felt so alone and lonely, so utterly by myself, and so absolutely isolated in my life—a feeling that prevailed not for days or even weeks, but for months! An almost unbearable loneliness and sadness of spirit that threatened to overwhelm me; yet, I had to keep up a brave front. I had to develop coping mechanisms and battle the demons of loneliness. It was a psychological battle that had to be waged simultaneously with the one against my life-threatening illness.

I consciously made a social survival decision. I devised a team approach to wage war on this front. I came to view my support as consisting of two teams. The first was the hospital staff, and by that I mean all staff, both healthcare and support staff, because I needed all the support I could muster. I consciously and strategically, if I can use that word in this context, created a new social world for myself. I worked at developing cordial friendships with the staff. We interacted, we consulted and we joked. I got to know them. Whether I was making dessert suggestions for Jennifer's Christmas dinner table, discussing fishing with Arnell, or probing Victor about his vacation trip to Las Vegas, I was interacting with the inhabitants of my new world and making new friends. It gave me a sense of social stability and interaction, a necessary "course of treatment" to sustain my psychological health.

Team #2, as I came to think of them (and if this sounds like The Amazing Race, with all of the detours and roadblocks I faced, perhaps it was) were the tried and true friends and relatives who continued to call and visit, offering me, and just as importantly, Allison, their support throughout my hospital stay. Their concern and good wishes were unwavering, and they provided me with at least a social salt and peppering of my old life. They breathed new life into me, helping to sustain my outlook and positive perspective. I came to look forward to their calls and visits; regardless of how lousy I was feeling. I have never been big on "social media", but this social network was a life saver!

Allison was, of course, the centre piece of my support teams. Her unfailing presence was the pillar I leaned on, the never-ending beacon in my dark wilderness that shone brightly to repeatedly guide me to a safe haven. I have never been alone when I am with this special woman! But, I have certainly felt lonely when I am without her!

Donald Gordon Ross

"I'll Be Home For Christmas"
Bing Crosby, 1951

So, at long last, after 8 ½ months of hospitalization, I was starting to feel half human. Gone was the vomiting. Gone was the nausea. Gone was one drainage tube. I actually felt like reading, and watching TV and having visitors. I felt well enough now that I actually cared about what I was missing in my former world, and it felt wonderful to care! I had Christmas music playing all day from CHFI on a radio that Tracey found for me. I wrote our Christmas cards. Upon request, a nurse would unhook me from my tubes, as I could now transfer myself from bed to the wheelchair, another feat considered impossible only a few short weeks before! I would cruise up and down the halls and out into the common areas, chatting up patients and staff.

Sam, Jennifer and Joyce would come for me every day for my exercises in the gym. I had to learn to walk all over again. I had little strength and less balance. I was motivated by their encouragement and my steady progress. I could now put on shorts, a T-shirt and running shoes and walk myself down to the gym with the aid of my walker—diaper tightly fastened, I might add! Each day I would perform various exercises between the parallel bars—squats, knee bends, standing on one foot, walking a few steps without holding on to the bars, and, with immense difficulty, trying to walk up stairs. This activity was particularly challenging in that one leg had to lift up my entire weight with every step. I desperately held on to the railings, willing myself to raise one foot up to the next step.

Every week I was weighed. Every time it was a keen disappointment, as my weight continued to drop. We were all getting terribly worried, for weight gain was one of the last pieces needed, if I was to recover. My weight had bottomed out at 122 pounds, down 83 pounds from my weight nine months before. But, there have to be easier ways to lose weight! As the nausea finally subsided, and the vomiting at last ceased, I could gradually accept a higher dosage of my feeds which had been keeping me alive for months. Now my feeds were starting to provide an amount of nutrition approaching the daily minimum caloric intake that I required to actually start gaining weight. Add to that the fact that finally the thought of food was no longer abhorrent and that my body and digestive system had begun to accept a little soup and spaghetti. I was finally on my way, and near the end of my stay at Providence I had been gaining a pound or two a week. I had much ground to gain in that department!

There were several corners turned on my road to recovery. A huge one was my ability to go home for the day on Christmas day, return to Providence for the night, and return home for the day on Boxing Day! I will never forget the wild anticipation the night before, and morning of, as the nurses, staff and I all made preparations for my first venture home in over 8 ½ months! I was like an excited kid awaiting the arrival of Santa, as I waited for my wheelchair-friendly taxi to collect me. Amid the application of last minute medications, I nervously struggled into new clothes, which Kate bought especially for me to wear, as absolutely nothing fit me anymore. As I was wheeled out to the front of the hospital to my awaiting chariot, I wished anyone, and everyone who would listen to me, a Merry Christmas!

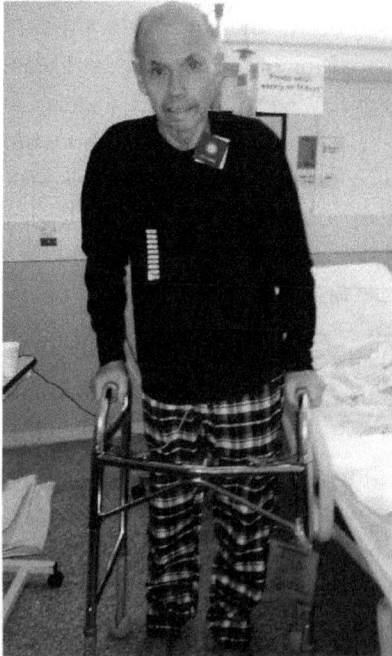

Standing with my walker, trying on new clothes to go home for Christmas

When I arrived home, it was an occasion of overwhelming emotion.
The 8 ½ months of a seemingly interminable, and almost terminal,
ordeal were shaken off almost instantly, as I reclined on the chesterfield
in our living room on Christmas morn with the love of my life sitting
beside me! I thought I had gone to heaven! I could almost believe the
ordeal I had gone through had never happened. I wanted nothing
more for Christmas than to be at home with my family one more time.
Clearly, there really is a Santa Claus!

Allison and I spent Christmas day together, alone. But we weren't
alone, for we revelled in the strength of our love and our journey of
incredible intimacy, and celebrated just being together. Never have
truer words been spoken than, "There's no place like home!" The
healing and motivational power of that visit was incredible for me,
especially when, only a couple of months before, I wondered if I would
ever again see home.

On Boxing Day, Matt and Natasha, and Kate and Kevin arrived with
the grandchildren, Kylie, Kody and Lukas to celebrate Christmas.
They were all amazed to see me at home and in clothes. I didn't yet
have the strength to lift our cat, let alone my 3 month old grandson, or
even to get up off the couch by myself, but that was okay. The kids
had requested it and I had a goal of making my famous pancakes from
scratch from my carefully guarded secret recipe. With much effort, I
stood leaning at the counter with my walker, assembled the mix and
started to cook the batch on the griddle. My strength did not allow me
to finish, and I did not eat a thing that day, as I was too concerned that
I could regress and get sick while away from the hospital; but, it didn't
matter to me. I didn't even think about it. I gazed in wonder at my
children and grandchildren, as we all sat at the dining room table. I
was deliriously happy just to be there. I was alive. I had survived. I
was getting better. Now there was no stopping me!

Everyone at Providence remarked on the change in me after my
Christmas visit home. My motivation to continue improving was sky
high. I began eating, not much hospital food, as I could never bring
myself to eat much more than the jellies and juices; but Allison brought
in my soups and spaghetti, and some delicious chocolate mousse from
our neighbor, Linda Hutson. Within a couple of more weeks my

weight had rocketed up to 131 pounds. My God, I was a heavyweight! As I slowly grew a little stronger, I started new exercises such as standing and folding laundry, learning how to get into a shower stall and how to move around the kitchen, all in preparation for going home. I even persuaded my team to have me visit the driving centre to learn how to get in and out of a car with an aid. There were, however, no guarantees about the extent of recovery that was possible for me, so I didn't even know when, or even whether, I could drive a car again.

2013   A Repurposed Man!

"Homeward Bound"
Simon and Garfunkel, 1966

On January 7, 2013, Allison and I attended a family meeting called to assess my status. Jannette, my day nurse, and Joyce, my rehab team leader, were present, as was the social worker/discharge planner. We discussed my terrific progress in recent weeks. I was asked when I thought that I would be functional enough to go home to resume my activities of daily living with continuing therapy. I said in another month. They replied that they thought I was close to being ready. How did I feel about going home sooner? I regarded the wall clock and replied that I could be ready in 30 minutes! That got a laugh, but Allison and I were both caught off guard when they set my discharge date for the next week!

This meant that everyone at Providence had to go into "hurry up offence mode" to get everything ready for a smooth hand-off to CCAC (Community Care Access Centre) which would now be in charge of my continued rehabilitation. On January 15, 2013, two hundred and ninety-one days after entering hospital, I was, amid fond farewells and good wishes, discharged for home. The extensive preparation and attention to detail by the Providence rehab, nursing and discharge planning group was clearly instrumental in a smooth transition from Providence to CCAC. The ball was not dropped anywhere. We were contacted by a CCAC nurse, dietician, physiotherapist and case worker either before I was actually discharged, or within a day of arriving at home, and all of the various medical equipment I needed arrived within 2 hours of my arrival home.

It may not be perfect, but you will never get me complaining about our health care system. I think if I had lived in the United States, given the costs of my hospitalization and treatments that I would personally have had to financially bear, I would have told them just to shoot me!

When I entered our front hall on my walker, it was hard to believe that I was actually coming home to stay, to recuperate. In one sense it was

265

almost unfathomable that I had been away for the better part of a year. The months of illness, pain, setbacks, emotional stress, dependency and fear started to fall away almost immediately. I received the shock of my life though when, for the first time, I saw the effects of the ravages of my illness on my body as I stared, naked and horrified, at the person in the mirror. I gawked at my emaciated body in a full length mirror. Could this human being who resembled a Biafran refugee be me! Skin and bones and no hair—I had aged 15 years! No wonder hospitals don't place mirrors in a patient's room!

Three generations of Ross men – Matt, Lukas and me

I still needed my feeds at home, as I was just starting to eat regular food again, and thoroughly enjoying the experience. I was restricted in moving around because of the feeding tube running into my abdomen and two remaining drainage tubes for infection. I expressed my wish to the dietician that I would like to be weaned off my feeds by March 1.

I beat that date by two weeks! And by the end of February Dr. Coburn had removed my one remaining drainage tube. Finally I was tubeless and unplugged! My weight had now soared to 147 pounds! I was feeling pretty good and hardly needed my walker around the condo.

The next big goal was to see if I was able to drive. My main concern was an intense neuropathy in my feet, the result of being bedridden for so long. A neuropathy is constant numbness/pins and needles. The feeling is akin to when your arm or leg falls asleep, only the feeling persists 24/7! Imagine that feeling and try to learn to walk and develop your balance again when your feet have lost their sensation! I wondered if I could feel the pedals on my van. I wondered how my driving reflexes would be on the Don Valley Parkway. I had loaned my van to Kate for the months I was in hospital. Assuming I could drive safely, I wanted to be driving by April 1. One Sunday Allison took me out in the van to a quiet street. I slipped behind the wheel. I held my breath while I shifted the car into gear and put my foot on the accelerator. Off I went. It was just like I had driven the van the day before. Up the Parkway I travelled. No problem. It was March 2!

Being a sole proprietor, my retail art business was now non-existent. Two weeks after I was out of hospital, Allison and my friend and associate, Rick Brooker, wheeled me around our industry trade show— the CGTA—where I visited with all of my suppliers from my wheelchair. I further went out on a limb and committed to exhibit at the 10 day National Home Show at Exhibition Place in March in order to try to move some of the extensive artwork inventory that had been in storage for a year. I had younger arms and legs do the set up and man the booth much of the time, and I was on site in a wheelchair for the weekends. Tiring, but I was getting stronger.

As April rolled in I started to think about getting up to the cottage. I've had many wonderful times up there on weekends from May through October every year for half a century. My grandchildren are now becoming the 5th generation to use it. It is very close to my heart. Allison and I missed all of 2012 at the cottage which was its 50th anniversary. I had a goal to get back up there by the long weekend in May. On May 3 Allison and I went up to the cottage in Haliburton, and I drove both ways.

This was a very emotional experience for me, given what I had been through the past year. On the Saturday morning at 7:15, I was lying in bed, wide awake, with tears running down my cheeks. And I knew what I had to do. I got out of bed (no Hoyer Lift for me anymore), got dressed and slipped out the back door. Allison was still sleeping. And I stared up at our driveway which has a 200 foot hill with a 40 degree incline. I had figured that, until my legs were strong enough, I would be driving to the top of the hill for the first half of the summer in order to go for walks on the road with Allison.

So, staring at that hill, I thought to myself, "I can do this!" And I put one foot in front of the other, and with tears streaming down my face, I walked up that hill. And, when I reached the top I felt like Rocky Balboa in the Rocky movie running up all those steps. And with one great fist pump I said, "Yes-s-s!!!" I felt as if I had won the lottery! And as I walked back down the hill, I thought to myself, "You know, when I landed at the doorsteps of first Sunnybrook, and then Providence, I did win the lottery. I just didn't know it yet! "

Able to work around the cottage again

"The Gift"
Jim Brickman, 1997

This past year has been a personal journey of perseverance, survival and remarkable recovery. It has been a questioning of the purpose of an ordeal, if not life, and it has been about the discovery of answers. It is a story of profound awareness. It is a story of inspiration, and it is a love story.

Being deathly ill isn't pretty. It's about tubes and needles, infection and drugs, shit and vomit. It is about pain and fear, suffering and heartbreak. It is about loneliness and being alone. It is about suddenly being cut off and isolated from your world, ripped out of your comfort zone and torn from your loved ones. And it is about experiencing every emotional nook and cranny, and *crevice*, in between.

It strips away Maslow's Hierarchy of Needs, quickly shedding all wants and reducing the patient's requirements to their most fundamental level of outright survival—breathing, eating, drinking, walking, thinking, speaking, keeping warm. Petty upsets, disagreements, squabbles, estrangements, relationship failures, career disappointments, financial troubles, the inability to have children, or cold soup, don't even show up on the radar! It is about staring down death. It is your own personal *Heart of Darkness*. It is Hell, and I've been there and back!

Sickness is the great equalizer. Shed are all trappings of material success. The person in the bed next to you may be a custodian or a financier, but you are now neighbours, physically separated by only four feet, united by a common situation of having a serious, or perhaps life-threatening, health condition. Your shared goal is to experience less pain, feel better than the day before, receive the treatment you need, get through another day, and hopefully inch closer to going home and resuming the life you know and desire more than anything to return to.

I have always considered that I led a very average sort of life. I'm just an ordinary human being who happened to have extraordinary circumstances thrust upon me. Many people have called me brave and courageous for how I coped with this ordeal. And I can accept that. I wasn't brave or courageous in the sense of those who perform acts of heroism, such as spontaneously rushing into a burning building to rescue a child, or saving a compatriot while under fire from the enemy on a battlefield. Those are decisions which are made spontaneously without time to really think through issues of personal safety or placing yourself in harm's way. They are part of your nature as a human being and instinctive as part of *who you are*. I have certainly never had the opportunity to see whether I could be courageous in that way. I honestly don't know how I would respond in such a situation.

I do accept that fighting this battle in the face of formidable adversity, staring down death, not giving up, bending but not breaking, literally putting one foot in front of the other, day after day, month after month, despite setback after punishing setback, did require bravery and courage. And I'm proud of that. I am proud that I persevered and did not give up. "Giving up" is *not in my vocabulary*!

Change usually happens out of a significant, sometimes catastrophic, event and then you respond. You find out who you really are and what your strengths are. I believe that the events, experiences and influences on my life's journey to date were all in preparation to allow me to at first survive the ordeal I went through, and now to thrive, as a result of it! I can now reflect back upon my life's journey with hindsight and insight. In a way, facing my illness meant facing me. Conquering those demons gave me affirmation of what I always believed about who I am.

My enduring positive attitude and my irrepressible sense of humour didn't fail me when I needed them the most. You have to believe in yourself. I believed that keeping a positive attitude was half the battle to staying alive. My philosophy of being patient, persevering and not giving up kept me going, when I kept being kicked when I was already down. What is it about the resilience of the human spirit that we keep getting up when we get knocked down? And it takes a particular learned mindset to be able to adapt to a confined 12' x 15' world for almost a year. I may have been a physical prisoner, but it was my mental and emotional outlook that got me through this ordeal and prevented me from just seeing bars!

I am not a particularly religious person; but, I do believe that what happened to me happened for a reason. It was not my time. Out of the physical and emotional ordeal that I went through, I believe that I was given a gift. I believe that what happened to me was so that I could be here, in this world today, entrusted with a new perspective on life and equipped with the tools to make a difference. Let me try to explain further.

Clearly what I went through was traumatic. In fact it was life-threatening; but, what I got out of it is a special ability, and an opportunity to use it! Of course it is all a matter of how you view the circumstances. It is all a matter of attitude. I could dwell on losing a year of my life, being torn from my loved ones, my business in ruins, the physical devastation of my body and the devastating toll my ordeal took on Allison and me emotionally. But, *I choose* not to look at it that way.

I believe that what I went through has provided me with the ability to make a difference in this life in a way that is completely different from any impact on others that I may have had before. Sure, I helped make people happy with their art selections, and I have managed and directed people in business. But let me share with the reader the impact which my remarkable, if not miraculous, recovery has had.

When I left both Sunnybrook and Providence I told the staff that I would come back to thank them properly when I could walk in under my own steam. I needed to pay it forward and show all of the staff exactly what their exceptional care did for me and how they helped me. I realize, as patients move through the health care system to the next stage of recovery, that, as health care professionals, they don't often get to see the end results of their outstanding efforts. I wanted all of them who were so instrumental in my recovery to see the happy ending they helped give me.

On March 28 I walked through the doors of Providence Healthcare—in street clothes, without a walker and weighing 147 pounds. It was a grand and emotional reunion that I will never forget. There were hugs and there were tears. Jaws literally dropped in amazement at the progress I had made. Jannette ran up and down the hall grabbing staff to show me off. She interrupted Dr. Papadopoulos from a meeting and he came tearing around the corner thinking there was an emergency. He stopped dead in his tracks and we embraced. I saw an immediate reaffirmation in the staff's eyes of the career choice they had made. I watched batteries instantly recharge. This walking miracle was living proof that they could help change lives! And, it felt so wonderful to say thank you to the people who I now considered to be my friends.

Jannette and me

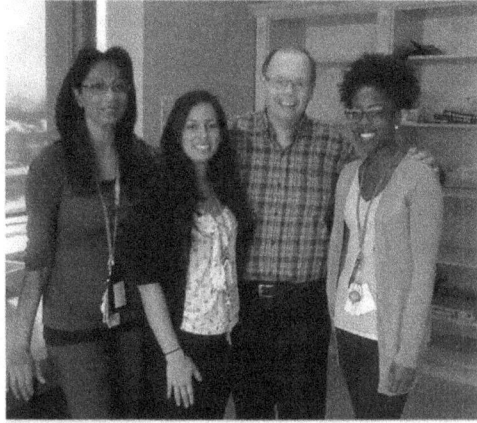

Joyce, Sam, me, and Jennifer

In subsequent weeks I went back to Providence to try to catch all of the staff. If my recovery could have this kind of impact, it was a very small thing for me to do to try to show everyone living proof of the good work that they do. I also walked back into Sunnybrook. This was now 6 months after I had left their care, so the difference that they noticed in me was even more striking. My visit had the same emotional impact as my visits to Providence, and I had to go back a number of times trying to catch as many doctors and nurses as I could. I didn't mind at all. I had never in my life had the kind of impact that I was clearly having on people. Now *I* was really making a difference! And I could see that, by being re-energized, the staff would go back out and continue to make a difference themselves by positively affecting the lives of others—the ripple effect! Maybe, just maybe, there was a greater purpose to the ordeal that I went through.

I was asked by my rehab team to speak at Providence Healthcare's

Educational Day Grand Rounds on May 28 addressing about 80 of the
professional healthcare staff and management of the complex. Allison
was by my side for this extremely emotional moment for me
personally, while I told them my story of recovery and the role they
played in giving me back my life. While I did have one table in
particular as my private cheering section, I could see that not one pair
of eyes in the entire audience wavered while I spoke. My message had
the desired effect—a story of inspiration and hope, a story of success
that they were instrumental in making happen. Proof positive of the
difference each one of them can make.

On June 26 I was the testimonial speaker to about 80 of Providence's
board members and major donors at their annual Appreciation
Reception on the 68th floor of First Canadian Place. My story
obviously inspired and motivated. I received a spontaneous standing
ovation! What an amazing feeling to receive instantaneous feedback
that I was making such a powerful difference!

As testimonial speaker at Providence Healthcare's Appreciation Reception

Allison and me with Josie Walsh, President, Providence Healthcare

Isn't part of what life is all about that we want to make a difference? After 65 years, that is what I am doing today in a different way than I have ever done before. I was given a "gift" when I survived this life-threatening illness, and that gift I am sharing with others in the hopes of providing my insight into life and possibly impacting others at an earlier stage of life's journey than I was at. I am told that many people wouldn't recognize they have been handed a gift, as hard fought for as it was. Few would feel comfortable sharing their very personal and intimate experience. Fewer still would be able to articulate that gift, and only a handful would choose to do something with it. I've been told that I fall into that last category. My reaction is, "Why wouldn't I?"

"Talk To Me"
Stevie Nicks, 1985

So, how can I at 65 years of age suddenly know how to write, or be an effective public speaker? My start in public speaking, as it were, was a personal disaster. I was repeatedly thrust onto centre stage when I had to make speeches in public school. In those early years I was a basket case with incredible stage fright. I hated with a passion having to stand in front of the class or being the centre of attention. My nervousness, self-consciousness, insecurity and lack of confidence were overwhelming!

I remember once writing a speech on the life of Albert Schweitzer that was pretty good. In fact it was too good as, much to my dismay, I kept moving on in the public speaking competition. It was a good experience, but the worst nightmare for someone with my degree of stage fright! I also remember (in even earlier years) preparing a speech on alligators (because I thought they were cool) that I had only half written when I had to deliver the darn thing. I had to stop while making the speech and own up to the fact that I had only written half a speech! How embarrassing! I wished at that point that the floor would open and swallow me up like an alligator!

So, I have come a long way since "back in the day". How did that happen? How did I eventually become comfortable and confident in front of an audience, able to speak and present effectively? Well, the progression is all there in my life experiences. My ability to speak and get comfortable got started in Grade 8 when I reluctantly took on the role of Artaban, in *The Other Wise Man*, our Grade 8 school play, and had to perform in front of a gym full of parents and students. My comfort level further improved when, in university, I willingly performed as part of the cast in *The Music Man*.

My material organization, and presentation, delivery and projection skills were developed and honed in many marketing plan and corporate strategy presentations throughout my business career. As a consultant, I gained group facilitation and seminar experience with different organizations. More recently, as an art retailer, I have interacted firsthand and frontline with customers, developing a personal selling style that tends to be relational, putting my audience at ease and instilling receptivity to the message with my confidence, credibility and sincerity. In other words, grinding through years of various practical experiences to become, as they say, an "overnight success"! Because I sure wasn't a natural when I started!

I have always derived tremendous pleasure (and I am convinced, escapism) from reading. I devoured books from a very young age. I got this from my mother who was a voracious reader! My parents would always take me to a Bayview Avenue bookstore at the end of June to pick out a couple of Hardy Boy, Tom Swift or Ken Holt adventure books to take away with me for our July cottaging vacations. As I would consume these within a few short days, I would supplement my hunger for adventure story reading with a visit to the Leaside Library where I would load up with the maximum number of books a student was allowed to take out at one time—eight, I think.

If I loved to read, I guess it might naturally follow that I would eventually love to write. And I did…that is, I do. I went on to major in English at U of T. And write I did...essays, that is. Tons of them, at least in terms of the weight of the paper, as there were, as I have mentioned, no computers invented yet. Boy, does that date me as a technological dinosaur, or what?

At Ryerson I had numerous assignments to prepare. In business I had those marketing and business plans to write, and presentations to make. I had to write in an organized, clear, easy to understand and articulate style to effectively and successfully communicate to my various audiences. So, I guess after all of these years, I have developed a certain "style" of writing and speaking that works for me and seems to be quite effective, and at times, impactful.

Isn't it absolutely amazing how your experiences in life prepare you for what's ahead? In my wildest dreams I would never have imagined that I would ever come to actually embrace speaking in public; that I would enjoy having attention focused on *me*. And that I would be speaking on a topic that would have been the last one I would ever choose to talk about—namely *me*, of all things! What could I offer others? What could I say that would be significant enough for crowds of people to actually want to sit there and listen to what I had to say? I never would have imagined during my public school days that I would be speaking in the future in such an impassioned way about *my* own story and *my* life experiences!

Donald Gordon Ross

"Que Sera Sera"
Doris Day, 1956

I have mentioned that I am not by any stretch of the imagination a religious person. I will grant that there was a greater power at work than any of us understands in the case of my miraculous recovery. I was on that slippery slope and going downhill to an inevitable end. The doctors had done all they could do. On my part, I had hung in there. It wasn't "my time". I do believe that, if there is a God, that indeed He or She does work in mysterious ways. I do believe that the ordeal that I went through perhaps did have a purpose. And if at least part of life's purpose is to make a difference in this world, then I have just received a Master's Degree! Perhaps I have been repurposed.

After learning of the life-altering health ordeal that I went through for a year, people have commented to me that I must have had a strong faith. And, indeed I did. I had a strong faith in myself. I believed in myself. After 63 years I knew myself. I knew that I could patiently persevere, that I could "dig deep", as they say. I wasn't a natural academic. If I studied, I got good marks. I f I didn't, I failed. It was that simple. Remember my experience in first year university! I had to patiently work at things. Nothing came easily.

I don't give up easily—sometimes to a fault. I persevered trying to make a broken marriage work, largely for the kids, but, in reality, I should have bailed long before. I have persevered in business several times, sometimes to advantage, and sometimes not. I believe that it's not how many times you fall down, but, rather, whether you keep getting up! You can conquer your own personal Mount Everest!

My story, the formidable trials that I went through, my remarkable recovery, the self- knowledge and awareness that I gained, opened my eyes. It presented an opportunity; it gave me a "gift". And that gift is the ability to make a difference by telling my story of hope and inspiration—whether that is through writing, one on one dialogues, or speaking to a group. It is the rare ability to motivate others and impact their thinking and behaviour. And that places me in a unique position. It is probably sacrilege to say it, but I feel that I am, in a way, acting almost in the role of a disciple, or at least as a teacher and communicator—clearly not in a religious sense. I do not consider myself to have religious convictions, although this whole experience has given me pause to wonder whether I should.

This experience has also given me reason to consider the notion of "fate". Do we have a preordained fate, a destiny, as it were? I wonder. I don't have an answer. In thinking back over my life's journey though, I can, however, now see several instances where an important decision—the choice—made by others many years before, has had a direct impact on significant future events that affected me personally and dramatically. In 1966, for example, my parents made the decision to move from our Rykert Avenue home in Leaside, where we had lived and grown up as a family for fourteen years, to Bayview Village. Had they not made that move, I firmly believe that, 46 years later, I could not have survived my illness in 2012 and gone on to impact people's lives with my story!

The reader may ask, "How is that possible?" That's a fair question. Here's how the connections work. If we had not moved to Bayview Village, my brother would not have gone to Earl Haig High School in Willowdale, and he would not have met Blair Forsyth who became one of his best friends. Blair ultimately married Sandy, and over the years I came to know them. Sandy, as the years rolled on, became good friends with Allison, and in 1999 she played matchmaker, setting Allison and me up at a dinner at their home. And the rest, as they say, is history! We married in 2003 and without Allison by my side I am convinced I would not have pulled through last year—46 years after my parents made the key decision to move from Leaside to Bayview Village. Is it coincidence or fate?

Here's another incidence, equally significant in its life-altering impact. If my parents had not built the cottage on Grass Lake in 1963, I would not have the four beautiful grandchildren that I have today—50 years later! "How does that work?" you might ask. Well, my parents could have built a cottage anywhere in southern Ontario. My Aunt Marge and Uncle Al had built one in Buckhorn. My parents were very close to them and that area was a consideration; but Haliburton captured their hearts for its beautiful hilly terrain. In 1965, I worked at Chateau Woodland on Lake Kashagawigamog for the summer, and it was there that Pam and I met through mutual friends. We went on to eventually marry and had two children—Matt and Kate. They in turn went on to marry and now have four children between them—our grandchildren. Coincidence, or fate? These connections are certainly fascinating, to say the least!

Okay, one more. Good things come in threes. If Pam and I hadn't moved to Brimwood Blvd. in Scarborough in 1976, I would not have been in the art business today, or spearheading a fund-raising initiative for hospitals and charities! As I have mentioned, one of our neighbours turned out to be renowned wildlife artist, Glen Loates. Pam and I developed a close friendship with Glen and Sally. Almost twenty years later, Glen and Sally asked me to work with them to help market Glen's art. I ultimately started my own art business, as I have documented, and was, of course still operating it when I took ill.

One of the strategies that I devised to reboot my business after I recovered from my illness was to initiate a fundraising initiative utilizing art in a sealed bid process. This program has hospitals and charities as the fundraising beneficiaries, allowing me to give back to the health care system which had saved my life—all 37 years after we moved to Brimwood Boulevard! Chance, fate, serendipity? Or what will be, will be? You be the judge.

Donald Gordon Ross

"Little Children"
Billy J. Kramer, 1964

There is a second "gift" which I have received which is most precious to me—my four grandchildren. This was not unexpected in the sense that I knew Matt and Kate both wanted to have children. And, while the successive arrival of four such little bundles in the span of four years was unexpected, what was really unexpected was the sheer amount of joy that these little critters have brought into our world. Their lives are truly a "gift"!

Certainly I have myself been blessed to experience the exquisite joy and privilege of bringing two children into the world, and watching them both grow up through childhood, into their teens, and then into adulthood as caring, responsible adults themselves. (My God, their mother and I must have done something right after all!) As Allison never had children of her own, this experience of "grandparenting" from day one is both a new one for her and one which we are experiencing together for the first time from inception, so to speak. Having little children around again for me is a wonderful experience, particularly as either they go home after a visit, or we go home after a visit. Never mind that home or cottage looks like a cyclone went through it about 15 minutes after they arrive, or that life is organized chaos, and daily activities are driven by the little ones' schedules. It's all good!

I am revelling in the role of grandfather and have Kylie, Kody and Lukas call me Poppa, of course, after my most adored grandfather. And in a year or two Norah will too. They call Allison Gramma. It did take me a while to get my head around the moniker of Poppa, but not long to adjust to the role itself. I know what a wonderful and enriching experience that a child, not to mention the adult, can have in a relationship with grandparents. I definitely wanted my grandchildren to experience that relationship, particularly as my own children did not have an opportunity to even meet their grandfathers! My Poppa taught me, by example, how cherished and enriching that relationship can be. It is, oh so very special!

Lukas, Kylie and Kody (The Three Amigos!)

Our first grandchild to be born was Kylie, a girl, to my daughter Kate and her husband, Kevin. She is now three years of age. Allison and I attended her birth. I think the first born is always extra special. My mother would have called Kylie a pixilated pixie—wispy blonde hair, blue eyes and her mom's rosy cheeks. One minute she is be-bopping around pushing a stroller with one of her dolls, the next minute playing in her kitchen, serving Poppa and Gramma strawberries or gold fish crackers, and then settling down to watch a *Tinker Bell* movie on her dad's iPad. She is very definite about what she likes and dislikes, wants and doesn't want. That will be interesting to see if that trait carries through as she grows older. In the meantime, she is fascinated that her Poppa has four belly buttons!

My heart melts every time she says, "Poppa come", as she puts her little hand in mine and pulls me along on an excursion around her house, down the steps to the beach at the cottage, or into our condo bedroom to look for Mr. Dickens hiding under the bed. At the cottage at Thanksgiving, I taught her how to swing her little arm back to throw pebbles in the lake. And Kylie and I danced in the cottage living room as she kept saying, "Shake your booty."

Second up was Lukas, born to my son, Matt, and his wife, Natasha, and he is now two years of age. I kidded Matt that it was thoughtful of him to get out of the way the ticklish issue of carrying on the Ross family name with his firstborn child, a boy, for up until that time, Matt was the last Ross. That little piece of family business has now been dealt with for another generation! I also felt most honoured when Lukas was given Donald as one of his middle names. I think it is also a nice nod of family recognition to my Uncle Don, my namesake, who died in World War II.

Once Lukas got his sea legs and started walking, that kid just hasn't stopped. He parades around non-stop investigating absolutely everything, and always with something in each hand. Early on his aunts have likened his gait to Mick Jagger's strut! I call him the Property Manager as he wanders all over the property—definitely the little "man in motion". He is always very focused on what he is doing, much like his father, I believe. He may not have the vocabulary yet, but he certainly understands what you say; he's a bright little fellow who delights in seeing what he can get away with!

Most recently, my daughter, Kate gave birth to a boy, Kody, who is almost two years old. Kody was born when I was in hospital. Blonde, blue-eyes and rosy cheeks, just like his sister. And like his cousin who never stops walking, Kody never stops smiling! I have never seen a kid smile so much. You smile at him and he breaks into the biggest grin you have ever seen. A strong little fella, he gets his little arms moving so rapidly up and down, it makes me wonder whether he may have a calling as a professional drummer!

Kody always greets us upon our arrival by calling out our names and immediately making a beeline to the children's bookshelf where he selects a book, trundles over to one of us, and asks to be placed on our lap while we read through the picture book to him! He points and gesticulates, imitating all sorts of animal noises at each one we point out. Might this be an early indication that 60 years from now another family member might have the interest and motivation to write! Wouldn't that be something!

Matt and Natasha announced this past Christmas Eve that they were expecting their second child. And indeed, as this book 'goes to press',

Norah Violet Natasha Ross arrived with much celebration on July 30, 2014. Little Lukas is now a big brother! That's four grandchildren in less than three and a half years. Oh my!! Perhaps my kids have been reading up on the prolific ways of my great grandparents!

What I am especially proud of is that my children, and their partners, have become such involved and responsible parents since assuming the mantle of parenthood. They are patient and interactive, and firm when they need to be. It's all about the kids!

Kylie and Poppa making pancakes

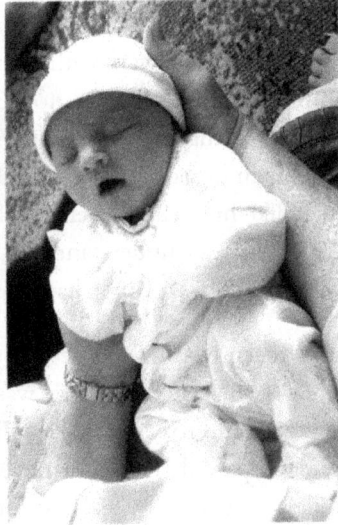

Two day old Norah held by Gramma Allison

"Life's Lessons"
Lynryd Skynyrd, 2003

So, now that I have written about my life's journey (so far) I get asked what advice I would give to others about how to live their lives, or how to cope with great adversity. Given my unassuming nature, I find it rather presumptuous of me to serve up a recipe for anyone on this topic. However, I will try to summarize some fundamental tenets and principles that underlie how I live *my* life and how I conduct *my*self? What beliefs, practices and core values underscored my ability to survive the fight of my life in the hospital? What principles of behaviour am I guided by?

If you, as reader, have stuck with me this far, then you (through my related experiences and life lessons learned) have picked up on the personal approaches that I have developed and meshed with my own personality traits to at times survive, and at times to thrive, on the path of life. If the lessons I have learned can be a useful approach for others to draw upon and employ on their life's journey, then I am delighted and honoured to share them. So, at the risk of preaching, here are ten fundamental underpinnings that support the way I live my life.

Learn from your mistakes. We all make them. The trick is to not make the same ones again. They are valuable learning experiences which can serve you well in life's education. I think of how I failed my first year of university and failed in my first marriage, as two of my most obvious miscues! I am pleased to report that in those two instances I didn't make the same mistake twice!

Get life's priorities straight. This, admittedly, can take time, and sometimes only comes with maturity, and after experiencing a great loss. The death of my father rocked my world and made me re-evaluate my life's priorities. I also eventually came to the conclusion that my career was my job and what I did to earn a living. It did not define who I was. It is easy at a young age to get so wrapped up in developing your career, that you lose sight of what is truly important. Readjust your priorities as required. Balance in life is the key!

Appreciate what you have, while you have it. For example, you only get one mother and one father. I have always regretted not spending more time with my father in the years leading up to his death. As a result, I maximized my time with my mother afterwards. It didn't take a protracted life-threatening situation in hospital to make me appreciate family, friends and the everyday pleasures of life, as I had developed that appreciation through the years. However, my time in hospital certainly accentuated that appreciation. Cherish, appreciate and savour what *you* have.

Recognize and acknowledge your passion. Don't hesitate to dream. As a laid back guy, I'm not sure that I had a driving passion about anything in particular (other than the cottage) until my creative side was awakened later in life when I fell into working in the business world of art. And, even today, I have just discovered how passionately I feel about writing. I now realize that I very much enjoyed writing essays in university and business plans throughout my career; but only now, at 65 years of age, and as a result of what I went through with my illness, have I been motivated to write a book, and even more recently a series of short stories based on recent experiences! I haven't enjoyed a project so much, or felt such a sense of personal accomplishment in years! Listen to your heart, as well as your head.

The Golden Rule: Do unto others as you would have them do unto you. Treat everyone the way that you would like to be treated. Learn to get along with everyone. Develop social and relational skills. Particularly through a wide variety of summer jobs and various companies that I worked for during my career, I was always meeting new people, or sometimes landing in working relationships with people totally out of my realm of experience or very different from me in personality and approach. There has also been more than one occasion where my first impression of an individual has been totally wrong. I have learned not to jump to conclusions too hastily in my evaluation of others. You meet all kinds, so learn to get along with all kinds, particularly in today's world of not just socio-economic differences, but cultural differences as well. As I noted, this approach stood me in good stead during my hospital stay.

Carefully evaluate your choices. Weigh the potential outcomes—gains or adverse consequences. We all face tough choices. It may be a decision to disconnect your mother's feeding tube, end a marriage, or decide on the surgery risks you are prepared to take to improve your own quality of life. You have to live with your decisions.

Take responsibility for your choices and actions. If you screw up, man up and own it. It's not whether you mess up. All of us do. It's how you respond and handle the screw up that defines us and on how we will be judged.

Believe in yourself. Don't always take the easiest path. I did in high school and university before I started to find my way, and I regret that. Take some chances. Yes, we always run the risk of failing, or being burned or hurt; however, nothing in life is a sure thing. With mistakes comes experience, and with experience comes growing confidence— unless, of course, you are fortunate enough to have that attribute naturally built into your character make-up. Pick yourself up, dust yourself off and try again, whether it is in business or in love.

Get comfortable in your own skin. This can take time, and there are some people who never do. Don't try to be someone you are not. Some self-assessment of your personality and character traits can go a long way towards helping you to understand and build upon your unique strengths. I finally realized that I could never be my father. I can only be me.

The power of love—the most powerful emotion we have, whether it be felt for your parents, your children or your life partner. There are more songs written about love than any other subject. The heart influences every action. And, when it comes to your partner, love can, at the same time, be both the most exhilarating and frustrating of emotions. It can run the gamut from looking through the world with rose-coloured glasses at the height of passion, to the depths of depression over its loss. But, when you find true love, it is a treasure to be cherished and nurtured for as long as you live. It enriches your life immeasurably; it is your nourishment and life blood, and you are so much more for it. It does indeed "raise you up". It certainly has for me with Allison.

Now, what key character traits saw me through the ordeal of my illness? I believe that a combination of my innate personality, my life experiences and the influence of certain significant individuals shaped me into who I am today. They prepared me to be able to at first survive my illness and prolonged hospitalization, and then to thrive coming out of it. I can boil this list down to five critical attributes.

A positive attitude. There is no question that throughout my life I have always seen the bottle as being half full, not half empty. I always try to see the best in people and situations. And that is a conscious choice. I choose to be a positive person. I put as positive a spin on life as I could, even when I endured the relentless series of setbacks of my illness. A positive attitude is half the battle in any fight. Your outlook towards your circumstances will ultimately make the difference in the outcome. Don't have your circumstances dictate how you feel; it's how you react to them that is key. *You* choose your attitude.

A sense of humour. Going hand in hand with a positive attitude is my indefatigable sense of humour. Sometimes it is a disguised way to deal with stress; other times it serves me well in lightening the load. It can break the tension and help make the best of a funny or serious situation over which I may have no control. Again, it's a choice.

Just do it. Like the Nike slogan says. I was taught by my parent's example to just do whatever has to be done. Whatever circumstances are thrown your way, just deal with it. In particular, having to deal with my father's death, telling my mother that her husband had died and being devastated by the failure of my marriage and separation from my children, come to mind as some of the more notable examples of just having to get on with it regardless of the circumstances. I am a firm believer that you may not be able to control the hand you are dealt, *but you can control how you play the hand.* And, *it's how you play the hand that counts!*

Develop the ability to adapt to change. I hate change; but there have been so many times in my life where I have had to deal with change, starting from when I was dropped off at Big Doe Camp as a child, to making the leap to university, or to finding myself without a partner or a job, that ironically I have developed the ability to adapt to change. And, that was never more evident than when I so unexpectedly underwent my recent medical ordeal. I had to call upon every fiber of fortitude and resilience that I could muster to get through that period.

And last, but not by any means least...

Don't give up. How we react and go head to head with life's incredible tests will sway the balance. Call it persistence or determination, but I have weathered many trials throughout my life's journey. As I said before, giving up is *not in my vocabulary!*

So, there you have it. Some insight into what makes this father, grandfather, husband and friend tick. These are some of the principles and behaviours that guide this particular human being. These are the traits and strategies that allowed me to literally live to fight another day. This is my best thinking from a 65 year run at getting educated on life. And yes, I am still making mistakes, as *my* learning curve continues.

Allison and me take our first dance since my release from hospital

Donald Gordon Ross

Epilogue—A Contented Man

"The Homecoming"
Hagood Hardy, 1975

So many people have impacted me on my life's journey—my father, Poppa, my mother, my brother, Uncle Al, my first boss, many friends, my treasured wife Allison, and yes, my children and grandchildren. Some taught me amazing things, others opened my eyes to the world, and still others provided guidance. And certainly the experiences on the path of my journey have indeed run the gamut to include happiness and joy…grief and sorrow…success and failure…pain and regret…ordeal and recovery. These experiences, both good and bad, have influenced and shaped me into who I am today. They have given me confidence, credibility and belief in myself, qualifying me, I believe, without having to get a PHD, to venture opinions, get life's priorities straight and learn how to live life more fully.

I look at the second chances I have been given throughout my life—in university, in my career, in marriage and especially in love. And now, most importantly a second chance at life itself. I appreciate the beauty of everyday life. We only get to live once, and I am grateful for everything that I have today. I am acutely aware of what is right in my life.

And indeed, life itself is a gift. Arriving safely to your destination is a gift. Waking up tomorrow to see your grandchildren is a gift, and it is a gift that you have the opportunity to make a positive contribution to other people's lives. Sometimes the path of your journey winds in directions you weren't expecting, and you have no idea what is coming around the next bend. We never really know where life is going to take us. We don't always get what we want, but we also get things we weren't looking for.

I can now reflect with insight upon the choices that I have made throughout my life and see the impact—the ramifications, or consequences—that they have had on my journey. Hindsight is truly 20/20! Someone once asked me, "How did you become so wise?"

And, although I had never considered myself to be wise, without stopping to think, I responded, "Because I made a lot of mistakes." That's how we gain experience. That's how we learn. Through a combination of successes and mistakes we can better manage our life experience.

I would submit that there are three things which we all ultimately want out of life, although, and I will be the first to admit it, it may take many people most of their life to discover them.

The first thing I believe that we all want out of life, and on which I have already expounded, is that we all want to make a difference. But, the second and third things that (sooner or later) we realize that we want out of life are "to love" and "to be loved". Very simple! Didn't we all dream at some point of finding that special person with whom we would become part of the greatest love story ever told? Even most guys will grudgingly admit that! But, what's that saying, "You have to kiss a lot of frogs to find a prince." Love someone for the qualities they possess; accept that they are not perfect. Nobody, and I mean no-o-body, is perfect. It's all about fit, complementing one another, being realistic, and developing unconditional love.

I met my wife, Allison, 15 years ago and we celebrated our 10th anniversary this past year. It was her first marriage and my second. Allison makes it easy to love her. I believe that we are more alive when we are in love. I wish that everyone could have what Allison and I have. I wish that everyone could love their partner the way that Allison and I love each other. She always tells me it was worth the wait!

Two years ago we were seriously concerned that we would not see our 9th anniversary, let alone our 10th! After I had been in hospital five months, we were planning my funeral and I was writing final letters to my children. We knew there was a good chance that I would die. During my 291 days in hospital we cried a lot, we hugged a lot, and we even laughed a lot. Now, we rejoice a lot! We celebrate the gift of life! We count our blessings. Be sure to count *yours*. It's a wonder-filled world!

This past Thanksgiving at the cottage was particularly special, as we all had more than the usual to be thankful for, after the ordeal of my illness that we went through. Allison and I were fortunate enough to spend six days at the cottage over Thanksgiving weekend. And what a glorious time we had! But, on the Thursday leading into Thanksgiving weekend, we were given the surprise of our lives when we visited my cousins, Sherry and Sean, in Buckhorn. As we were chatting away in their living room about 2:30 in the afternoon, we heard someone come in the door behind us calling out for directions to Haliburton! Imagine our complete surprise when we turned around and saw my brother standing there!

My brother Al, who lives in San Diego, flew into Buffalo on a redeye, rented a car and drove to Buckhorn to surprise us for the weekend. And, boy, did he ever! It was the surprise of my life! The last time he had seen me was in hospital the year before! What a difference! We emotionally embraced. Sherry and Al had conspired to pull off the surprise. Al had wanted to get back to the cottage for Thanksgiving for years, and this seemed the perfect year. As he said, "I have my brother back." The kids love their always entertaining Uncle Al, and we all thoroughly enjoyed and appreciated being together as a family. What a homecoming!

As I recline in my favourite arm chair in the corner of the cottage living room by the stone fireplace (I'm so literally a hearth and home kind of guy) I often glance at the sign hanging over the kitchen counter which says, "Gord's Bar". I wonder what my father would say, and know that he would be thrilled that the cottage is a gathering place for the family, and so well enjoyed by his grandchildren, and now his great-grandchildren. That's what both he and my mother would think if they could see us!

I ask very little out of life and savour simple everyday pleasures. I am happiest when surrounded by my bride, my children and my grandchildren. So Thanksgiving is nirvana for me! When the cottage living room looks like a tornado has gone through it, and duffel bags are stacked condominium-style high, furniture rearranged and a mattress placed beside our bed for our little granddaughter Kylie to sleep on—do I care? Not one bit! In fact, I love it. I am alive. I survived an extraordinary ordeal. I was handed a second chance at life itself. I am with my family, and that is all important. *Nothing else matters!*

Thanksgiving family photo at the cottage.
Back Row: Allison, Matt, Al, Kylie, Kevin, me
Front Row: Lukas, Natasha, Kate, Kody